R D QUENTIN

LONGMAN ILLUSTRATED DICTIONARY OF COMPUTING SCIENCE

computers and their application

LONGMAN   YORK PRESS

YORK PRESS
Immeuble Esseily, Place Riad Solh, Beirut.

LONGMAN GROUP UK LIMITED
Burnt Mill, Harlow, Essex.

First published 1987

ISBN 0 582 89335 6

Illustrations by Jane Cheswright
Photocomposed in Britain by Prima Graphics, Camberley, Surrey, England.
Printed and bound in Lebanon by Typopress, Beirut

ASCII 7-bit code

0 NUL 00	1 SOH 01	2 STX 02	3 ETX 03	4 EOT 04	5 ENQ 05	6 ACK 06	7 BEL 07	8 BS 08	9 HT 09	10 LF 0A	11 VT 0B	12 FF 0C	13 CR 0D	14 SO 0E	15 SI 0F
16 DLE 10	17 DC1 11	18 DC2 12	19 DC3 13	20 DC4 14	21 NAK 15	22 SYN 16	23 ETB 17	24 CAN 18	25 EM 19	26 SUB 1A	27 ESC 1B	28 FS 1C	29 GS 1D	30 RS 1E	31 US 1F
32 space 20	33 ! 21	34 " 22	35 # 23	36 $ 24	37 % 25	38 & 26	39 ' 27	40 (28	41) 29	42 * 2A	43 + 2B	44 , 2C	45 - 2D	46 . 2E	47 / 2F
48 0 30	49 1 31	50 2 32	51 3 33	52 4 34	53 5 35	54 6 36	55 7 37	56 8 38	57 9 39	58 : 3A	59 ; 3B	60 < 3C	61 = 3D	62 > 3E	63 ? 3F
64 @ 40	65 A 41	66 B 42	67 C 43	68 D 44	69 E 45	70 F 46	71 G 47	72 H 48	73 I 49	74 J 4A	75 K 4B	76 L 4C	77 M 4D	78 N 4E	79 O 4F
80 P 50	81 Q 51	82 R 52	83 S 53	84 T 54	85 U 55	86 V 56	87 W 57	88 X 58	89 Y 59	90 Z 5A	91 [5B	92 \ 5C	93] 5D	94 ^ 5E	95 _ 5F
96 ` 60	97 a 61	98 b 62	99 c 63	100 d 64	101 e 65	102 f 66	103 g 67	104 h 68	105 i 69	106 j 6A	107 k 6B	108 l 6C	109 m 6D	110 n 6E	111 o 6F
112 p 70	113 q 71	114 r 72	115 s 73	116 t 74	117 u 75	118 v 76	119 w 77	120 x 78	121 y 79	122 z 7A	123 { 7B	124 | 7C	125 } 7D	126 ~ 7E	127 DEL 7F

Contents

How to use the dictionary

This dictionary contains nearly 1500 words used in computing science. These are arranged in groups under the main headings listed on pp. 3–4. The entries are grouped according to the meaning of the words to help the reader to obtain a broad understanding of the subject.

At the top of each page the subject is shown in bold type and the part of the subject in lighter type. For example, on pp. 90 and 91:

90 · **LANGUAGES**/ASSEMBLER

LANGUAGES/COBOL · **91**

In the definitions the words used have been limited so far as possible to about 1500 words in common use. These words are those listed in the 'defining vocabulary' in the *New Method English Dictionary* (fifth edition) by M. West and J. G. Endicott (Longman 1976). Words closely related to these words are also used: for example, *characteristics*, defined under *character* in West's *Dictionary*.

The dictionary has an appendix entitled *Note on computer working* which contains an introduction to computers and their methods of working. If you are not familiar with the basic ideas involved in computing you may find it helpful to read this appendix before using the dictionary.

1. To find the meaning of a word

Look for a word in the alphabetical index at the end of the book, then turn to the page number listed.

In the index you may find words with a number at the end. These only occur where the same word appears more than once in the dictionary in different contexts. For example, **chain**

chain[1] is a set of slugs in a printer;

chain[2] is a method of dealing with collisions.

The description of the word may contain some words with arrows in brackets (parentheses) after them. This shows that the words with arrows are defined near by.

(↑) means that the related word appears above or on the facing page;

(↓) means that the related word appears below or on the facing page.

A word with a page number in brackets after it is defined elsewhere in the dictionary on the page indicated. Looking up the words referred to may help in understanding the meaning of the word that is being defined.

In some cases more than one meaning is given for the same word. Where this is so, the first definition given is the more (or most) common usage of the word. The explanation of each word usually depends on knowing the meaning of a word or words above it. For example, on p. 21 the meaning of *AND gate*, *NOT gate*, and the words that follow depends on the meaning of the word *gate*, which appears above them. Once the earlier words are understood those that follow become easier to understand. The illustrations have been designed to help the reader understand the definitions but the definitions are not dependent on the illustrations.

2. To find related words

Look at the index for the word you are starting from and turn to the page number shown. Because this dictionary is arranged by ideas, related words will be found in a set on that page or one near by. The illustrations will also help to show how words relate to one another.

For example, words relating to systems analysis are on pp. 191–194. On p. 191 *systems analysis* is followed by words used to describe analysis and data flow and illustrations showing the steps in the life of a system and a data flow diagram; p. 192 continues to explain and illustrate systems analysis, explaining problem definition and system specification; p. 193 explains and illustrates parallel and pilot runs and p. 194 gathers together the remaining words relating to systems analysis.

3. As an aid to studying or revising

The dictionary can be used for studying or revising a topic. For example, to revise your knowledge of memory, you would look up *memory* in the alphabetical index. Turning to the page indicated, p. 41, you would find *main memory*, *internal memory*, *immediate access store*, *core memory*, and so on. Turning over to p. 42 you would find *cache memory*, *scratch pad*, *associative memory*, and so on; on p. 43 you would find non-destructive read out etc.

In this way, by starting with one word in a topic you can revise all the words that are important to this topic.

4. To find a word to fit a required meaning

It is almost impossible to find a word to fit a meaning in most dictionaries, but it is easy with this book. For example, if you had forgotten the word for the first or top entry in a tree, all you would have to do would be to look up *tree* in the alphabetical index and turn to the page indicated, p. 149. There you would find the word *root* with a diagram to illustrate its meaning.

5. Abbreviations used in the definitions

abbr	abbreviated as	p.	page
adj	adjective	pl	plural
e.g.	*exempli gratia* (for example)	pp.	pages
etc	*et cetera* (and so on)	sing.	singular
i.e.	*id est* (that is to say)	v	verb
n	noun	=	the same as

THE DICTIONARY

general purpose computer a computer which can be used for a number of different types of work rather than one which is mainly intended for a special purpose such as scientific calculation.

digital watch

digital computer the commonest type of computer, dealing with data in the form of numbers or characters rather than continuous signals (p. 22). It contains a CPU (p. 31) in which the control and calculation functions (p. 18) are performed. Connected to the CPU are one or more peripheral devices (p. 12) used to feed data to the CPU and display or store the results.

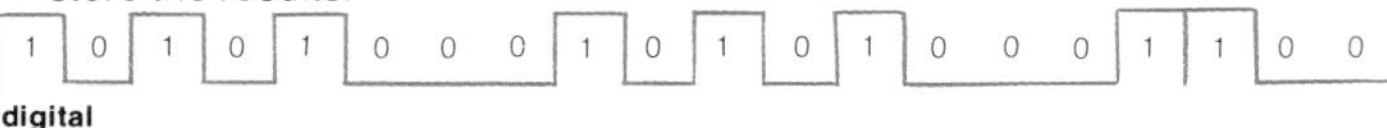

digital

analog

analog computer a computer which deals with data in the form of continuous signals (p. 22) that measure the changing size of something, e.g. the amount of electricity flowing through a circuit, rather than data in the form of numbers or letters.

analog watch

hybrid computer a computer which combines in some manner the ability to handle the data partly as if it were a digital computer (↑) and partly as if it were an analog computer (↑). It often consists of several small computers, analog and digital connected together, whose main purpose is to control the operation of another machine.

mainframe (*n*) a medium to large-sized computer, usually with a number of peripheral devices (p. 12), rather than a mini (↓) or micro-computer (↓). It can usually run several programs at the same time and may have several smaller computers connected to it.

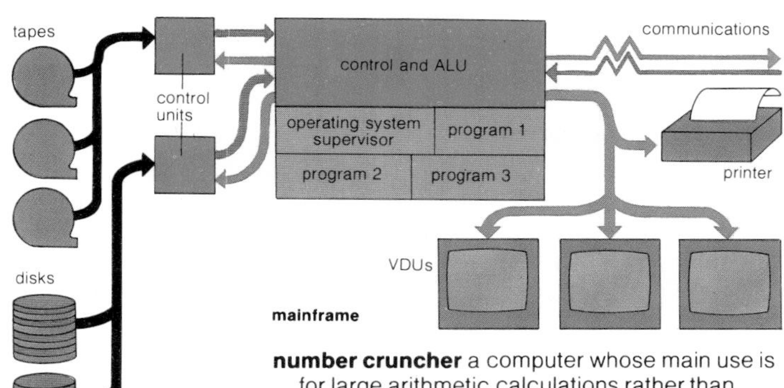

mainframe

number cruncher a computer whose main use is for large arithmetic calculations rather than general purpose work.

character oriented of a computer which is mainly used for data which changes in length and is therefore handled in groups of bytes (p. 17) rather than words (p. 47), which is the usual manner for handling numbers. Some computers can handle data easily only when it is in the form of computer words, others can handle either characters or words equally well.

micro

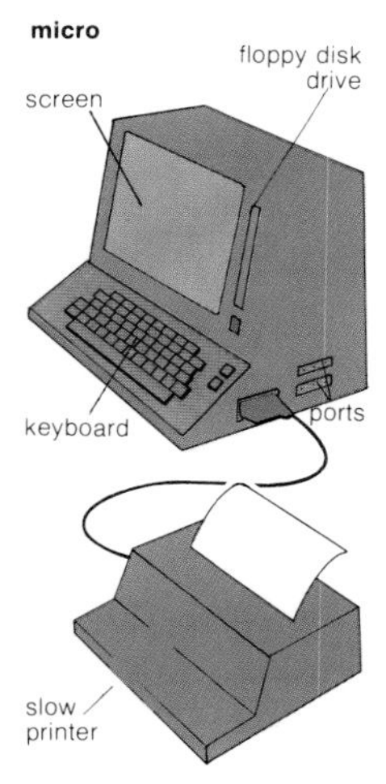

mini-computer (*n*) a computer which is usually larger than a micro-computer (↓) but with not so much power as a mainframe (↑) and with fewer peripheral devices (p. 12). The word size (p. 47) can be 8, 16 or 32 bits (p. 17) and it can be used by more than one person at a time.

mini (*n*) = mini-computer (↑).

micro-computer (*n*) a small computer usually used by only one person at a time. The word size (p. 47) is usually 8 or 16 but can be 32 bits (p. 17). It may have a printer, one or two floppy disks (p. 67) and perhaps a hard disk (p. 67) but sometimes just a keyboard and a screen (p. 84).

micro (*n*) = micro-computer (↑).

PC Personal Computer. A micro-computer (↑) intended for a single user.

host (*n*) a computer with one or more computers connected to it. It is the main computer and controls the others which usually do less important work, such as preparing data for processing by the host computer, or printing out the results.

slave computer a computer connected to, and controlled by, a larger computer called the host (p. 9). It does work such as reading cards (p. 52), printing results, etc, which would waste the time of the host computer.

multi-access (*adj*) of a computer which is used by two or more persons at the same time. Each person usually has the use of a terminal (p. 79).

generation (*n*) (1) a class of computers made about the same time and using similar ideas. The early computers were first generation, present-day computers, using micro chips (p. 24), are either third or fourth generation. Also applied to languages; (2) the process of taking programs, or parts of programs, and joining them to make a working system – usually an operating system (p. 130); (3) a copy of a file (p. 153). Successive copies are numbered in the order they are produced.

configuration (*n*) a list or diagram of all the parts of a computer, e.g. CPU (p. 31), tapes (p. 71), disks (p. 66), etc, which may also show the way in which they are connected. **configure** (*v*).

compatible (*adj*) of computers, devices, or programs, which can be connected without any special arrangements having to be made. The programs written for one computer will run on the other, either without change or with only small changes. Files (p. 153) from one computer can be read on another, etc. **compatibility** (*n*).

computer installation (1) all the units which are part of a computer, including units which are not connected to the computer but are needed to support its work, e.g. card punches (p. 54), tape library (p. 190), etc.; (2) the room or building in which a computer, especially a mainframe (p. 8), is placed.

installation (*n*) (1) = computer installation (↑); (2) the act of putting together all the parts of a computer at the place where it is going to be used. **install** (*v*).

plug-in unit a device which can be attached to a computer or another device as a complete unit without the need for any change to the device or the computer.

on-line and off-line

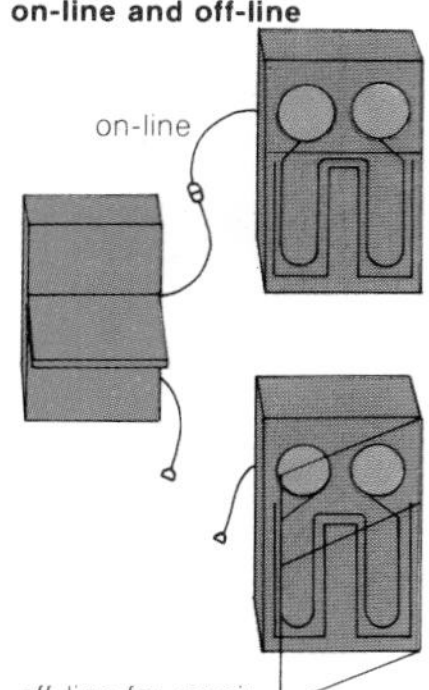

installation

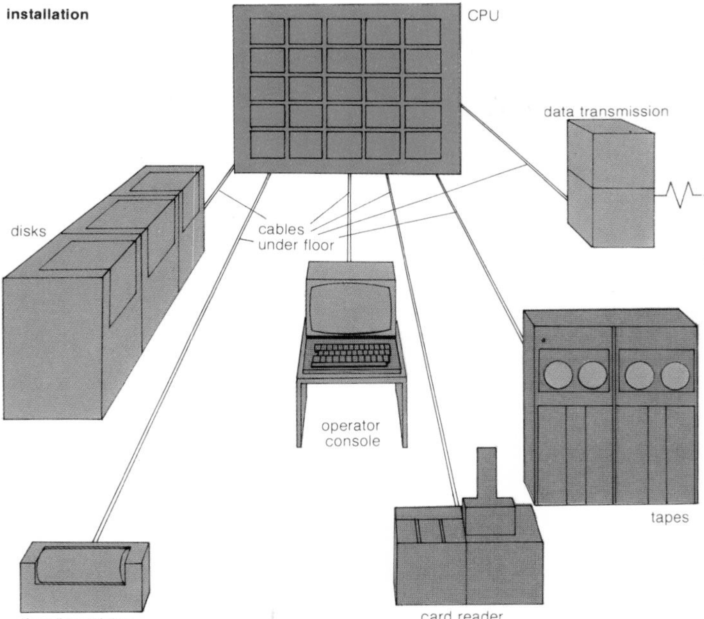

CPU

data transmission

disks

cables under floor

operator console

tapes

fast line printer

card reader

off-line

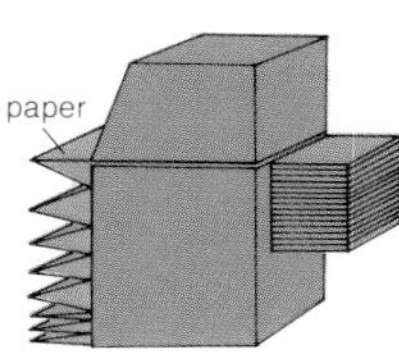

guillotine always off-line

plug compatible of a plug-in unit (↑) which has been made by a different manufacturer from the one who made the device that the unit is replacing.

off-line (*adj*) of a device which is either not connected to a computer or is not controlled by it. Devices can be off-line all the time, or may be taken off-line for small periods of time for maintenance (p. 188).

on-line (*adj*) of a device which is connected to and controlled by a computer.

ancillary equipment equipment such as a key punch (p. 56) or burster (p. 63) which is part of a computer installation (↑) but is not connected to the computer.

auxiliary equipment = ancillary equipment (↑).

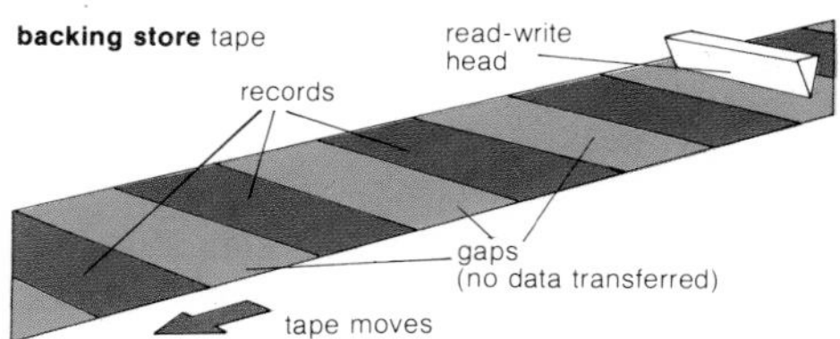

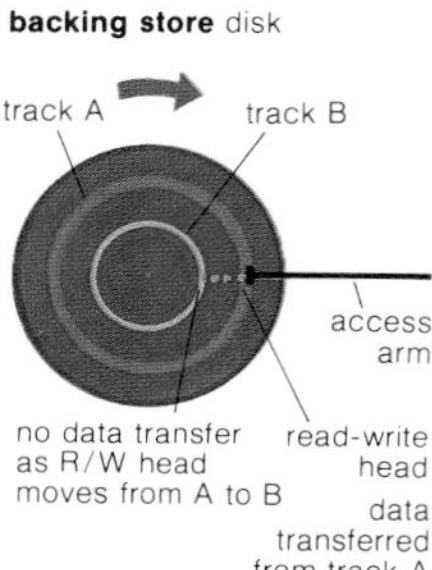

backing store storage other than memory. It means storage on units such as tapes (p. 71) or disks (p. 66). These hold much more data than memory but the data has to be read into memory before it can be used by a computer.

backing storage = backing store (↑).

auxiliary storage = backing store (↑).

secondary storage = backing store (↑).

peripheral device a device, such as a printer or a disk (p. 66), which is a part of a computer but is separate from the CPU (p. 31) although connected to it and controlled by it. The device can be used to feed data to the CPU, or to store the data for further processing at a later time, or to produce results in a form which can be read by human beings, e.g. printing.

peripheral equipment peripheral devices (↑) which are, or can be, connected to the CPU (p. 31).

peripheral transfer the movement of data between two peripheral devices (↑).

actual transfer rate the amount of data which can be transferred to or from a peripheral device (↑) divided by the time taken, provided that the transfer of data is continuous, i.e. there are no pauses while some part of the device, such as a disk access arm (p. 70), is moved.

effective transfer rate the total amount of data transferred to or from a peripheral device (↑) divided by the total time taken, including any time during which data is not being moved, for example, during a seek (p. 70).

input device a peripheral device (↑) which can hold or accept data in a form which can be read by a computer. Some devices can only provide input, e.g. card readers (p. 54). Some input devices can also accept output, e.g. a disk (p. 66).

input unit = input device (↑).

synchronous and asynchronous

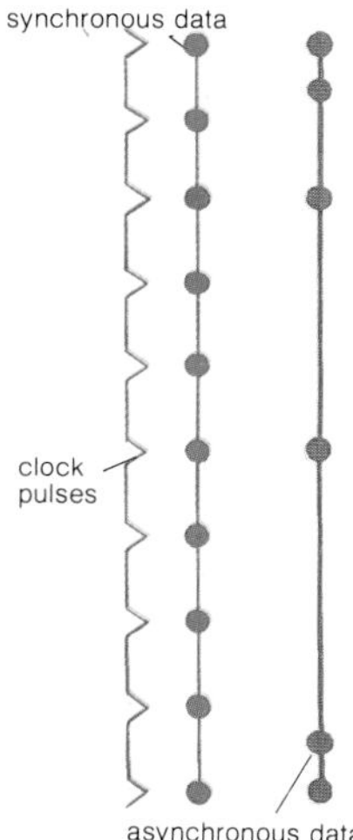

output device a peripheral device (↑) which can accept data from a computer either for storage, e.g. disk (p. 66), or for display on a screen (p. 84) or printer.

output unit = output device (↑).

port (*n*) a point where it is possible to connect an input-output device to a computer or a channel (p. 27).

synchronous (*adj*) of a method of working in which operations, such as transferring data, are done at fixed intervals of time rather than as soon as the preceding operation is completed. The times are controlled by some form of clock (p. 23) or timer (p. 24). **synchronize** (*v*).

asynchronous (*adj*) of a method of working in which an operation, such as transferring data, is started as soon as the preceding one is finished.

feed (*v*) to enter data into a computer. **feed** (*n*).

volume (*n*) (1) a single tape reel (p. 71) or disk pack (p. 66) or any other device, on which data can be stored, and which can be treated as a single unit. In a computer installation (p. 10) each reel or pack is usually given a separate number called the volume number; (2) the amount of something such as the number of transactions (p. 162), or the number of source documents (p. 183).

error correction the process of correcting data which has been found to be in error, usually on transmission (p. 76) between two devices. It can sometimes be carried out by a device without the need for any action by a human.

error detection the process of testing or checking data, usually on transmission (p. 76) between two devices, to find out whether the data has been transferred correctly. It does not mean that the error is corrected.

redundancy check extra data added to a record (p. 154) or other data so that a device can detect any errors in reading or writing the data. The use of a parity bit (p. 29) is a simple example and the idea is widely used on tapes (p. 71) and disks (p. 66) both to detect and correct errors.

sequential access a method of access where it is necessary to examine every address or record (p. 154) in sequence, i.e. one after the other, in order to find the one you want.

random access[1] a method of access to a single memory location, or a single record (p. 154) on a direct access device (p. 67), either by the use of an address or a key (p. 156), without having to access any other memory location or record.

direct access[1] = random access (↑).

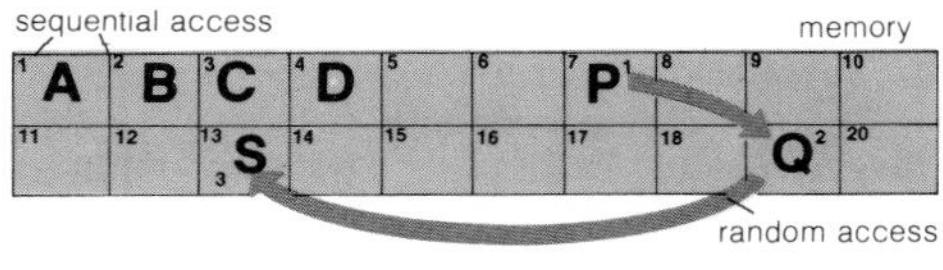

sequential and random access

hardware (*n*) the parts of a computer made from materials such as metal, glass, etc and which can be seen and handled, i.e. not programs.

software (*n*) the programs which a computer needs and uses in order to carry out its work.

firmware (*n*) the special programs which are fixed in ROM (p. 42) and usually allow a machine to perform specific actions. The machine need not be a computer, it could, for example, be a printer.

register (*n*) a part of a computer, usually in the control unit (p. 27) or the ALU (p. 31), which can be used for calculations rather than just the storing of data. The calculations can be performed on quantities which may be binary numbers (p. 49) or the addresses of memory locations. Some registers are for general use, others are used only for special purposes. Registers are also used in the control units of peripheral devices (p. 12) for special purposes such as counting the number of characters read or written during the transfer of data.

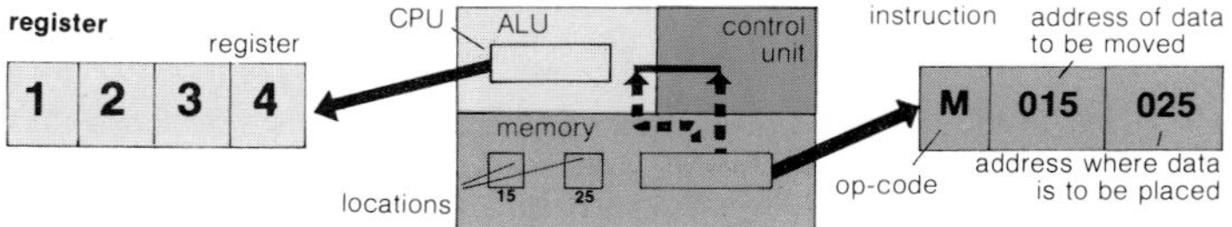

register

alphanumeric

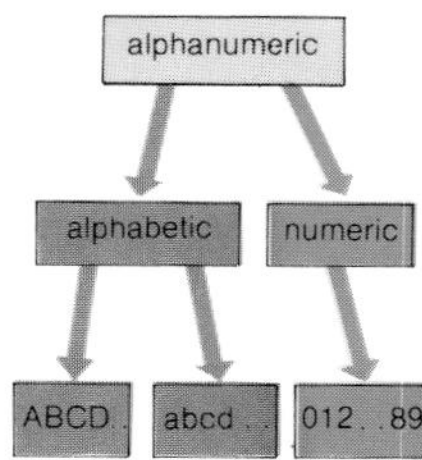

accumulator (*n*) (1) = a register (↑); (2) = a part of memory which is being used to hold the results of a calculation. **accumulate** (*v*).

instruction format the way an instruction is set out, usually consisting of an op-code (↓) with one or more addresses. The format depends on the particular computer and, for a particular computer, it usually depends on the op-code.

counter (*n*) a register (↑) or an accumulator (↑) being used to keep a count of the number of times something is done in a program. For example, it may count the number of lines printed or the number of times a group of instructions is performed.

op-code (*n*) a part of an instruction which says what action is to be carried out, e.g. an addition or a move of some data. A computer usually has between 40–150 op-codes, depending on size, one for each instruction in its instruction set (p. 34).

operation code = op-code (↑).

operand (*n*) (1) the part of an instruction which says where the data is to be found or where the result is to be placed. There may be several operands, usually two, and they are normally addresses which point to the location of the data. Only occasionally are the operands the actual data themselves; (2) one of the things on which an operation is done. For example, if we add the numbers 3 and 4 then the operation is addition, and the operands are the numbers.

reverse Polish notation a method of writing arithmetic expressions in which the operation follows the operands (↑), e.g. a + b would be written as a b +. The method is commonly used in computing to handle arithmetic expressions held as binary trees (p. 149).

alphanumeric (*adj*) of a set of characters consisting of all the letters A to Z, the digits (p. 16) 0 to 9 and blank. It does not include special characters (p. 46) such as $, & : + [? etc.

alphameric (*adj*) = alphanumeric (↑).

numeric (*adj*) of data held in the form of numbers, usually either decimal (p. 16) or binary (p. 16).

decimal number

3 decimal digits → must be 0 to 9

binary number

0000 1110 ≡ $[1 \times 2^3 + 1 \times 2^2 + 1 \times 2^1 = 14]$

8 bits → must be 0 or 1

hexadecimal number

0E ≡ $[0 \times 16^1 + 14 \times 16^0 = 14]$

2 hex digits → must be 0 to 9 A to F

octal number

016 ≡ $[0 \times 8^2 + 1 \times 8^1 + 6 \times 8^0 = 14]$

3 octal digits → must be 0 to 7

decimal number a number which uses the decimal digits (↓) 0 to 9. It is the common form of number which people use every day.

decimal digit any one of the numbers 0 to 9.

decimal (*n*) (1) a decimal number (↑) as opposed to a number in one of the other forms, binary (↓), octal (↓) or hexadecimal (↓); (2) the part of a number which is between two whole numbers, e.g. the number 1.25 lies between 1 and 2 and .25 is the decimal part. **decimal** (*adj*).

decimal point the character which separates the two parts of a decimal number (↑). In some countries a full stop is used, e.g. 1.25 but in others a comma is used e.g. 1,25.

digit (*n*) a single number. The possible values of a digit depend upon the range of radix (p. 48) being used. For example, for decimal numbers (↑) the values are 0 to 9, but for binary numbers (p. 49) a digit is either 0 or 1.

binary (*adj*) two. It is often used to mean binary arithmetic or binary numbers (p. 49).

binary digit one of the two digits 0 and 1, which are used in binary (↑) arithmetic. It is commonly called a bit (↓).

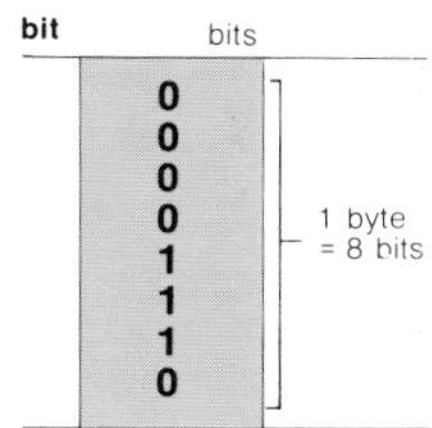

bit (*n*) a binary digit (↑). It is the smallest piece of information that a computer can deal with. All data is stored in a number of bits each of which has the value 0 or 1. It is the particular arrangement of the bits which is used by the computer to decide what the meaning of the data is, i.e. whether it is a number, a letter, or a special character (p. 46). Most computers cannot address a bit, they can only address bytes (↓), which contain 8 bits, but they have instructions which can change the value of any bit within the byte. Some large computers are able to address any bit in memory.

byte (*n*) a group of 8 bits (↑), making up a single memory location.

nibble (*n*) a group of four bits (↑), i.e. half a byte (↑). It is mainly used in relation to micro-computers (p. 9).

hexadecimal (*adj*) of numbers counted in groups of sixteen, by using the digits (↑) 0 to 9 and the letters A to F, instead of the usual decimal (↑) groups of ten. Thus each single hexadecimal character can represent (p. 45) a decimal number (↑) from 0 to 15. These are the possible values that can be held by four bits (↑) - 0000 to 1111. It is the most common method of describing data where it is held in bytes (↑). Each byte, i.e. 8 bits, can be represented by two hexadecimal characters. **hex** (*abbr*).

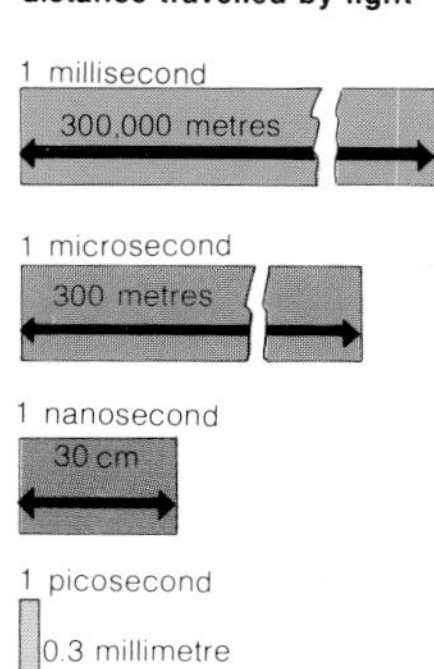

octal (*adj*) of numbers counted in groups of eight, by using the digits (↑) 0 to 7, rather than using the usual decimal (↑) groups of ten. The decimal number (↑) eight would be shown as 10 in octal. Octal is used to show all the values which can be held by three bits (↑).

millisecond (*n*) one thousandth of a second.

microsecond (*n*) one millionth of a second.

nanosecond (*n*) one thousand millionth of a second.

picosecond (*n*) one million millionth of a second.

K (*n*) (1) of data, 1000, thus 10K is the same as 10,000; (2) of memory, 1024, which is the multiple of 2 nearest to 1000, so 64K of memory means 64 × 1024 = 65536 memory locations.

kilo (*n*) = K(↑).

mega (*adj*) one million. It is used to describe large amounts, e.g. a mega-byte of memory means a million bytes (p. 17) of memory.
giga (*adj*) one thousand million.
default option the meaning or value that is used if a person does not say which particular meaning or value is wanted. For example, number, by default, means a decimal number (p. 16) and not a binary (p. 16) or a hexadecimal (p. 17) one. **default** (*n*).
connector (*n*) (1) a shape used in diagrams and flowcharts (p. 121) to show paths from one point to another especially from one page to another; (2) a piece of equipment which allows two machines to be joined together so that data or signals (p. 22) can be passed between them. **connect** (*v*), **connection** (*n*).
expression (*n*) an arrangement of numbers and symbols (p. 98) usually mathematical e.g. ((1 + 2) × 3) or logical, e.g. (A and B) or (C and D).

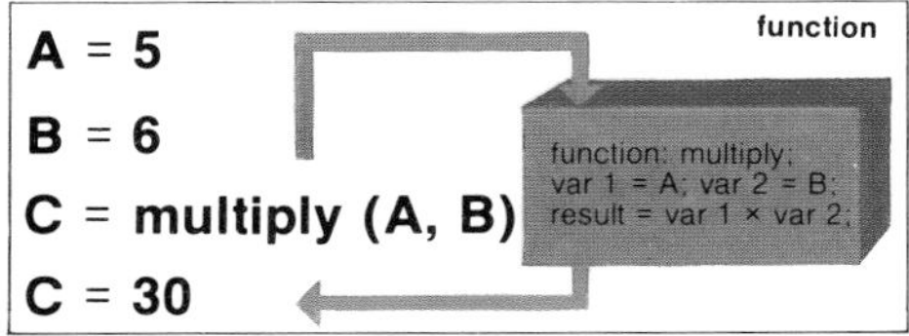

function[1] (*n*) (1) an op-code (p. 15). It specifies the instruction to be carried out; (2) an expression (↑) which includes an equal sign, e.g. if F = b + c, then F is said to be a function of b and c. If either b or c changes then so does F; (3) a routine (p. 111) which accepts the values for the items on the right-hand side of an expression and returns a value for the expression as a whole.
function[2] (*v*) to work or to be capable of working or being used.
malfunction (*n*) the result when something has gone wrong; i.e. a fault in a piece of equipment or an error in a program.
hang-up (*n*) the result when a program or a computer has stopped because some part is not working correctly.

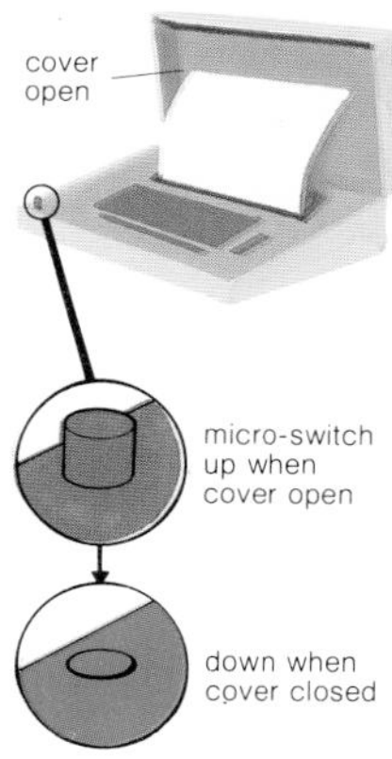

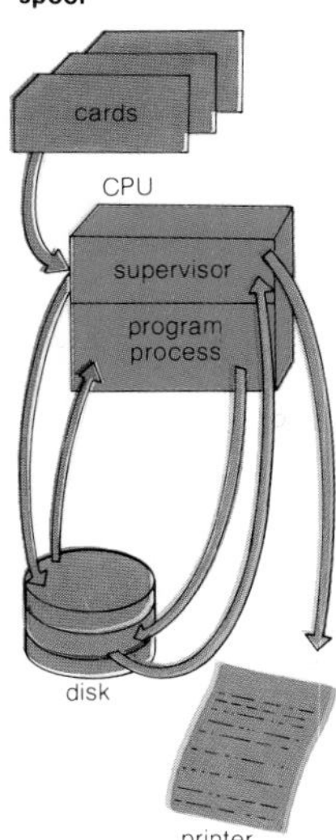

micro-switch (*n*) a small switch (p. 24) used to control the working of a machine, or part of a machine. Usually it prevents the machine from working if a safety cover is not in place.

overlap (*v*) to do two or more things at the same time by using the spare time in between the steps of one action to do the other. For example, computers can overlap the execution of programs with printing. After receiving an instruction to print a line a printer will take e.g. a tenth of a second before it is ready to print the next line. During this time the computer will do other work.

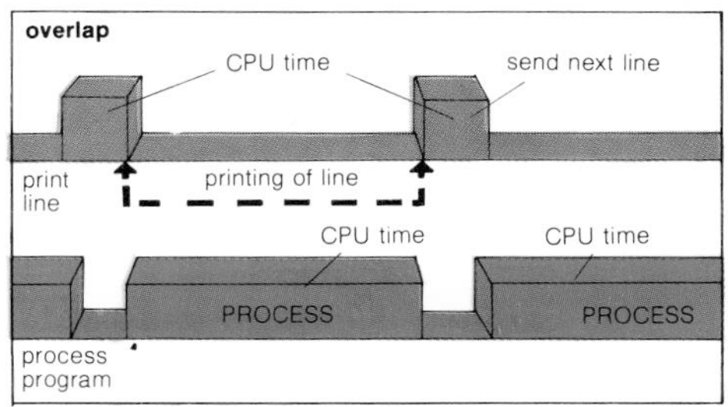

print-out (*n*) a printed report (p. 185) or listing produced by a computer program.

spool[1] *s*imultaneous *p*eripheral *o*perations *o*n-*l*ine. Of certain input-output operations, especially card (p. 52) reading and printing, which are overlapped (↑) with each other. On some mini (p. 9) and most mainframe (p. 8) computers it is not usual for a program to print its results directly. Instead they are placed on a disk (p. 66) and the operating system (p. 130) will use one of its programs to perform the printing. This is called spooling. **spool** (*v*).

medium (*n*) the material on which data can be stored e.g. punch cards (p. 52), paper tape (p. 64), or magnetic tape (p. 71).

manual (*n*) a printed paper book which describes how to use a program language (p. 103) or some part of the computer. Usually provided by the company which wrote the program or manufactured the computer.

monadic (*adj*) of an operation on a single operand (p. 15). The most common example is the NOT (p. 35) operation.

dyadic (*adj*) of an operation on two operands (p. 15) to produce a result. It is almost the same as a binary operation (↓) except that the result is not limited to two possible values.

Boolean[1] (*adj*) (1) of something especially a variable (p. 119), which has two possible values, true or false; (2) connected with Boolean algebra (↓).

Boolean[2] (*n*) a program variable (p. 119) or a switch (p. 120) which can have only two possible values, such as true or false, or 1 or 0.

Boolean algebra a set of rules for dealing with operands (p. 15) which can have one of only two possible values, i.e. they are either true or false. The results are also limited to two possible values. The rules were discovered by Boole in the 19th century and have proved to be very useful in handling special types of computer problem.

Boolean operation an operation which uses rules of Boolean algebra (↑) on its operands (p. 15).

binary operation (1) an operation which needs two operands (p. 15). For example addition is an operation which needs two numbers to be added together; (2) an operation which uses Boolean algebra (↑); (3) an operation using binary (p. 16) arithmetic.

complementary operation the result of a Boolean operation (↑) is one of two possible values, true or false. If a particular operation produces one result then the complementary operation, using the same operands (p. 15) will give the opposite result.

truth table a table which shows how logical operators (p. 34) will work. It examines all possible values of the inputs, setting them to 1 if they are present, 0 if not and then follows the rules of Boolean algebra (↑) to decide the outputs which will be produced from each arrangement of the inputs. Often used to decide how a circuit will work.

boolean operations

monadic

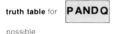

NOT **0** = **1**
NOT **1** = **0**

dyadic

0 AND **0** = **0**
1 AND **0** = **0**
1 OR **0** = **1**

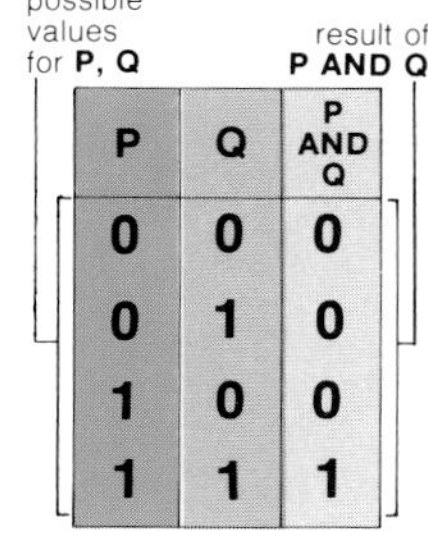

P	Q	P AND Q
0	0	0
0	1	0
1	0	0
1	1	1

gate (*n*) a simple circuit which has more than one input but only one output. The gate examines the input signals (p. 22) and, if they are the right ones for the particular type of gate, then it is opened and an output signal allowed through. Otherwise the gate is closed and no signal is sent out. Most circuits are groups of different types of gates.

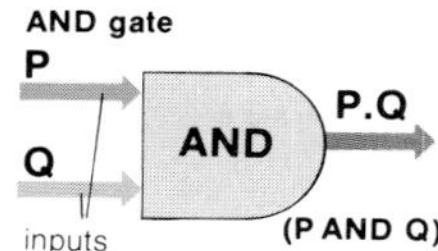

AND gate a gate (↑) which has at least two inputs, each of which can be 0 or 1, and one output. It will produce an output of 1 if all inputs are 1, but if any of the inputs is 0 then the output is 0.

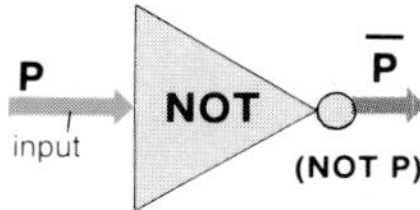

NOT gate a gate (↑) which produces an output which is the opposite of the input, i.e. if the input is 1 then the output is 0. Also known as a **negator**.

negator (*n*) = NOT gate (↑).

inverter (*n*) a device or circuit which is similar to a NOT gate (↑). It produces an output which is the opposite of the input, e.g. an input of 1 would be changed to 0. **invert** (*v*).

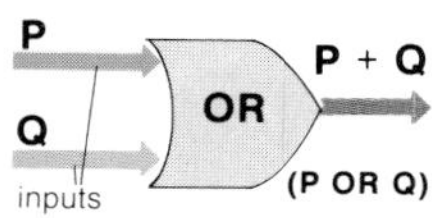

OR gate a gate (↑) which has at least two inputs each of which can be 0 or 1, and one output. It will produce an output of 1 if any of the inputs is 1, but will produce an output of 0 if all the inputs are 0.

NAND gate a gate (↑) which acts like a NOT gate (↑) with an AND gate (↑). It has at least two inputs which can each have the value 0 or 1. The gate will produce an output of 1 if at least one of the inputs is 0, but will give an output of 0 if all the inputs are 1.

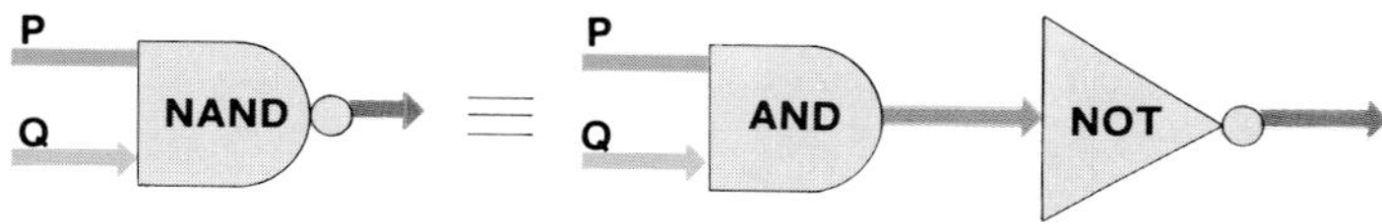

NOR gate a gate (↑) which acts like a NOT gate (↑) with an OR gate (↑). It has at least two inputs which can each have the value 0 or 1. The gate will produce an output of 1 if all the inputs are 0, but will produce an output of 0 if any one of the inputs is 1.

interface (*n*) the place where two devices or two programs meet or join. For devices the interface is usually a special piece of circuitry so that data can pass from one device to the other; for programs it is usually a special routine (p. 111) which changes the data in some way so that one program can accept the output of the other. **interface** (*v*).

monostable (*adj*) of a circuit which has only one possible value, i.e. it is always either 0 or 1.

bistable (*adj*) of a circuit which can have two possible values, i.e. either 0 or 1. It will hold its value until it receives a command signal (↓) to change; or it can accept another input which may cause it to change.

flip-flop (*n*) a circuit or device which can have one of two possible values, i.e. either 0 or 1, and which can be changed from one to the other. **flip-flop** (*adj*).

logic element a simple circuit which can hold one of two possible values, for example, a flip flop (↑).

drive (*v*) to send signals (↓) through a circuit so that it will operate.

signal (*n*) a steady or changing stream of electric current (p. 24) in a circuit or communications link (p. 76). It is possible for parts of a circuit to detect a signal and it may cause some action to be taken. It can also mean simply that there is a current as opposed to there not being one, or that there is a marked change in the size of the current for a very short time. **signal** (*v*).

pulse (*n*) a change in the strength of a signal (↑) for a short amount of time. It can be detected by the device to which it is sent. It usually causes the device to take some particular action.

digital (*adj*) of signals (↑) or data in which information is sent not as a continuous stream but as a set of pulses (↑) which are used to represent (p. 45) the binary digits (p. 16) 0 and 1.

signal regeneration the process of giving a fresh pulse (↑) to a signal (↑) so that it is brought up to its correct strength.

flip-flop

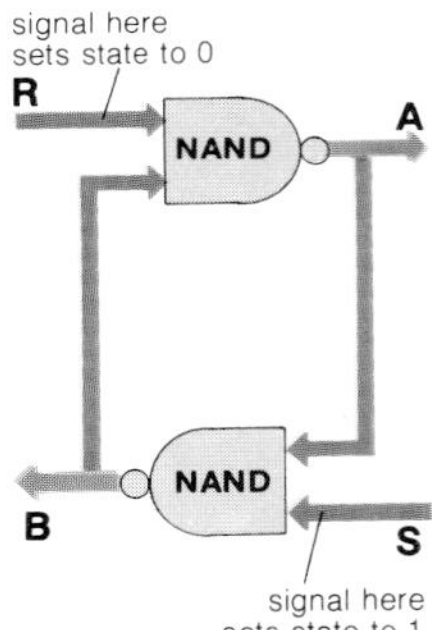

signal

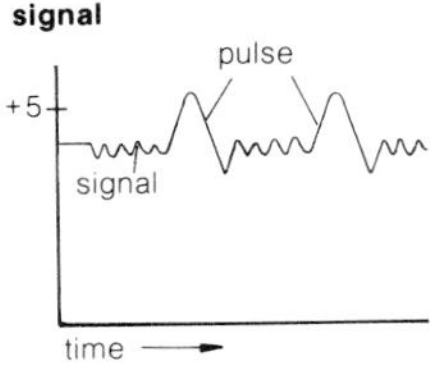

command signal a signal (↑) or pulse (↑), usually sent by the CPU (p. 31), which forces some part of the circuitry of the machine to perform its work.

sensing signal a signal (↑) which is sent in front of data so that the device to which it is sent can be made ready to receive the data which follows.

handshake (*n*) a set of signals (↑) whose purpose is to synchronize (p. 13) the transfer of data between two devices.

converter (*n*) a type of circuit which can change signals (↑) from one form to another, e.g. an analog-to-digital converter (↓).

converter

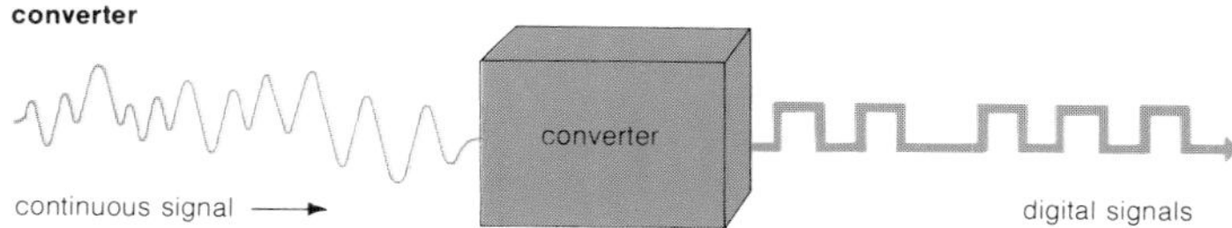

delay line a device or circuit which can receive a signal (↑) and then send out the same signal after a very short interval of time. Commonly used in earlier computers.

analog-digital converter a circuit which changes continuous signals (↑) into digital (↑) ones.

Hamming code an error checking (p. 30) code which uses the distance between signals (↑) to detect errors. It can also sometimes correct the errors.

clock (*n*) (1) a circuit which sends out signals (↑) or pulses (↑) so that there is exactly the same interval of time between them. It is used to make sure that a computer operates its other circuits at the correct time; (2) = timer (p. 24).

clock signal a signal (↑) or pulse (↑) sent out by a clock (↑). Also known as **clock pulse**.

master clock the main, or only, clock (↑) in a CPU (p. 31).

clock track a track (p. 68) on which clock (↑) pulses or signals (↑) are stored and which can be used by a computer either to check or to operate the device which contains the track.

cycle (*n*) a fixed interval of time between two signals (↑). **cycle** (*v*).

timer (*n*) a part of a computer, usually a special register (p. 14), which is used to hold the time of day, commonly to the nearest hundredth of a second. Programs can use it either to print out the time at which they run, or to measure the amount of time which the user is allowed. It can be used to control when programs can be run.

cycle time (1) the time taken to read a unit of data, usually either a byte (p. 17) or a word (p. 47), from memory and into the CPU (p. 31); (2) = cycle (p. 23).

switch[1] (*n*) (1) a part of a circuit which can be set to on or off, or which can be used in some way to change the path by which data or signals (p. 22) can pass through the circuits in a computer; (2) a small arm which can be set to on or off, similar to an electric light switch.

electronic switch a circuit which performs in the same way as a switch (↑), i.e. it can be set to one of usually two positions, and can change the flow of signals (p. 22) through a circuit. It works very quickly, in about a microsecond.

current (*n*) the flow of electrical charge or power from one point to another along a path, called a conductor. The conductor is usually a metal but other substances can be used.

conductor (*n*) a material, e.g. a metal, which allows an electric current (↑) to pass.

semiconductor (*n*) a material which will allow an electric current (↑) to pass, but not so well as a metal would. It is particularly useful in the circuits needed for computers and is used in almost all the circuits in modern computers.

silicon (*n*) a material which can be used with metals to make a semiconductor (↑). There are other materials which can be used but this is the most common one for computer circuits.

chip (*n*) a very small piece of silicon (↑) or a wafer (↓) which contains a number of circuits. The circuits are usually ones which can carry out some particular action required by a computer. The circuits of modern computers consist of large numbers of chips which are placed on boards and connected together. Also known as **silicon chip**, **micro chip**.

switch manual

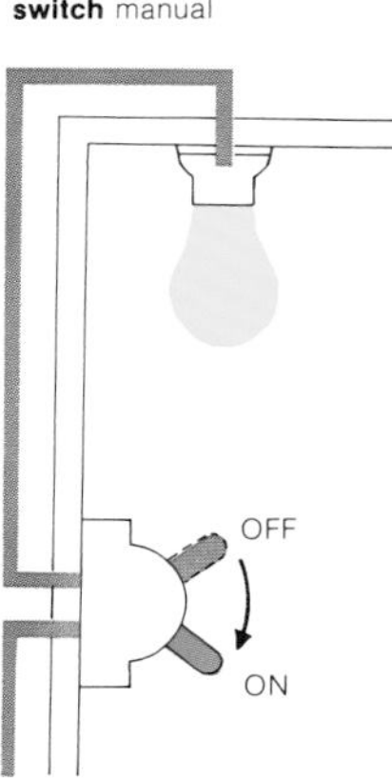

simple electronic switch

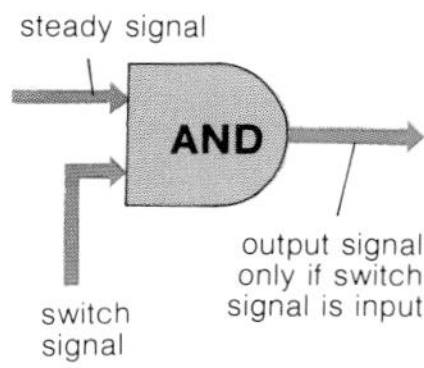

wafer (*n*) a very thin piece of material, usually silicon (↑), which has a number of very small circuits placed on it.

transistor (*n*) a small device or circuit which is a semiconductor (↑) and is used in the circuits of a computer.

solid state of a circuit whose parts consist of solid elements, usually semiconductors (↑) such as transistors (↑). Such circuits are not easily broken accidently. In early computers the materials for circuits included materials, such as glass, which were easily damaged.

integrated circuit a number of simple circuits joined together so that they act as a single circuit which can perform more difficult work.

MSI medium scale integration. It is similar to LSI (↓) but the number of circuits grouped together is smaller.

LSI large scale integration. A large number of circuits are grouped together and placed on a wafer (↑) and then covered and sealed against damp or dust. Commonly it simply means the use of chips (↑).

VLSI very large scale integration.

transputer (*n*) a processor on a single chip (↑).

adder (*n*) a circuit which takes two digits (p. 16) as inputs and outputs their sum. Also known as **digital adder**.

subtracter (*n*) a circuit which takes two digits as inputs and outputs their difference.

adder-subtracter (*n*) a circuit which can act as an adder (↑) or a subtracter (↑) depending on the command signal (p. 23) which it receives.

two-input adder a circuit which has two inputs and two outputs. The inputs are digits (p. 16) to be added and the outputs are the sum of the digits and any carry-bit (p. 26) which is produced. Also known as **half adder**.

two-input adder

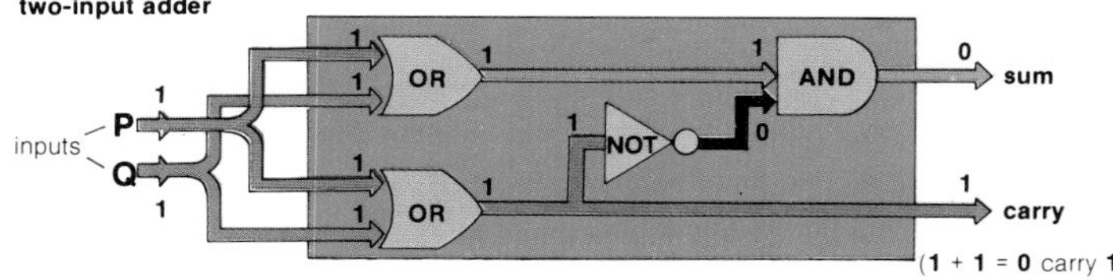

(**1** + **1** = **0** carry **1**)

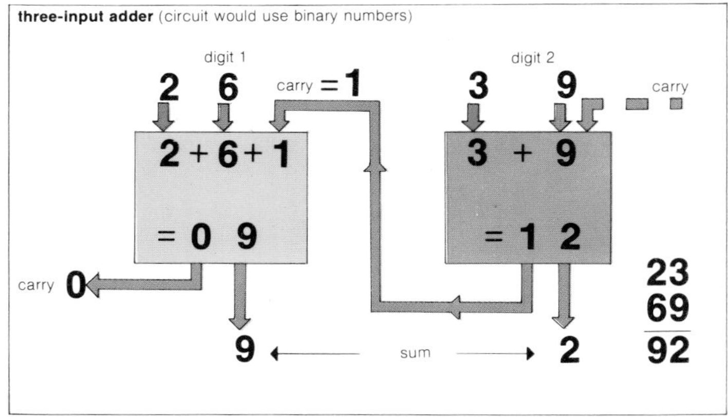

three-input adder a circuit which has three inputs. Two of these are digits (p. 16) to be added together, the third is a carry-bit (↓) from the addition of two earlier digits. There are two outputs, the digit which results from the addition and any carry-bit which may be produced. Also known as **full adder**.

carry-bit (*n*) a bit (p. 17) which is produced when two digits (p. 16) are added and the result is too large to be stored as a single digit. The part of the sum which is too large is carried into the next position by setting the carry-bit to a value of 1.

end-around carry a carry-bit (↑) which is produced in the high-order (p. 50) position and causes a bit to be fed into the low-order (p. 50) position.

addend (*n*) one of the two operands (p. 15) used in an adder (p. 25) circuit. The other is often called the augend (↓). The value in the addend is not changed by the addition.

augend (*n*) one of the two operands (p. 15) used in addition in an adder (p. 25) circuit, the other being the addend (↑). The sum resulting from the addition usually replaces the original value in the augend.

control unit and channels

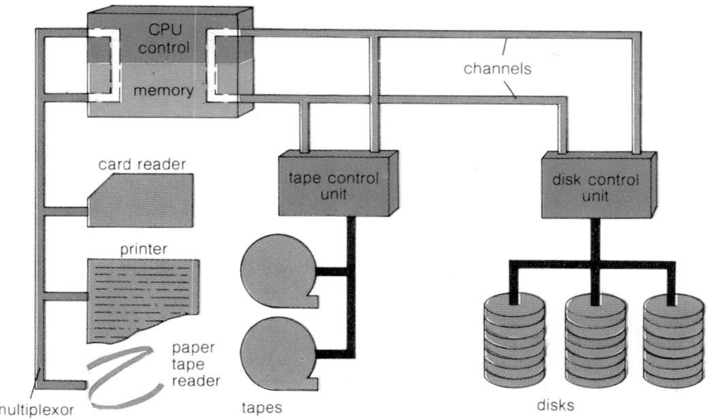

control unit a device which controls the transfer of data along a channel (↓) to another device. The unit may have its own separate circuits or it may be operated by a program in a computer. The CPU (p. 31) contains a control unit which may also control the peripheral devices (p. 12) in addition to the memory and the ALU (p. 31), but it is usual for each group of tapes (p. 71) or disks (p. 66) to have a control unit of their own which is separate from the CPU. These control units have their own registers (p. 14) together with their own circuits for error detection (p. 13) and error correction (p. 13). Also known as **controller**.

decoder (*n*) a circuit which changes the data, usually control data, received by the CPU (p. 31) into another form so that the CPU can use it to operate its other circuits.

channel (*n*) a wire, or a group of wires or other form of conductor along which data or signals (p. 22) can be sent from one part of a computer to another, e.g. from the CPU (p. 31) to a peripheral device (p. 12). Also known as a **bus** or **highway**.

bus (*n*) = channel (↑).

highway (*n*) = channel (↑).

data channel a channel (p. 27) along which data can pass between the CPU (p. 31) and a peripheral device (p. 12). Also known as **input-output channel**.

multiplexor (*n*) a data channel (↑) which allows more than one device to send data along it at the same time. The devices are usually slow speed ones such as printers.

selector channel a data channel (↑) which allows data to pass at high speed but deals only with one device at a time. It is used to transfer data from devices such as tapes (p. 71) or disks (p. 66).

mass bus = selector channel (↑).

trunk (*n*) a data channel (↑) between two devices which can carry a number of streams of data. The devices are usually switching (p. 24) circuits, e.g. telephone exchanges. **trunk** (*v*).

path (*n*) (1) a channel (p. 27) or connected channels along which data or signals (p. 22) can be moved between two devices; (2) the route through a directory (p. 107).

burst mode a condition in which data is transferred in separate groups and not in a continuous stream. Most data is transferred in this manner but the word usually means that the data is being transferred from a high speed device, e.g. a tape (p. 71) or disk (p. 66), not from a slow one such as a printer.

interleave[1] (*v*) to transfer data from two peripheral devices (p. 12) at the same time. A small amount of data from one device is transferred followed by the transfer of a small amount from the other device and so on. It is possible to do this if the devices are slow, e.g. a printer and a card reader (p. 54), because there are pauses between the individual pieces of data from each device.

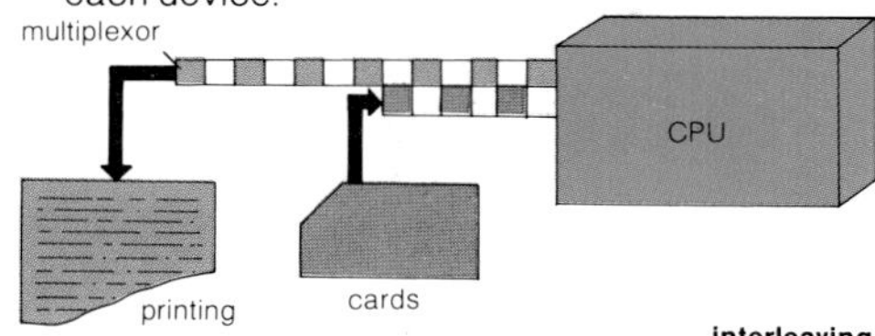

interleaving

drop-out (*n*) an error condition which is caused by one or more bits (p. 17) being accidentally lost during the transfer of data.

cycle stealing a process in which one device, usually a control unit (p. 27), uses spare cycles (p. 23) from another device, usually the CPU (p. 31), to transfer data. By using spare CPU cycles it is possible to speed up the movement of data.

channel status word a word (p. 47) in memory which holds information about the results of an input-output operation. At the end of the operation the computer examines the contents of the word for a number of things, e.g. to see how much data was transferred by the operation, whether there were any errors etc.

standard interface an interface (p. 22) which has been made in such a way that it is possible to join together different parts of a computer e.g. a control unit (p. 27) to a peripheral device (p. 12) without having to provide more circuits. It can also mean a way of connecting programs, or parts of programs, without the need to provide any more instructions.

check bit a bit (p. 17) which is attached to some data but is not part of the data. It is used to check that the data is correct. A common way is to set it equal to 1 if the number of bits in the data is odd, but equal to 0 if the number of bits is even.

parity bit

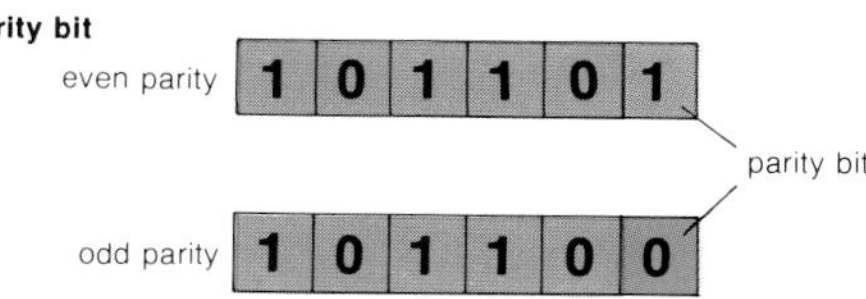

parity bit a bit (p. 17) attached to data and set either to 0 or 1 so that the total number of bits which are equal to 1 is either even, known as *even-parity*, or odd, known as *odd-parity*. It is used to make sure that a bit which is part of the data does not accidentally change in value when the data is transferred.

parity check (1) the detection of an error using a parity bit (p. 29); (2) a method which uses one or more parity bits to detect, and possibly correct, errors.

error check a condition which can be set in a circuit if it detects an error either in the working of the circuit or in the data being sent.

check register a register (p. 14) where data is placed and is then compared to the same data in a different register to make sure that it has been received correctly.

start and stop bits

start bit a bit (p. 17) or signal (p. 22) which causes the device which receives it to prepare to perform its work. Usually the device is one which is going to receive data but it can be any device which stops and starts.

stop bit a bit (p. 17) or signal (p. 22) which causes a device to stop working. Usually the device is one which receives data but it can be any device which stops and starts.

enable (*v*) to allow something to be possible when it had been prevented. For example, a terminal (p. 79) which had been disabled (↓) could be enabled. It could then transmit and receive data.

disable (*v*) to prevent a device or circuit from doing something which it could otherwise do. For example, a terminal (p. 79) could be prevented from sending or receiving data to or from the CPU (↓).

inhibit (*v*) = disable (↑).

servo-mechanism (*n*) a circuit or piece of equipment which continuously measures the results of the actions of part of a machine and uses the results to decide whether to continue the action or to change it.

structure of a computer

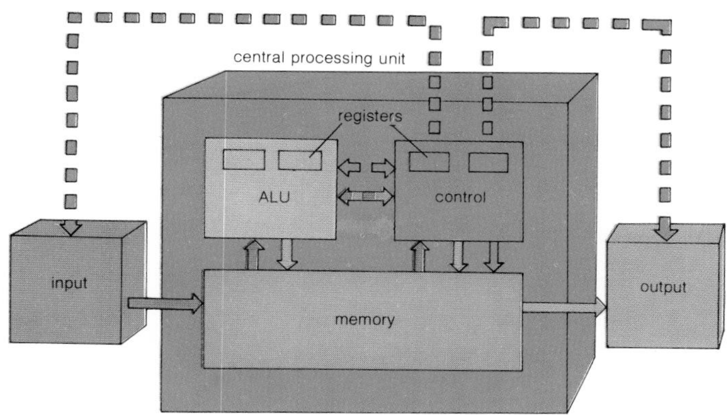

CPU central processing unit. The main part of a computer which has three sections; memory, an arithmetic logic unit (↓), and a control unit (p. 27). The memory holds instructions and data, the control unit takes the instructions and arranges for them to be carried out using the arithmetic logic unit where necessary. The control unit also starts the transfer of data between memory and any peripheral device (p. 12), e.g. a printer which is connected to the CPU.

central processing unit = CPU (↑).

central processor = CPU (↑).

processor = CPU (↑).

arithmetic logic unit ALU. The part of the CPU (↑) in which all arithmetical instructions (p. 35) and logical instructions (p. 34) are actually carried out. Data is held in memory and passed to the ALU when necessary and the results are then usually stored in memory.

ALU = arithmetic logic unit (↑).

general purpose register a register (p. 14) in the CPU (↑) which can be used by programs for calculations, or for storing addresses. A computer usually has 4 to 16 such registers.

register size the amount of data that a register (p. 14) can hold. For general purpose registers (p. 31) it is normally the same as the word length (p. 47) of the machine and the size is said to be the number of bits (p. 17) it will hold. Usual sizes are 8, 16 or 32 bits, depending on the size of the computer. Registers which have a special purpose, e.g. floating-point registers (↓), usually have a different size which depends on their use.

address register a register (p. 14) which is used only to hold addresses.

memory address register MAR. A special register (p. 14) in the CPU (p. 31). It is used to hold in memory the address of a location whose data is being read or written.

MAR = memory address register (↑).

memory buffer register MBR. A special register (p. 14) in the CPU (p. 31). When data is being moved between memory and other parts of the computer the address is held in the memory address register (↑) but the actual data is transferred using the memory buffer register.

MBR = memory buffer register (↑).

program counter a special register (p. 14) in the CPU (p. 31). It holds the address of the location of the next instruction to be carried out after the present one is completed.

instruction address register = program counter (↑).

sequence control register = program counter (↑).

instruction register a special register (p. 14) in the CPU (p. 31). It holds the complete instruction, i.e. op-code (p. 15) and operands (p. 15), which is actually being carried out.

control register (1) = program counter (↑); (2) a special register (p. 14) as opposed to a general purpose register (p. 31); (3) = instruction register (↑).

buffer register a register (p. 14) used to hold data during its transfer from one part of the computer to another.

floating-point register a register (p. 14) in the CPU (p. 31) which is used for calculations but can deal only with numbers in floating-point (p. 51) form.

register sizes

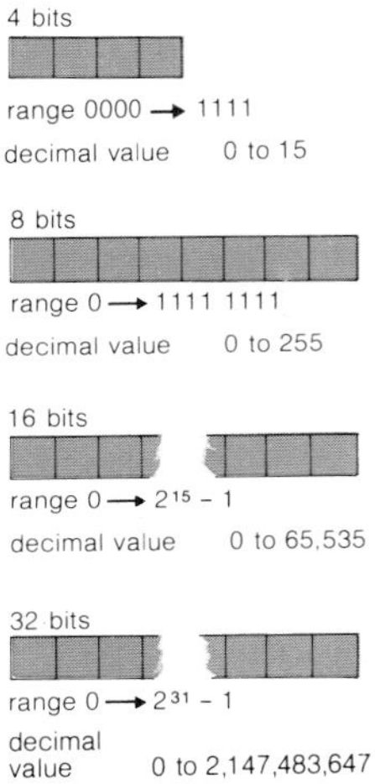

4 bits

range 0000 → 1111

decimal value 0 to 15

8 bits

range 0 → 1111 1111

decimal value 0 to 255

16 bits

range 0 → $2^{15} - 1$

decimal value 0 to 65,535

32 bits

range 0 → $2^{31} - 1$

decimal value 0 to 2,147,483,647

micro-instruction (*n*) the simplest form of a computer instruction. It is provided by the action of a circuit. The micro-instruction may be one of the computer's instruction set (p. 34) but more often a number of such micro-instructions have to be carried out in order to do a single computer instruction.

micro-code (*n*) instructions which can be carried out by selecting some of the circuits from a group of micro-instruction (↑) circuits. The instruction set (p. 34) for a computer is now usually provided in this way rather than by a separate circuit for each instruction.

fetch cycle the steps which a CPU (p. 31) takes to get an instruction from memory and bring it into the control unit (p. 27) of the CPU in order to execute it. **fetch** (*n*), **fetch** (*v*).

fetch cycle

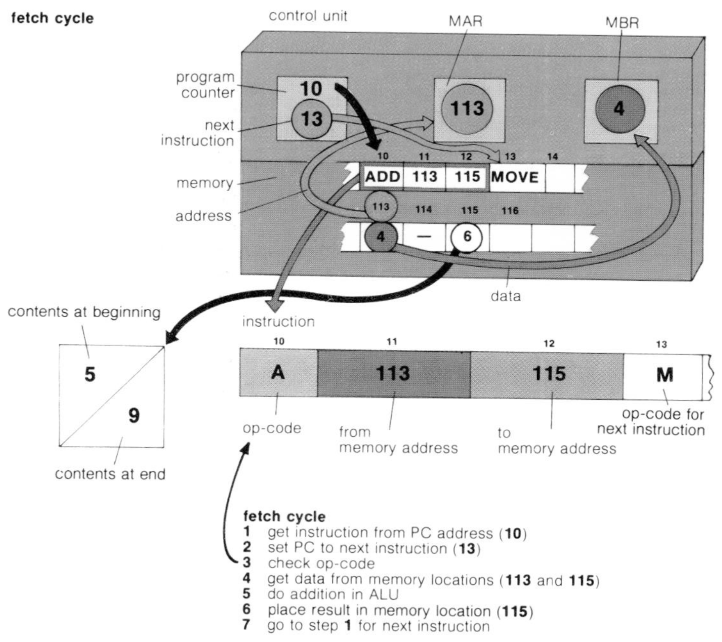

micro-program (*n*) a special type of program which uses micro-instructions (p. 33) to perform some act. It usually does the work needed to do one of the computer's instructions, e.g. a computer may do multiplication by a micro-program which does repeated addition.

instruction set the complete range of instructions which a particular computer can execute. The size of the range is different for different computers. The smallest machines have 40 to 50 separate instructions; the largest machines have 100 to 150. A small machine may therefore have to execute several instructions to do what a large machine could do in a single instruction. Machines are now being made with a reduced instruction set (RIS), that is around 50 to 60 instructions.

instruction time the time it takes for an instruction to be fetched (p. 33) and executed. Different instructions take different times to execute and computer manufacturers often print tables showing the time for each instruction, especially times for arithmetic instructions, because these are often used to compare the speed of different computers.

logical instruction an instruction which examines a statement to decide whether it is true or false, i.e. the answer must be yes or no. For example it might look to see whether a register (p. 14) is equal to 0. As a result of its examination it will set a circuit in the CPU (p. 31), or a switch (p. 120) in a program, to a value which can then be tested. It does not move or change the data being examined in any way.

logical operation a logical instruction (↑) or a group of them. The common ones are AND (↓), OR (↓) and NOT (↓).

logical operator one of the operators such as AND (↓) or NOT (↓).

AND (*n*) a logical instruction (↑) or operation (↑) which examines two or more inputs, and gives an answer of true only if all the inputs are true. Thus we might choose to do something only if A = 1 and B = 2; any different values of either A or B would mean the thing would not be done.

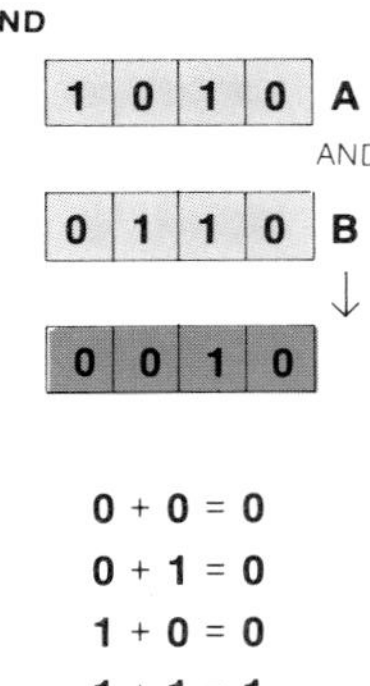

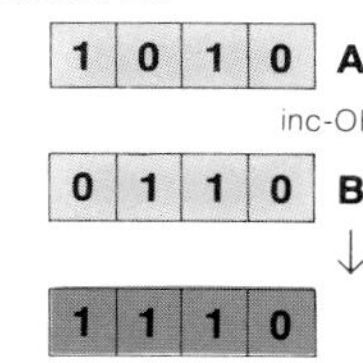

0 + 0 = 0
0 + 1 = 1
1 + 0 = 1
1 + 1 = 1

exclusive-OR

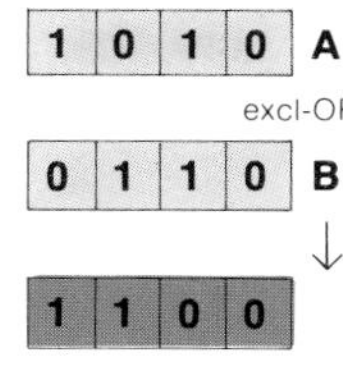

0 + 0 = 0
0 + 1 = 1
1 + 0 = 1
1 + 1 = 0

inclusive-OR (*n*) a logical instruction (↑) which gives a result of true if any one of the inputs is true. For example, if something is to be done
  if A = 1 or B = 2,
then it is done
  if A = 1, or B = 2, or
  if A = 1 and B = 2.
This is the common meaning of the OR (↓) instruction.

exclusive-OR (*n*) a logical instruction (↑) which gives a result of true if one, and only one, of the inputs is true. For example, if something is to be done
  if A = 1 or B = 2,
then it is done
  if A = 1 but B ≠ 2, or
  if B = 2 and A ≠ 1,
but not
  if A = 1 and B = 2.
This is the less common meaning of the OR (↓) instruction.

OR (*n*) (1) = inclusive-OR (↑); (2) = exclusive-OR (↑).

NOT (*n*) a logical operation (↑) which gives a result of true when the opposite of a statement is true. For example, the words 'If not A' mean that something is done only if A is not true.

equivalence (*n*) a logical operation (↑) which gives the result true if all the inputs are true or if they are all false.

arithmetic instruction an instruction which will perform arithmetic, e.g. an add instruction.

arithmetic operation an arithmetic instruction (↑) or group of instructions which will perform arithmetic calculations.

shift (*v*) to move all the digits (p. 16) or characters held in a register (p. 14), or occasionally in an area of memory, either to the right or the left. The characters or digits moved past the end of the register or area are usually lost, the spaces which appear at the other end are filled with 0s or 1s depending on the exact type of shift. **shift** (*n*).

shift register a special register (p. 14), usually in the ALU (p. 31), which is used only for shifting (↑).

arithmetic shift a process in which the digits (p. 16) in a register (p. 14) are moved either to the right or to the left. Digits shifted beyond the end of the register are dropped. If the shift is to the right, the sign bit (p. 49), which is in the high-order position, is used to fill the spaces which become empty. This is called *sign propagation*, and keeps the sign of the number the same. If the shift is to the left the sign bit may be lost, but the loss can be detected by the CPU (p. 31). For example, starting with + 1234 a shift to the right would produce ++ 123, a shift to the left would produce 12340. If the number is positive it has the same effect as multiplication or division of the register by the radix (p. 48) of the number.

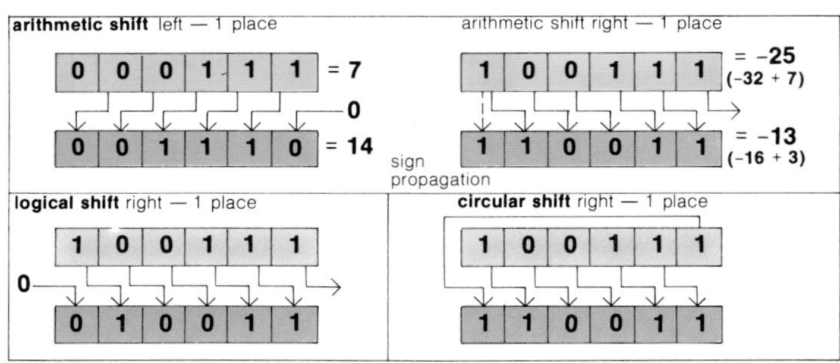

logical shift (1) a shift (p. 35) of data held in a register (p. 14), which moves the bits (p. 17) either to the right or to the left. Any bits moved beyond one end of the register are lost. No attempt is made to keep the sign; (2) = circular shift (↓).

circular shift a shift (p. 35) where any bits (p. 17) moved past one end of the register (p. 14) are moved into the other end of the register. At the end of the operation the original bits are still in the register but they have all moved the same number of places to the right, or left.

end-around shift = circular shift (↑).

rotational shift = circular shift (↑).

compare (*v*) to examine two things to see whether they are equal or whether one is larger than the other. The machine's collating sequence (p. 46) is used to make the decision. Computers have instructions which will compare the contents of variables (p. 119), registers (p. 14), etc in different ways in order to decide what to do next. **comparison** (*n*).

branch instruction A program consists of a sequence of instructions which are done one after the other. It is often necessary to carry out instructions which are not the next ones in the sequence but are at another part of the program. A branch instruction is one which tells the computer to go to a part of the program which is not the next in sequence. **branch** (*n*), **branch** (*v*).

jump instruction = branch instruction (↑).

execute instruction an instruction that causes a program to do another instruction which is not the next in sequence. The program then continues with the usual order. It allows a single instruction to be changed more easily than would otherwise be possible.

no-op (*n*) an instruction which does nothing, (although it may allow an address register (p. 32) to be set to a new value). It is often used by programs to allow other instructions to be placed correctly in memory.

no-operation = no-op (↑).

do-nothing instruction = no-op (↑).

halt (*n*) an instruction which stops a program from continuing. **halt** (*v*).

single step operation a process in which a computer is made to operate in a special manner so that it does only a single instruction and then waits. This makes it possible to examine the complete effect of an instruction. It is used when trying to find the cause of errors in programs, or faults in the computer.

simultaneous operation a process in which two or more operations happen at the same time. This is usually done by interleaving (p. 28) the operations but if there are two circuits then each can handle an operation at the same time.

von Neumann (1) an American who designed a very early form of computer; (2) a computer which operates by processing one instruction after another, instead of doing two or more instructions at the same time. Most present day computers are von Neumann machines.

parallel operation a process in which two operations can happen at the same time. It is not the same as simply interleaving (p. 28) two operations; the device must have two sets of circuits for parallel operation. Computers are now being made with CPUs (p. 31) which will work in this way.

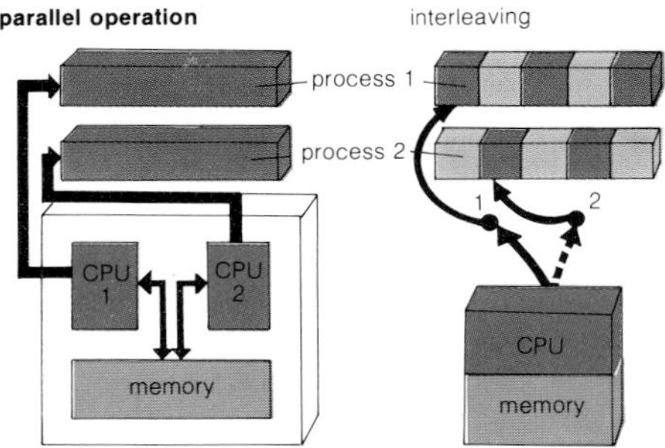

multi-processor (*n*) (1) a computer consisting of two or more CPUs (p. 31) which work together; (2) a computer with one CPU which can perform two or more programs at once by interleaving (p. 28) its work. This operation should be called multi-programming (p. 140).

I-O bound of a CPU (p. 31) not fully loaded. It could do more work, but cannot get any because the data channels (p. 28) are already transferring data as fast as they can.

compute bound of a CPU (p. 31) completely busy performing instructions and unable to go any faster even though the peripheral devices (p. 12) attached to it are not operating at full speed.

write inhibit to prevent a program from writing on to a storage device (p. 199) or possibly to memory. It is used to prevent accidental over-writing of data and can be done either by a special circuit or by instructions in a program.

protection (*n*) a means of preventing part of a computer from being used. For example, it may prevent part of memory used by one program from being accidentally used by another program which is in a different part of memory. Most machines which allow multi-programming (p. 140) or multi-access (p. 10) have circuits or software (p. 14) which provide protection for parts of the machine. **protect** (*v*).

interrupt (*n*) a special signal (p. 22) that can be sent by any device or program and which tells the CPU (p. 31) that something has happened which needs attention, e.g. an input-output operation has been completed and should be checked for possible errors, or a user may want to enter some data through a terminal (p. 79), or a program may want some data from a peripheral device (p. 12). The program that is being executed at the time is usually stopped while the operating system (p. 130) handles the cause of the interrupt. Once this has been done the program is allowed to continue. Computers make considerable use of interrupts to control the way they work. **interrupt** (*v*).

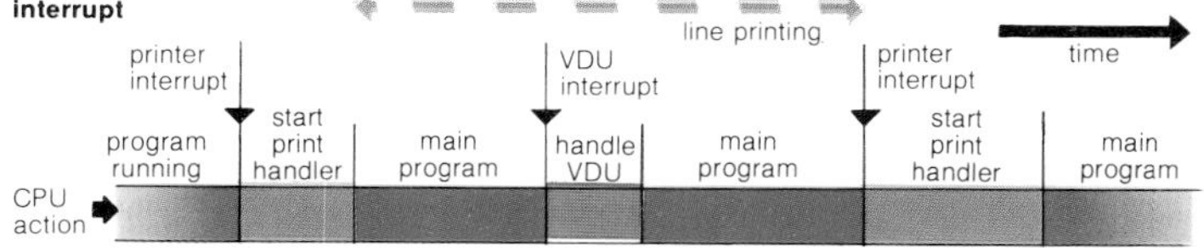

trap (*n*) a condition that happens when a program or a device does something which is not expected or allowed, e.g. an attempt to divide by 0. Such an event is detected by the CPU (p. 31) and the operating system (p. 130) will usually take some action to deal with it. **trap** (*v*).

mask[1] (*v*) to shut off, or inhibit (p. 30), interrupts (p. 39) so that they are not accepted or processed by an operating system (p. 130).

mask[2] (*n*) an arrangement of bits (p. 17) or characters which is used to pick out some, but not all, of the bits or characters in another bit pattern (p. 50).

program status word a word (p. 47) in memory which holds the information needed to continue a program after it has been halted to allow an interrupt (p. 39) to be handled. It will contain the address of the instruction where the program stopped, the state (↓) of special switches (p. 24), etc.

status word = program status word (↑).

state (*n*) the condition of a circuit or program at a particular point of time. Often used of a circuit which can have several possible values.

busy (*adj*) of a state (↑) when a device, such as a printer or a disk (p. 66), is working and cannot accept more work. This condition can be detected by the CPU (p. 31) and the operating system (p. 130) will cause programs which want to use the device to wait until it is free.

backspace[1] (*v*) to go backwards one space, or one record (p. 154), so that data which has been read or written can be re-read or re-written. It is possible to backspace some devices, e.g. a tape reel (p. 71), but not others, e.g. a card reader (p. 54) or a disk (p. 66).

re-set[1] (*v*) to put something back into the condition it was in at the start. It may be a device, e.g. a tape (p. 71) which is re-wound (p. 73) back to its starting point, or a computer after some fault has happened.

re-set[2] (*n*) the action of setting parts of memory, being used as counters (p. 15), or accumulators (p. 15), or switches (p. 24) back to the values they had at the beginning of a program.

busy test

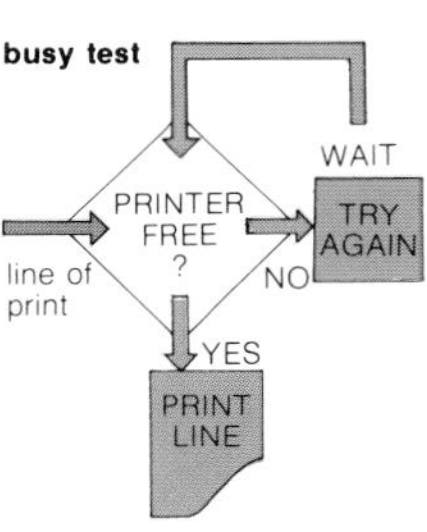

backspacing a tape

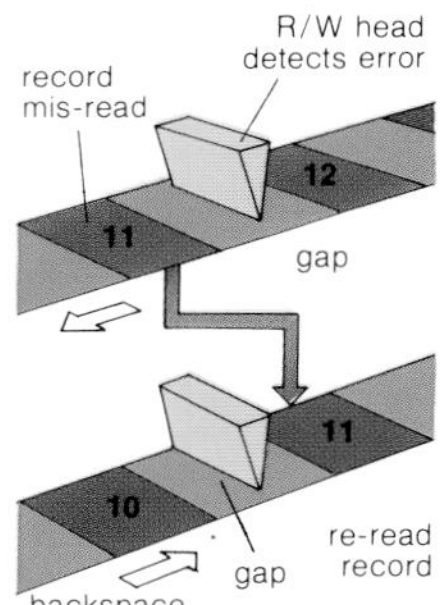

main memory the part of a computer that holds the instructions and data so that they are immediately available. The instructions are used by the control unit (p. 27) to act upon the data either by calculation, or by moving the data to other parts of memory or between the CPU (p. 31) and the peripheral devices (p. 12).

main store = main memory (↑).

primary storage = main memory (↑).

main storage = main memory (↑).

store[1] (*n*) = main memory (↑).

internal memory memory held in the CPU (p. 31). It usually means the same as main memory (↑) but can sometimes mean other forms such as cache memory (p. 42).

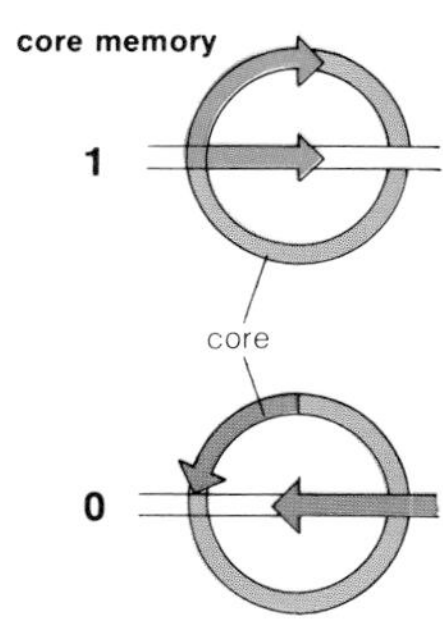

RAM random access memory = main memory (↑).

immediate access store a store such as main memory (↑), which can be accessed very quickly and without using a read-write head (p. 202).

core memory = main memory (↑). In early computers memory was made by using very small rings of metal called cores.

core (*n*) = core memory (↑).

ferrite core = core memory (↑).

core plane a board, part of which holds a piece of a core memory (↑), and which can be connected to the CPU (p. 31).

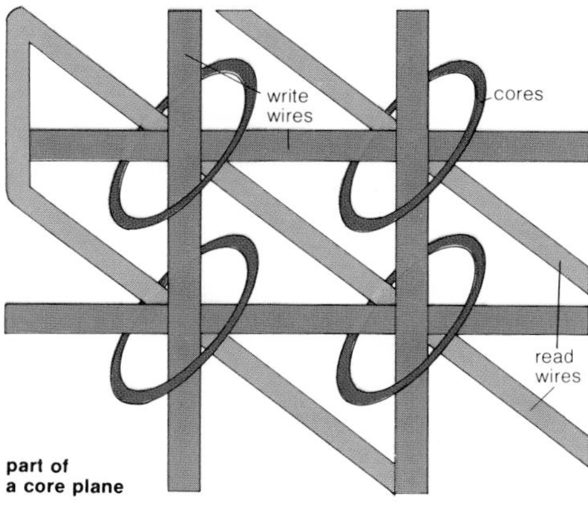

part of a core plane

cache memory memory which is held in the CPU (p. 31) and operates at a higher speed than the main memory (p. 41). It cannot be used by a programmer. It holds a copy of a small part of main memory which has just been used; if the same data is needed again, it can be found more quickly. It can hold data from I-0 devices.

scratch pad a special memory, usually faster than main memory (p. 41), which can hold the results of preceding instructions ready for use by later ones.

associative memory memory whose locations are found by using the contents of the locations instead of the memory address.

content addressable memory = associative memory (↑).

cryogenic store memory which works only at very low temperatures.

thin film memory which uses a magnetic material on a film. It is not generally used.

volatile memory

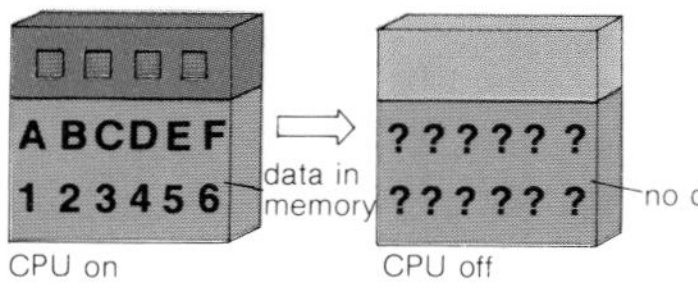

non-volatile memory

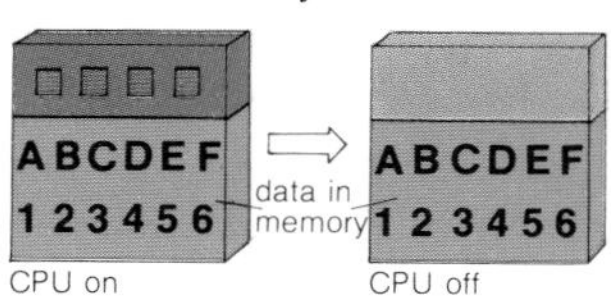

volatile memory memory in which the contents are lost if the computer is turned off.

non-volatile memory memory which continues to hold data if the computer is turned off.

non-erasable memory memory which can be read but not over-written or cleared.

read-only memory memory which can be read but not over-written.

ROM = read-only memory (↑).

PROM programmable read-only memory. A read-only memory (↑) whose contents are usually left unchanged but which can be changed by using a special circuit if necessary.

EPROM erasable programmable read-only memory. A memory whose contents are fixed: they can be read but it is only possible to over-write them by using special equipment.

non-destructive read-out the process of reading the contents of memory but leaving those contents unchanged.

destructive read the process of reading memory in a way that causes the contents to be lost.

memory cycle (1) the act of reading from or writing to main memory (p. 41); (2) the time taken to read or write a single memory location.

storage access cycle the time taken to complete the reading or writing of one location of memory.

memory protection the process by which memory is allowed to be read but not written. It can also mean that a part of memory cannot be accessed by any program except the one to which it belongs. This may be done either by hardware (p. 14) or software (p. 14) or the use of the two together.

memory protection

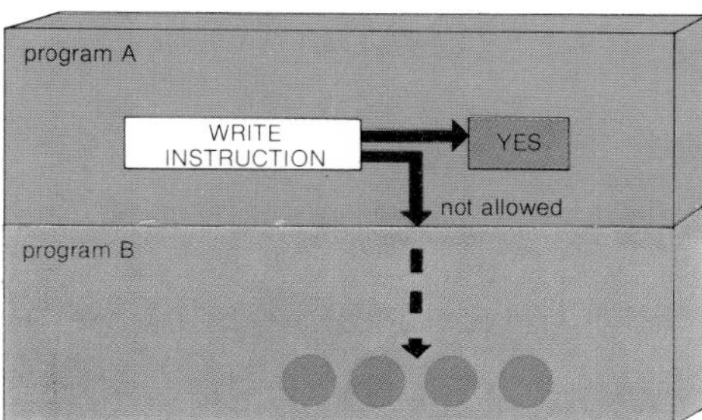

mass store a store usually in the form of a direct access device (p. 67). It can be a slow form of memory. It holds very large amounts of data which cannot be accessed as quickly as main memory (p. 41).

capacity (*n*) the amount of data that can be held in memory or on tape (p. 71) or disk (p. 66). The unit of measure is usually bytes (p. 17) or words (p. 47).

megabit (*n*) a million bits (p. 17). It is used as a measure of storage capacity (↑).

megabyte (*n*) a million bytes (p. 17). It is used as a unit of measure of storage capacity (↑).

gigabyte (*n*) a thousand million bytes (p. 17). It is used as a measure of storage capacity (↑).

virtual memory
16K program

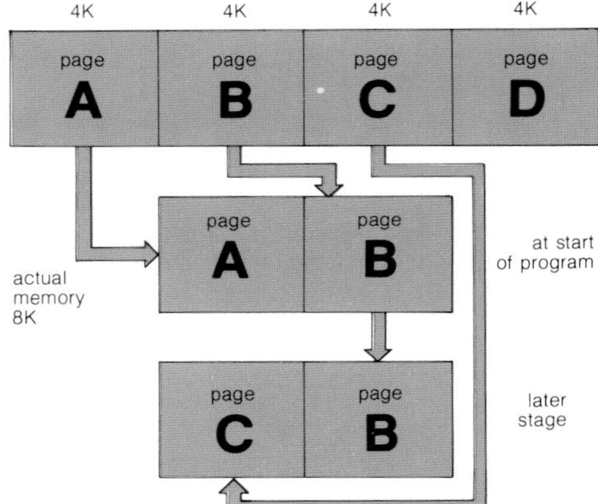

virtual memory a system where memory appears to be much larger than is actually available. The addresses of the virtual memory are mapped (p. 118) on to the actual memory. It allows programs to be written as if they were on a larger computer but the whole of the program is never in memory at the same time.

virtual storage = virtual memory (↑).

virtual address an address in virtual memory (↑).

virtual machine a computer and its peripheral devices (p. 12) which is simulated (p. 108) by another computer so that the simulated computer has no fixed memory size.

storage allocation the process of deciding which parts of memory can be allocated (p. 134) to each program that is being run. It also includes deciding how much memory can be used for general things which are used by more than one program, e.g. input-output buffers (p. 161).

storage protection a means of preventing the memory being used by one program from being either accidentally or purposely overwritten by another program. It is usually provided on medium or large computers.

storage allocation

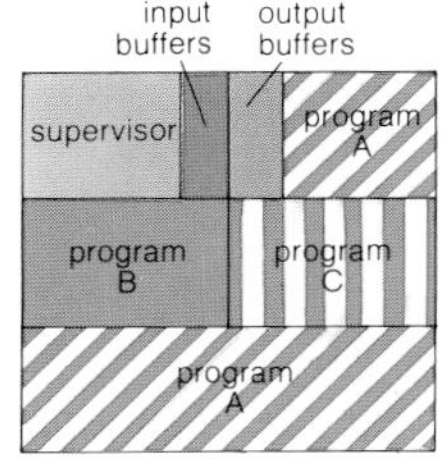

representation (*n*) the form in which data is held. For example, a number may be held in binary (p. 16) or in decimal (p. 16) form; each is a different representation of the same thing. **represent** (*v*).

code^2 (*n*) the complete set of characters which is contained in any particular representation (↑).

ASCII American Standard Code for Information Interchange. One of the two common ways of setting out all the available characters in a particular order in a computer. Each character has a binary (p. 16) value and when it is stored in memory or on a storage device (p. 199) each byte (p. 17) has its bits (p. 17) set to the value which matches the character's place in the order. For example, the letter A is the 66th character in the order so the byte which stores an A has its bits set to value 65 (the numbering starts from 0). The usual version has 128 possible characters. The other main way of ordering is EBCDIC (↓), which is similar but has 256 characters. Both codes are given in full on the endpapers.

EBCDIC Extended Binary Coded Decimal Interchange Code. One of the two common ways of setting out all the available characters in a particular order in a computer. It is similar to ASCII (↑) but the order of the characters is different and there are 256 characters instead of 128. Both codes are given in full on the endpapers.

binary coded decimal (1) a representation (↑) where each decimal digit (p. 16) is held as four binary digits (p. 16). For example, the decimal number (p. 16) 7 would be held as 0111; (2) a representation used on early computers. It uses 6 bits to hold digits, the letters A to Z, and some special characters (p. 46).

BCD = binary coded decimal (↑).

alphabet (*n*) (1) the letters a to z (or A to Z); (2) all the letters, numbers and special characters (p. 46) which can be used in a computer. For example, the ASCII (↑) set contains 128 characters in its alphabet, not all of which can be printed. **alphabet** (*adj*). (*See* endpapers).

special character one of the characters of a set which is neither alphabetic (p. 45) nor numeric (p. 15), e.g. $,?,[.

character set the complete arrangement of characters which a computer is able to use. The main ones are ASCII (p. 45) and EBCDIC (p. 45). Some computers can use either, others can only work with one particular set.

character string a group of characters which is of no particular length. Each word in a written sentence, such as this one, is a string of characters.

string[1] (*n*) a group of characters, or bits (p. 17), of no particular length. Computer operations are usually different for each type. The string may have no entries in which case it is generally called a *null string*.

space character a character which causes a space to appear when it is printed. The binary notation (p. 49) in ASCII (p. 45) and EBCDIC (p. 45) has a decimal value of 32, not 0, and the character comes just before the set of printing characters in a collating sequence (↓). **space** (*v*).

space = space character (↑).

blank (*n*) the character which produces a space (↑) when printed or shown on a screen (p. 84). **blank** (*v*).

collating sequence the sequence in which the characters of a character set (↑) will be arranged if they are placed in order of their binary (p. 16) values. The order depends on which character set the computer uses. For example, in ASCII (p. 45) the upper case letters (A-Z) come before the lower case (a-z) and so *A* is considered to be smaller than *a*. In EBCDIC (p. 45) they appear in the opposite order, and so *A* is considered to be larger than *a*. The collating sequence is used by a computer to decide whether one character is larger than another when data is being compared (p. 37) or sorted (p. 169).

collate (*v*) to put into proper order. In a computer it means to arrange data by keys (p. 156), which can be in records (p. 154) or punched cards (p. 52), in the order of the character set (↑).

character set

digits

0 1 2 3 4 5 6 7 8 9

alphabetic upper case

A B C D E F... X Y Z

alphabetic lower case

a b c d e f... x y z

special characters

$? + – ; < =

characters which do not print

parts of ASCII sequence of characters

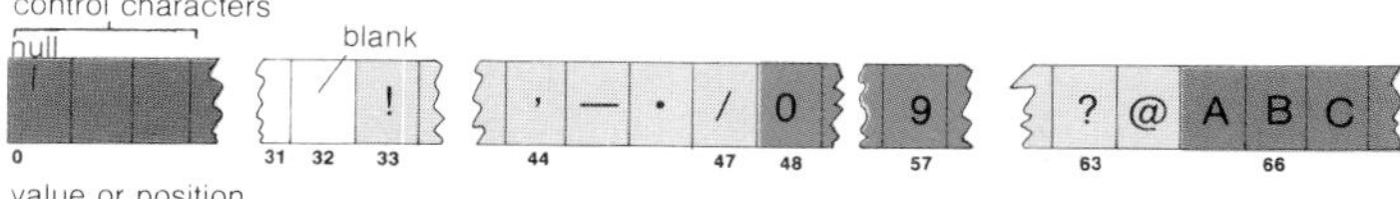

value or position

different collating sequence for ASCII and EBCDIC

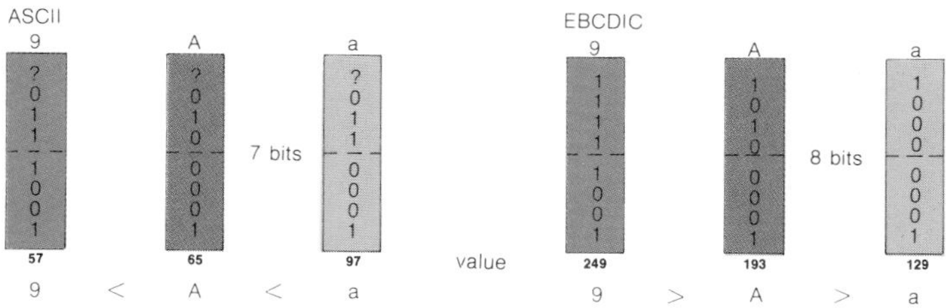

bytes and words
in 32 bit word machine

byte = 8 bits

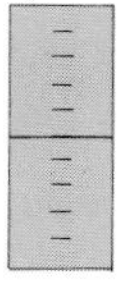

half word = 2 bytes = 16 bits

byte byte

word = 2 half words = 4 bytes = 32 bits

half word half word

upper case of a letter in capitals, e.g. A B C. Most printers will print upper case, some can print lower case (↓) as well.

lower case of a letter which is not in capitals, e.g. a b c. Some printers cannot print lower case.

word (*n*) a group of bytes (p. 17) which a computer can access. The number of bits (p. 17) in the group is usually the same as can be held in one of the general purpose registers (p. 31) of the computer. Common sizes are 8, 16, or 32 bits, i.e. 1, 2, or 4 bytes, depending on the size of the computer. Medium or large computers usually work with 32-bit words, mini (p. 9) or micro-computers (p. 9) with 8, 16 or 32-bit words.

word length the number of bits (p. 17), or bytes (p. 17), in a word (↑).

word size = word length (↑).

full word = word (↑). It is used when the computer is able to access half words (↓) or double words (p. 48).

half word the number of bits (p. 17) or bytes (p. 17) needed to make half of a full word (↑) in a computer. For example, in a 32-bit word there would be four bytes, a half word would be 2 bytes. Larger computers usually have instructions which can access a half word at one time.

double word two words (p. 47) in memory which are used together for some particular purpose especially for double precision (p. 210) calculations. In larger computers they can usually be accessed with a single address.

double word

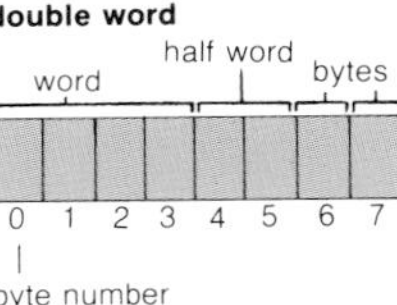

radix (*n*) the number of values which can be held in a single digit (p. 16) position. For example, in the decimal (p. 16) system the radix is 10 and so there are ten values which a single digit can have, i.e. 0–9. In the binary (p. 16) system the radix is two so a binary digit (p. 16) can have only one of the two values 0 or 1.

radix

system	radix	number	decimal value
decimal	10	$111 = 1 \times 10^2 + 1 \times 10^1 + 1 \times 10^0 = 100 + 10 + 1$	111
binary	2	$111 = 1 \times 2^2 + 1 \times 2^1 + 1 \times 2^0 = 4 + 2 + 1$	7
octal	8	$111 = 1 \times 8^2 + 1 \times 8^1 + 1 \times 8^0 = 64 + 8 + 1$	73
hexadecimal	16	$111 = 1 \times 16^2 + 1 \times 16^1 + 1 \times 16^0 = 256 + 16 + 1$	273

zoned decimal a representation (p. 45) in which decimal numbers (p. 16) are held so that there is one digit (p. 16) to each byte (p. 17). The lower four bits (p. 17) of the byte hold the value 0–9; the upper four bits have a value which places the whole byte in the correct place in the collating sequence (p. 46). The upper half byte can also have a value which is used as the sign. This way of storing decimal data is used for display or printing but not calculation.

zoned decimal

F	F	F	F	F
0	1	2	3	4

5 bytes (hex format)

packed decimal a representation (p. 45) in which decimal numbers (p. 16) are held as two decimal digits (p. 16) in each byte (p. 17) of a field (p. 155), except for the right-hand byte which holds one digit (p. 16) and the sign. For example, + 123 would be held in two bytes as 123 +. Some computers can do calculations on numbers held in this way; they do not need to change them into binary numbers (↓).

packed decimal

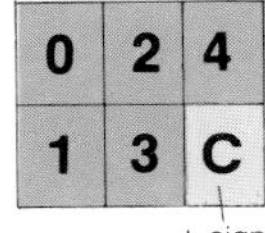

3 bytes (hex format)

unsigned binary
or +ve signed magnitude

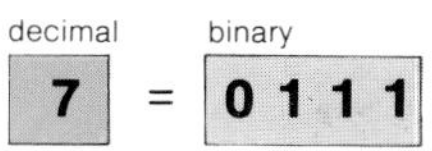

-ve signed binary

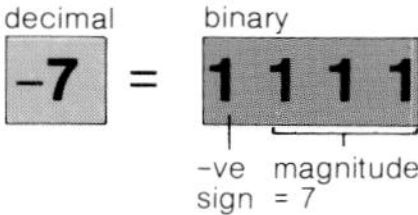

binary notation a representation (p. 45) which uses only the binary digits (p. 16) 0 and 1. It needs more digits (p. 16) than other methods, such as decimal (p. 16), but it is easier for a computer to use because a bit (p. 17) can hold either of the two binary digits.

binary number a number held in binary notation (↑).

magnitude (*n*) the size of number when the sign is not considered e.g. + 100 and - 100 have the same magnitude.

sign bit a bit (p. 17), usually the high-order bit (p. 50), which does not have a value but is used to hold the sign of a number.

signed magnitude a representation (p. 45) of a binary number (↑) where the bytes (p. 17) which hold the number have the high-order bit (p. 50) used for a sign and the remaining bits give the magnitude (↑) of the number. The sign bit is 0 for positive numbers and 1 for negative ones.

complement (*n*) a part needed to make a whole thing. With numbers, the complement of a number added to the number will always give the same result which depends on the radix (↑). For example, decimal numbers (p. 16) have a radix of 10, and to form the complement of the number 234, each digit (p. 16) is subtracted from nine which is one less than the radix. This gives 765 which is the nines complement (↓). If 1 is added to this we get the tens complement, i.e. 766. In a computer the usual radix is two and so the numbers are stored either in ones complement (↓) or twos complement (p. 50) form.

nines complement a number formed by taking a decimal digit (p. 16) and changing to the digit needed to make 9, e.g. the nines complement of 23 is 76. The complement (↑) of a number can be used by a computer to hold negative numbers without the use of a minus sign.

ones complement the binary number (↑) produced by changing all 0 bits (p. 17) to 1, and all 1 bits to 0. For example, 0110 (= decimal 6) has a ones complement of 1001. This method of storing binary numbers can be used to hold negative numbers without use of a minus sign.

forming twos complement

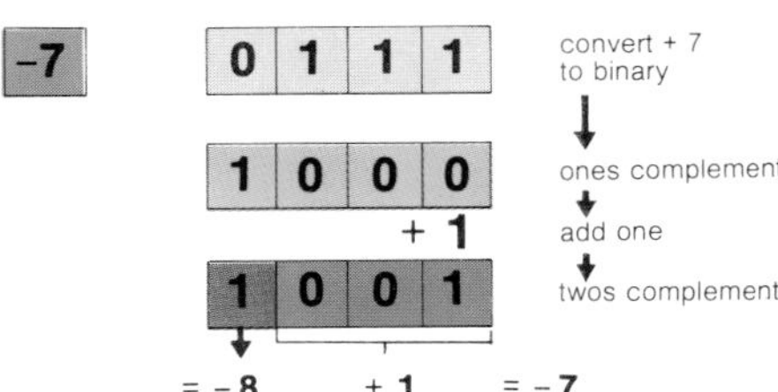

twos complement the number found by first finding the ones complement (p. 49) of a binary (p. 16) number and then adding 1. For example, 0110 has a ones complement of 1001 and so the twos complement is 1010. By giving a negative value to high-order bit (↓) it is possible to hold negative numbers without using a bit (p. 17) just for the minus sign. This is the most common way of holding numbers in a computer.

bit pattern an arrangement of bits (p. 17), usually 8, which is used to hold a particular value. The value may be a number, e.g. 00000100 would be equal to the decimal number (p. 16) 4, or it may be a character, e.g. 00100001, equal to 65 in decimal, is the way in which the ASCII (p. 45) code holds the letter A.

bit string a group of bits (p. 17) which is not of any particular length, i.e. it is not necessarily a byte (p. 17) or a word (p. 47). The string has no numeric (p. 15) value, instead each bit usually has a special meaning for some purpose in the computer.

bit position the number of a bit (p. 17) in a byte (p. 17), a word (p. 47) or a bit string (↑). The numbering is usually from the right and starts with 0 but it is sometimes from the left.

high-order bit the left-hand bit (p. 17) in a number of bits, the one which has the greatest value. For example, in a byte (p. 17), the high-order bit would be the bit with a value of 128.

low-order bit the right-hand bit (p. 17) in a number of bits, i.e. the one with the lowest value, normally 1.

high- and low-order bits

byte

1 0 1 1 0 1 1 0

high-order bit (bit 7)

low-order bit (bit 0)

floating point 32 bit floating point register (numbers in decimal)

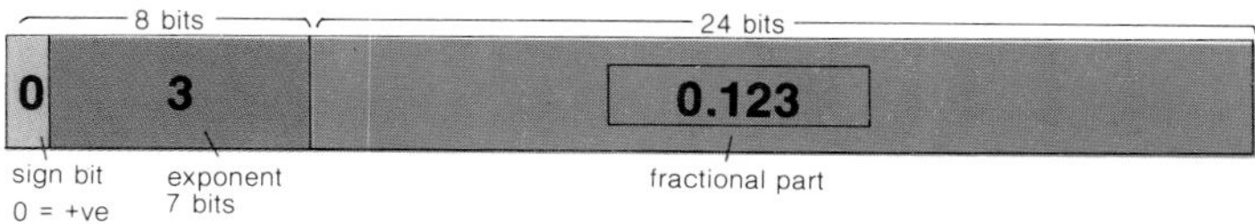

written as

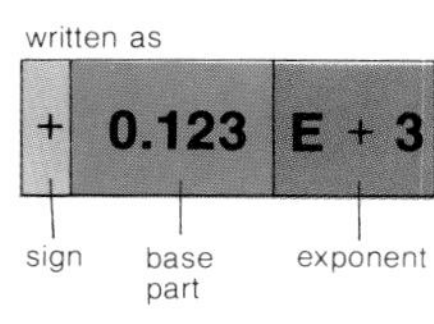

= + **0.123** × **10**^{3} = + **123**

floating-point (*adj*) of a number in two parts: a base part (↓) where the digits are shown as a decimal (p. 16) between 0 and 1, and an exponent (↓) which says how many times the base part is to be multiplied or divided by 10. For example, 0.123 with an exponent of 2 would be 12.3; with an exponent of −2 it would be 0.00123. This allows very large and very small numbers to be held in the same amount of memory. Special floating-point registers (p. 32) and instructions are used to handle numbers held in this form.

base part the first part of a floating-point (↑) number, it is always between 0 and 1.

exponent (*n*) a number which is used to show how many times another number is to be multiplied by the radix (p. 48). It is used in floating-point (↑) numbers to show how many times the base part (↑) is to be multiplied by 10.

characteristic (*n*) the part of a floating-point (↑) number that contains the exponent (↑).

external format the way in which data is stored when it is not held in memory. Data held on backing store (p. 12) or cards (p. 52) may be stored in a different way and need conversion (↓) either by hardware (p. 14) or software (p. 14) before it can be used in memory.

conversion[1] (*n*) (1) the process of changing data from one form to another, e.g. from decimal (p. 16) to binary (p. 16); (2) leaving the data in the same form but changing from one form of storage to another, e.g. taking data held on cards (p. 52) and transferring it to disk (p. 66); (3) changing data from one form of representation (p. 45) to another, e.g. from ASCII (p. 45) to EBCDIC (p. 45), for use on another machine. A conversion may include any or all of these changes. **convert** (*v*).

80 column punch card

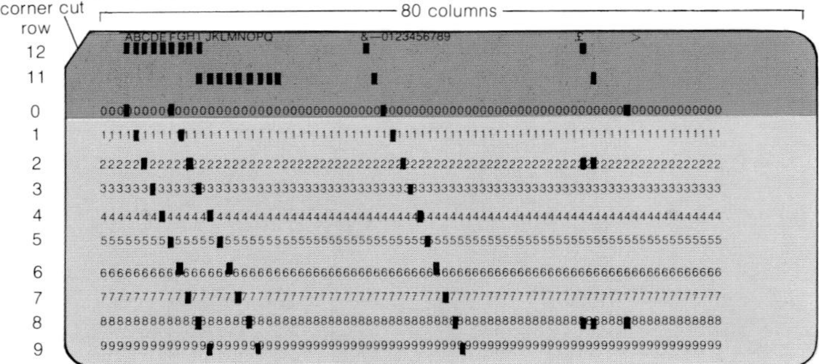

punch card a thin card into which holes can be punched (↓). The way the holes are arranged is used to represent (p. 45) data. The commonest form of punch card is about 19 centimetres by 8 centimetres and has 80 columns (↓) across the card and 12 rows (↓) from top to bottom; a smaller card which will hold 96 characters is also used. There are other sizes, e.g. 21 and 40 columns, but these are much less common.

card (*n*) = punch card (↑).

Hollerith (1) the man who produced the first 80-column punch card (↑); (2) a punch card with 80 columns (↓) and 12 rows (↓).

card code (1) the arrangement of the holes in a column (↓) of a punch card (↑) that is used to represent (p. 45) a particular character. In 80-column cards it is a single hole for the digits (p. 16), two holes for letters, and two or more for other characters; (2) one or more characters in a card which are used as a record code (p. 102).

punch[2] (*v*) to make a hole in a punch card (↑). The hole is usually almost a square in 80-column cards (↑) but in 96-column cards it is a small round hole. **punch** (*n*).

column (*n*) each character in a punch card (↑) is held as an arrangement of holes which are one above the other and this is called a column.

card column = column (↑).

column

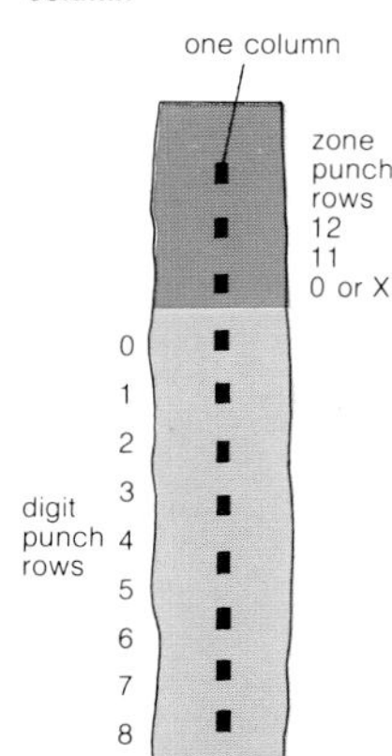

zone punch

alphabetic

special characters

12 11 0 zone punches

twelve punch

digits unsigned

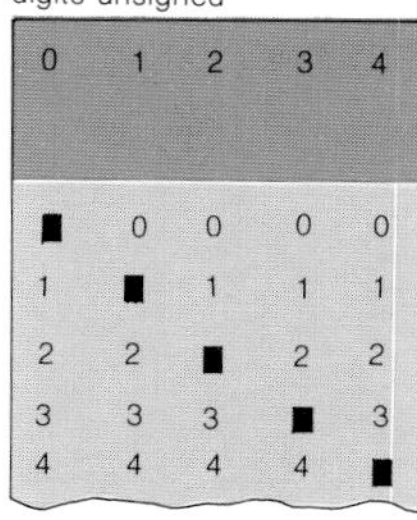

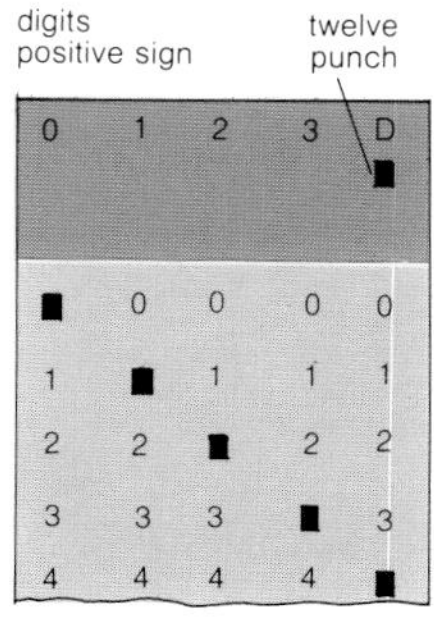

row (*n*) a line across a punch card (↑) where holes can be punched (↑). Each row has a different value. There are 12 rows on an 80-column card (↑). The top two are zone position (↓) rows, the *third row* may also be a zone position row, and the bottom ten rows record the digits (p. 16) 0 to 9.

twelve-edge the top edge of a punch card (↑).

nine-edge the bottom edge of a punch card (↑).

card file a file (p. 153) held in punch cards (↑). There may be one or more cards for each record (p. 154) in the file.

deck (*n*) = card file (↑).

card deck = card file (↑).

card format the way that the columns (↑) in a punch card (↑) are used, i.e. which columns are to be used for particular fields (p. 155) of the data.

zone position one of the top three rows (↑) of an 80-column card (↑). The names given to each of the rows differ between manufacturers.

zone punch to put a hole in one of the top three rows (↑) of a punch card (↑) when there is also another punch in the same column (↑), but in the rows used for digits (p. 16).

over-punch = zone punch (↑).

twelve punch a hole in the top row (↑) of a punch card (↑). It is used either as a part of a character, or as an over-punch (↑) to show a plus sign. It is sometimes used by itself as part of a record code (p. 102).

Y-punch (*n*) (1) = twelve punch (↑); (2) = eleven punch (↓).

eleven punch a hole in the second row (↑) of a punch card (↑). It is used either as a part of a character, or as an over-punch (↑) to show a minus sign. It is often used by itself as part of a record code (p. 102).

X-punch (*n*) (1) = eleven punch (↑); (2) = twelve punch (↑).

zero punch a hole in the third row (↑) of a punch card (↑). It is used either alone to show a value of 0, or as an over-punch (↑), e.g. a zero punch and another in row 2 would represent (p. 45) the letter *S*.

tens position (1) = twelve punch (p. 53); (2) = third row (p. 53).
punch[1] (*n*) (1) a hole made in a punch card (p. 52); (2) a machine which can punch holes in cards.
card punch (1) a device connected to a computer which can be used to punch cards (p. 52); (2) = key punch (p. 56).

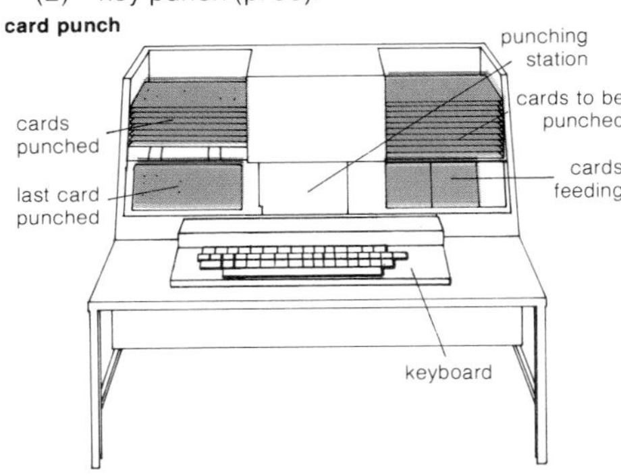

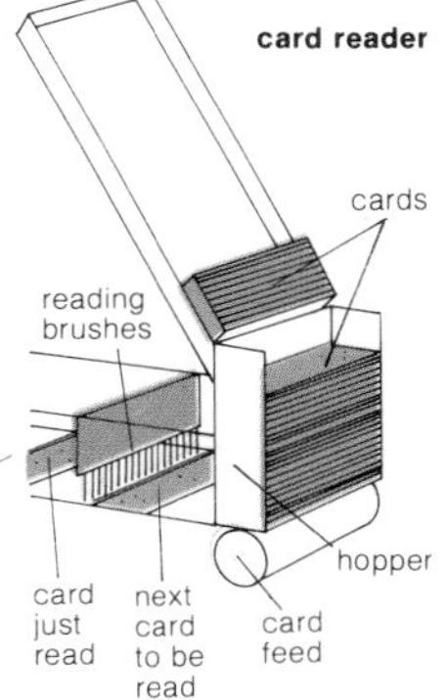

card reader a device, usually connected to a computer, which can read punch cards (p. 52) and transfer the data.
cpm cards per minute. A measure of the speed of a card reader (↑) or a card punch (↑).
card reproducer a machine which can take one card deck (p. 53) and either reproduce it in exactly the same form, or change the columns (p. 52) in which data is recorded. It can also produce two or more cards (p. 52) for each one in the original card deck and can add new data, such as a date, to each new card.
machine-cycle of punch card (p. 52) devices which perform a series of operations every time a card is read, or punched (p. 52).
hopper (*n*) the part of a card reader (↑) or card punch (↑) into which cards are placed so that they can fall into the card feed (↓).
card feed the part of a card reader (↑) or card punch (↑) where the cards (p. 52) are moved from the hopper (↑) into the part of the machine were they are read or punched (p. 52).

clutch point a point in time when the card (p. 52) can be moved from the card feed (↑) to be read or punched (p. 52). In each machine cycle (↑) there are only two or three points when a card can be read.

edge leading the edge of the card which the card reader (↑) or punch (↑) expects to be fed for correct use, i.e. whether the nine-edge (p. 53) or the twelve-edge (p. 53) has to go in first.

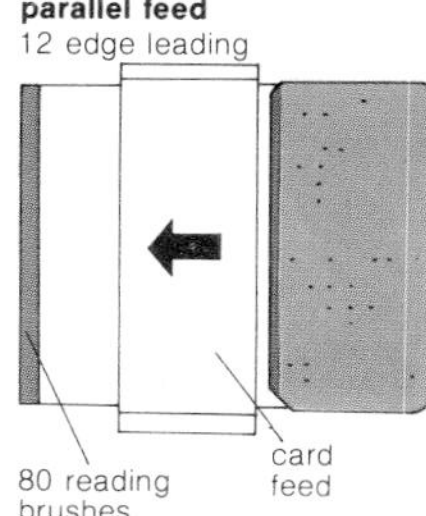

parallel feed of cards (p. 52) fed with the top or bottom edge leading (↑). All 80 columns (p. 52) are read or punched (p. 52) together.

serial feed of cards (p. 52) fed with the left side leading, and with each column (p. 52) read or punched (p. 52) before the next one.

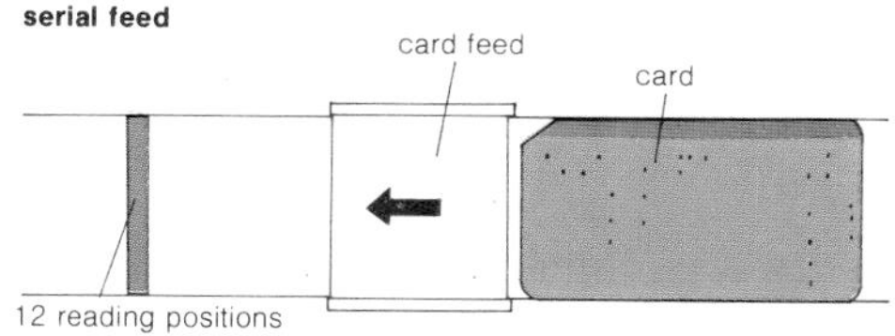

card stacker the part of a card reader (↑) or card punch (↑) where cards (p. 52) are placed after they have been read or punched (p. 52).

misfeed (*n*) a failure of a card (p. 52) to enter a card feed (↑) correctly. **misfeed** (*v*).

card wreck a situation in which a punch card (p. 52) has become torn while being fed and caused the card reader (↑) or punch (↑) to stop.

mark sense to mark data on cards (p. 52) with a special pencil. The marks are magnetic and can be read by a machine which punches (p. 52) the correct holes according to the data.

column binary a card code (p. 52) in which digits (p. 16) are held in binary (p. 16) form in a card column (p. 52); this allows two digits to be held in each column instead of one.

corner cut of a punch card (p. 52) with a part cut off one of the corners. It has no effect on the data in the card but helps to separate cards used for different purposes.

double punch to put more than one hole into the rows (p. 53) of a card column (p. 52) which hold the digits (p. 16) 0 to 9.

multi-punch (*v*) to put more than one hole in a single column (p. 52), e.g. to punch rows 0-6-8. The punch (p. 54) holes may be in any of the rows (p. 53).

end printing data printed on the end of the card (p. 52) so that a person can read it. Usually done on a card reproducer (p. 54).

end printing

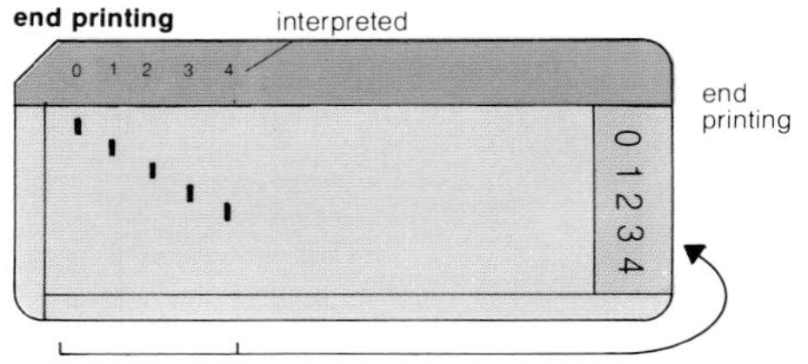

gang punch punching (p. 52) the contents of one card (p. 52), or a part of the card, into a group of cards. For example, a date might be punched into the first card and a card reproducer (p. 54) would punch the same date into all the following cards.

key punch a card punch (p. 54) which is not connected to a computer. It is used by a person who presses keys to cause the holes to be punched (p. 52) into a card (p. 52).

interpret (*v*) to print on the top edge of a punch card (p. 52) the character represented (p. 45) by the holes in a card column (p. 52).

interpreter[1] (*n*) a key punch (↑) which both punches (p. 52) the holes and also interprets (↑) them.

verifier (*n*) (1) a machine similar to a key punch (↑). Instead of punching (p. 52) a hole when a key is pressed it checks to see whether there is a hole already there; if not it gives a warning. It should also detect if the hole is there but is an off punch (↓). It is used to check that punching has been done correctly; (2) a person whose job is to use a verifier. **verify** (*v*).

double punch

interpreting

B

0 0 0

1 1 1

2 2

multi-punch columns

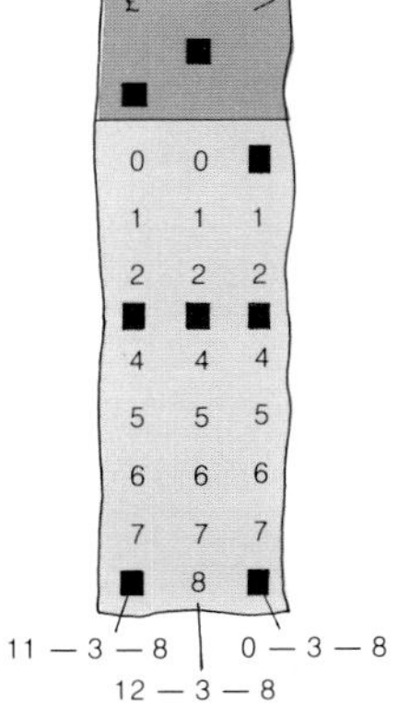

off punch a hole which is not in the exact place it should be, it is slightly out of position and will probably not be read correctly.

left zero fill a process in which a key punch (↑) will enter one or more zeros in front of other non-zero digits. For example, a user may enter 123 but if five columns (p. 52) were being used for the number then, although the user has not entered the zeros at the front, the card (p. 52) would be punched (p. 52) as 00123.

roller (*n*) a metal roller over which cards are passed in a card reader (p. 54). In some readers a wire brush (↓) will be able to touch the roller if there is a hole in the card (p. 52) and send a signal (p. 22) to the card reader.

wire brush a fine brush made with wire which is placed against a roller (↑). As cards (p. 52) feed into the machine the card moves between the roller and the brush and prevents them from touching but if there is a punched hole in the card then the wire touches the roller and this allows the reader to know where the holes appear in the card. There can be a brush for every column (p. 52).

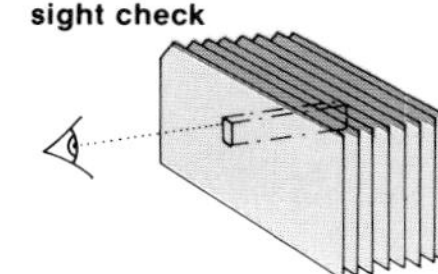

sight check to hold a group of cards (p. 52) up to a light. If every card is punched (p. 52) in the same position then it is possible to see the light through the holes.

unit record a machine which is used only for handling or processing punch cards (p. 52).

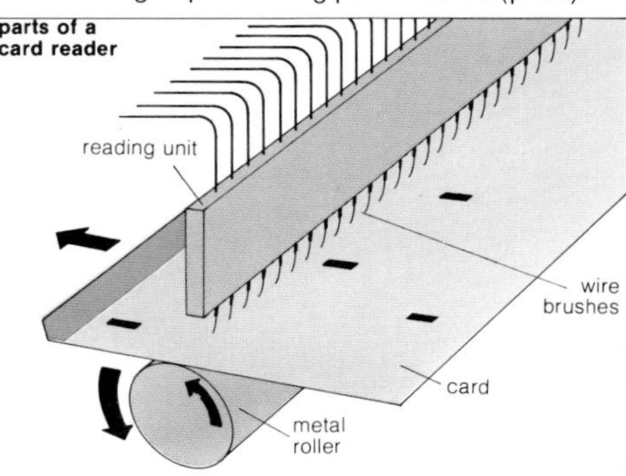

printer (*n*) a device which can print the results obtained from running a program. The range of characters which a printer can print varies; some have only upper case (p. 47) letters, the digits (p. 16) 0–9 and a few special characters (p. 46) such as $, %, ?. Others can also print lower case (p. 47) letters and a larger range of special characters. The number of positions that can be printed on a line is usually between 80 and 144, but the most common is 132.

line printer chain

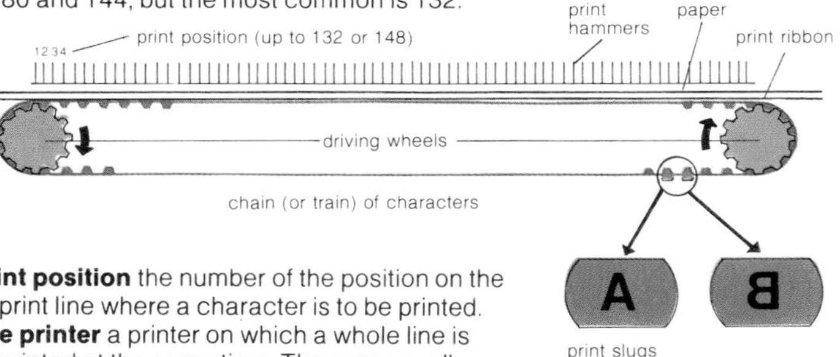

print position the number of the position on the print line where a character is to be printed.

line printer a printer on which a whole line is printed at the same time. They are usually faster than character printers (↓), with speeds ranging from 300 to 1200 lines a minute.

character printer a printer which prints a line one character at a time, rather than all the characters at once. It may print from left to right only, or from right to left as well (bi-directional printing). These printers are usually slow; their speeds range from 30 to 100 characters a second and their rate of printing depends on the number of characters printed, not on the number of lines.

chain[1] (*n*) a set of slugs (↓) which are joined together and which move along the line of print without touching the paper. Any character in the chain can be printed when it is hit by a hammer (↓).

train (*n*) a set of slugs (↓), next to each other but not joined, which move along the line of print without touching the paper. A slug will print when it is hit by a hammer (↓). It is possible to change a single character by replacing the slug.

fonts

0 1 2 3 4 $

0 1 2 3 4

slug (*n*) a small piece of metal in the form of a single printable character. When the slug is struck by a hammer (↓) in a printer the character on the slug is printed.

font (*n*) the style of printing produced by the printer. Also known as **fount**.

type face = font (↑).

hammer (*n*) a metal arm used in a printer. The hammer forces the paper and the print ribbon (p. 62) against the metal slug (↑) in order to make it print. Character printers (↑) may have a single hammer which moves along the print line. Line printers (↑) have a hammer for every print position (↑) which strikes only when the correct character is opposite the hammer.

barrel printer a line printer (↑) which has a full set of characters for every print position. The characters are on the outside of a hollow metal roller which is the same width as the page. The roller turns and when the correct character is level with the print line the hammer in that position strikes to produce the printed character.

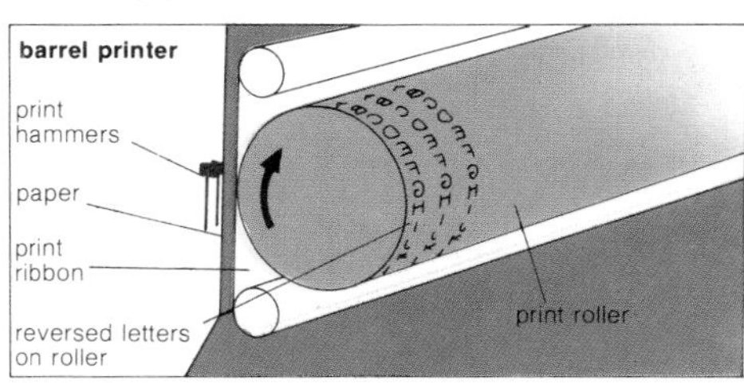

characters formed by matrix printer

matrix (7 × 5)

matrix printer a character printer (↑) in which each character is formed, not by a hammer (↑) striking a metal slug (↑) or a character on a barrel printer (↑) but by a series of metal pins which print the shape of the character required. Speeds range from 100 to 300 characters per second. The quality of print depends on the number of pins and the speed. Some printers take several passes over a single line to produce very high quality print.

dot printer = matrix printer (↑).

daisy-wheel printer a printer which uses a daisy-wheel (↓). The wheel turns and, when the correct character is at the top of the wheel, the printer's hammer (p. 59) strikes. It is a slow printer, about 30–60 characters a second and is used with mini-computers (p. 9) or word processors (p. 89). It gives a good print quality.

daisy-wheel (*n*) a flat circular plastic or metal wheel which has fine cuts running from the edge almost to the centre so that the wheel consists of very narrow pieces. On the end of each piece there is a printable character. In a printer the wheel turns round and when the correct character is at the top of the wheel a hammer (p. 59) strikes and prints it.

type-wheel (*n*) = daisy-wheel (↑).

print-wheel (*n*) = daisy-wheel (↑).

laser printer a printer in which fine, but powerful, beams of light are used to create the character which is to be printed. The printer may either print a whole page in one operation or operate as a line printer (p. 58).

thermal printer a high speed line printer (p. 58) in which heat is used to create the character on the paper.

carriage (*n*) the part of a printer which consists of the form-feed (p. 62), the printing characters, the print ribbon (p. 62) and the print hammers (p. 59).

daisy-wheel

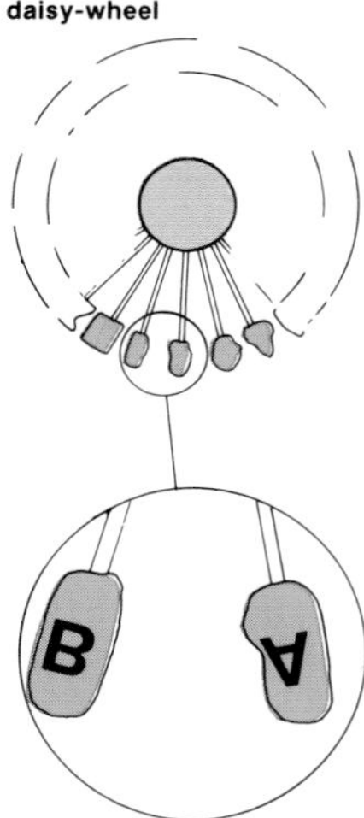

carriage

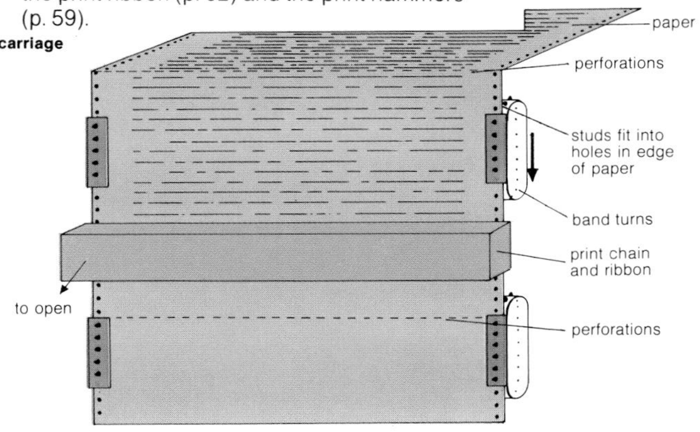

continuous stationery

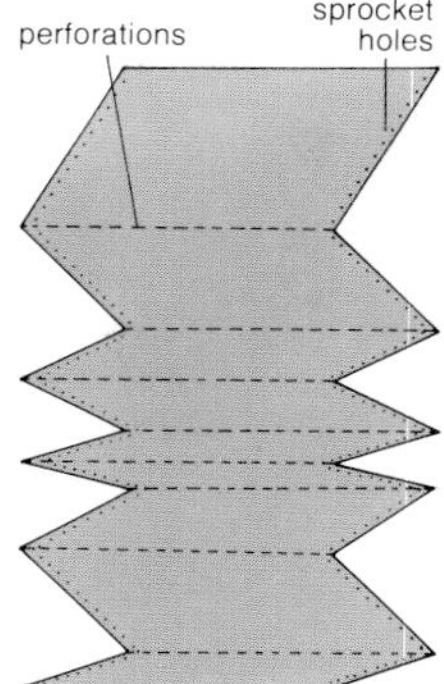

two-part paper

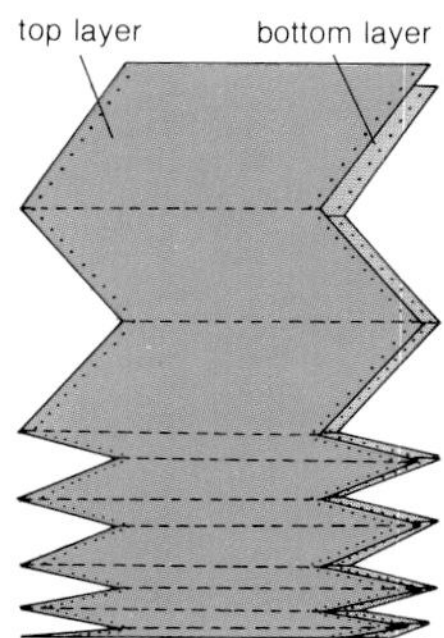

carriage control character a character which is next to the data to be printed but is not itself printed. Instead it is used by the program which is doing the printing to control the spacing and skipping (↓) of the lines being printed.

control character[1] = carriage control character (↑).

carriage control tape an endless loop of paper tape (p. 64) which has holes punched (p. 52) in it to control the skipping (↓) of blank lines between the printing, used especially when there are different numbers of blank lines between the printed lines.

skip (*v*) to move the paper more than one line when no printing is being done. It is a quicker way of positioning the paper to receive the next line of print. **skip** (*n*).

paper throw = skip (↑).

continuous stationery the connected sheets of paper used on computer printers. At the top and bottom of each sheet there are perforations (↓) which allow sheets to be easily separated after printing. There are sprocket holes (p. 62) at each side of the paper to allow it to be moved. There may be one or more layers of paper.

perforation[1] (*n*) a very small hole. A line of these holes goes from one side of the paper to the other to form the bottom of one sheet of continuous stationery (↑) and the top of the next. They allow continuous stationery to be easily torn into separate sheets. **perforate** (*v*).

single-part paper continuous stationery (↑) which consists of just one layer of paper.

two-part paper continuous stationery (↑) which consists of two layers of paper.

inter-leaved carbon set continuous stationery (↑) which consists of two or more layers of paper with sheets of carbon paper between which permit copies to be made of the print on the top layer. It is now less common than NCR (↓).

NCR no carbon required. Continuous stationery (↑) of two or more layers, of which the upper layers are specially treated so that they allow a character printed on the top sheet to appear also on the lower sheets. It provides more than one copy of a print-out (p. 19).

pre-printed stationery paper which has printing on it, e.g. a company's name and address.

form-feed (*n*) (1) the part of a printer which moves the paper when printing is taking place; (2) a code (p. 102) which causes the paper to be moved to the top of the next sheet.

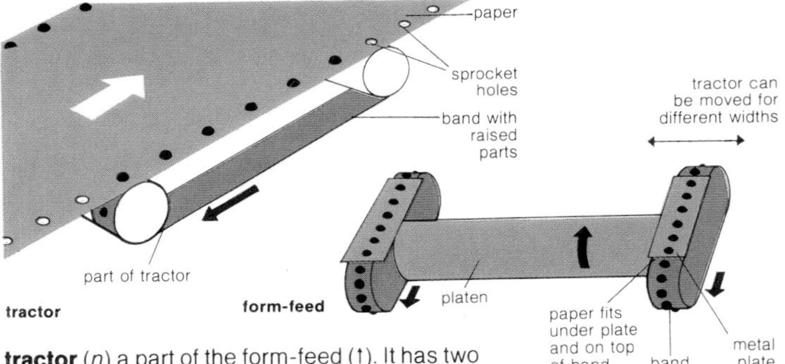

tractor **form-feed**

tractor (*n*) a part of the form-feed (↑). It has two bands, usually of hard rubber or similar material which have raised small smooth points, called studs, on their surface. The studs fit exactly into the sprocket holes (↓) on either side of sheets of continuous stationery (p. 61). The bands are turned by the printer and cause the paper to move. The bands can be moved across the printer to allow different widths of paper to be used.

sprocket hole[1] one of the holes at either side of sheets of continuous stationery (p. 61). The studs on the bands of the printer tractor (↑) fit into these and move the paper when printing is taking place.

platen (*n*) a metal roller which may be covered with hard rubber material. It lies across a printer underneath the paper. The hammers (p. 59) force the print character and the paper against it.

print ribbon material which is coated with ink in some way for use in a printer. When a hammer (p. 59) strikes a print character the ribbon is forced against the paper and prints the character.

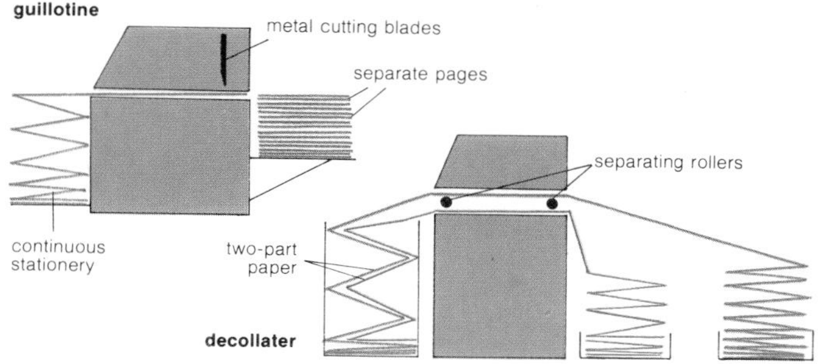

guillotine (*n*) a machine which cuts continuous stationery (p. 61) in order to separate the sheets. It may also be able to cut off the sprocket holes (↑). **guillotine** (*v*).

burster (*n*) a machine which separates continuous stationery (p. 61) into single sheets by tearing it along the perforations (p. 61) between the sheets. **burst** (*v*).

decollator (*n*) a machine which will separate continuous stationery (p. 61) that has more than one layer of paper into single layers.

COM computer output micro-film. A program, instead of printing, will write out on a tape (p. 71) the data it would have printed. The tape is then read by a special machine and a micro-film (↓) is produced either in the form of a roll of film or as a micro-fiche (↓).

micro-film (*n*) a film on which printed output can be held. It takes up much less space than the paper and is used where the information needs to be kept for a long time. **micro-film** (*v*).

micro-fiche (*n*) micro-film (↑) which is in the form of a small sheet of film about 12 centimetres by 10 centimetres. It can be read using a special viewing machine.

spacing chart a piece of paper with small blank squares, each the size of one printed character. It is used to show the way in which a user wants printed output to appear. A programmer will then write a program to produce the output the user wants.

micro-fiche

about 270 pages of print

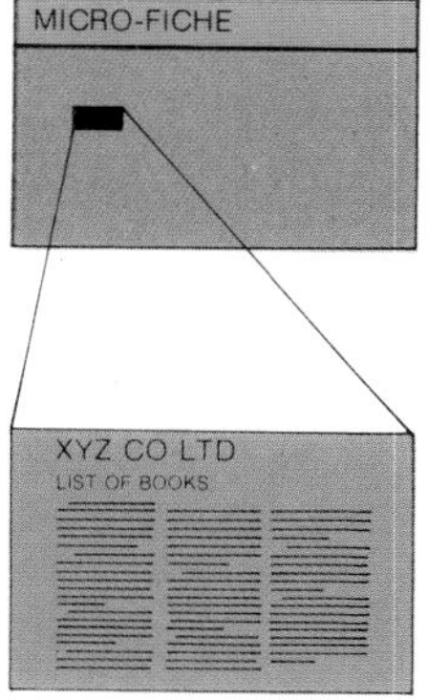

one of the pages on micro-fiche

paper tape 8 channel

erase character (all holes punched)

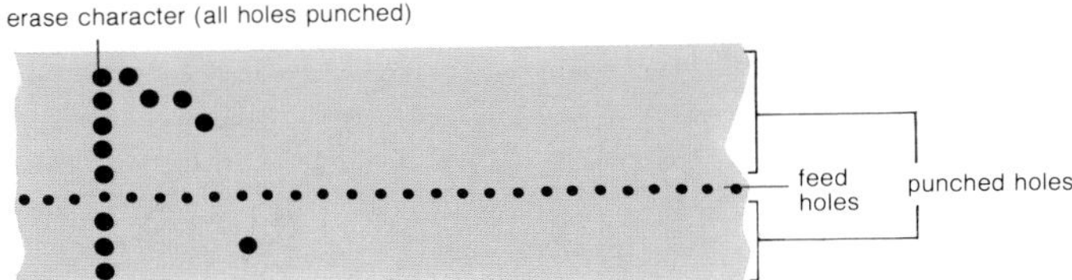

paper tape paper about 2 or 3 centimetres wide and of any length into which holes are punched (p. 52). There may be 5, 6, 7 or 8 holes across the width of the paper and the arrangement of the holes is a representation (p. 45) of a character.

punched tape = paper tape (↑).

punch tape code the arrangement of holes in a paper tape (↑). Each arrangement represents (p. 45) a character. A range of codes is used depending on whether there are 5, 6, 7 or 8 holes used to represent a character. Sometimes the representation can be either numeric (p. 15) or alphabetic (p. 45) depending on the shift character (↓).

erase character a special character (p. 46) which is used mainly on paper tape (↑). It has a hole punched (p. 52) in every track (p. 68) and the character is then passed by when the tape is read. A character which has been wrongly punched can be deleted by punching all the hole positions; it will then be ignored by the reader. The same idea is also used in data transmission (p. 76).

delete character = erase character (↑).

ignore character = erase character (↑).

shift character a character in a paper tape (↑) which says whether the following characters are numeric (p. 15) or alphabetic (p. 45). The same idea is used in data transmission (p. 76).

control character[2] = shift character (↑).

paper tape punch a machine which makes the holes in paper tape (↑). It can be one connected to a computer and which accepts the output from a program and punches (p. 52) it into paper tape. It can also mean a machine not connected to a computer which is used by a person who wants to enter data into a computer. The person uses a keyboard and when a key is pressed the representation (p. 45) of the character is punched into the paper tape.

paper tape reader a machine, usually connected to a computer, which will read paper tape (↑). Sometimes it is a small machine which just reads the paper tape and transfers the data on to a magnetic tape (p. 71) which can later be read into a computer.

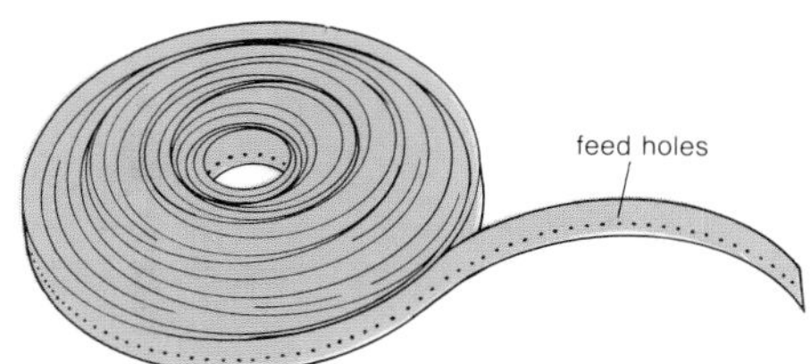

spool of paper tape

splice

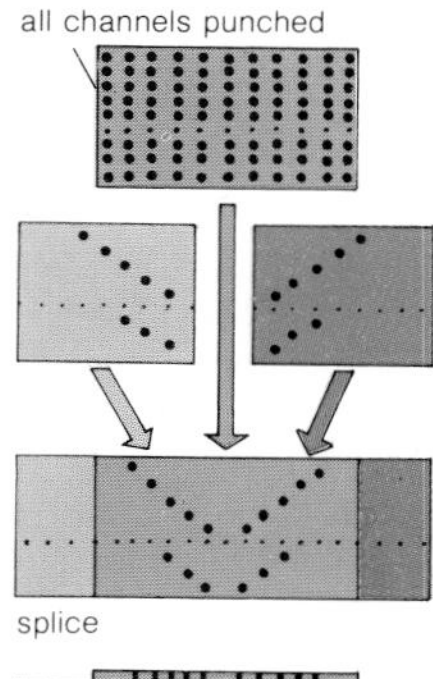

spool[2] (*n*) a length of paper tape (↑) which is curved round into a circular shape. **spool** (*v*).

perforation[2] (*n*) a hole punched into paper tape (↑). It is about a quarter of a centimetre across.

chad (*n*) a small piece of paper which comes out of the hole made by a paper tape punch (↑).

splice (*v*) to join together two separate pieces of paper tape (↑). **splice** (*n*).

feed hole a small hole which is used to move the paper tape (↑) in a paper tape reader (↑). There is a continuous line of these holes along a piece of paper tape, either in or close to the centre. Smooth points on the edge of a small wheel fit into these holes. When the wheel turns the paper tape is moved.

sprocket hole[2] = feed hole (↑).

disk drive

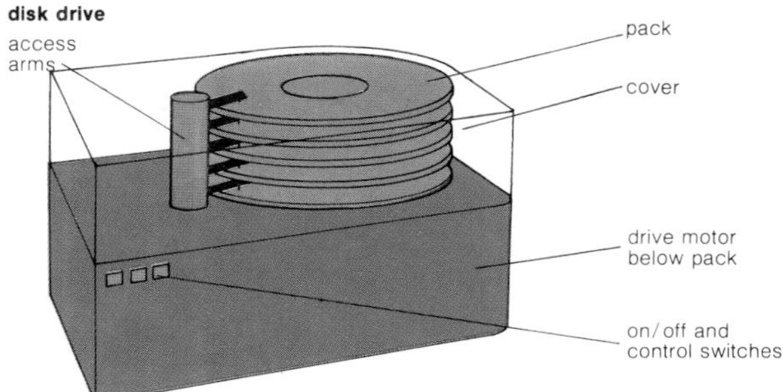

disk drive a device on which a disk pack (↓) can be placed. It turns the pack around and also has one or more access arms (p. 70) which can reach any part of the pack where data can be stored. The drive is connected to a control unit (p. 27) which in turn is connected to the CPU (p. 31).

disk pack a device which consists of from one to ten or eleven flat circular surfaces on which data can be recorded. The surfaces, called platters (p. 68), are joined to a spindle (p. 68). When placed on a disk drive (↑) the pack can be turned round at speeds between 20 and 50 times a second. Access arms (p. 70) on the drive have read-write heads (p. 202) which can be moved across the surfaces, without touching them, so that they can transfer data to or from any part of the pack. Very often the pack can be removed from the disk drive and stored away from the computer until it is needed again. It has a cover which is placed over the pack when it is not on the drive but which is usually removed when the pack is placed on the drive.

pack (*n*) = disk pack (↑).

disk (*n*) (1) = a disk drive (↑); (2) = a disk pack (↑).

disc (*n*) = disk (↑).

magnetic disk = disk (↑).

disk storage = disk (↑).

disk file a file (p. 153) held on a disk pack (↑).

disk pack

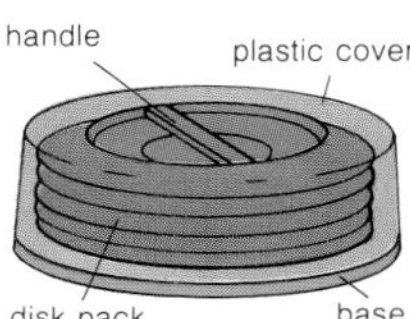

section through disk pack

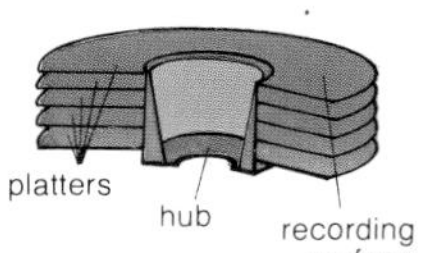

floppy disk

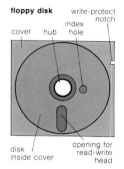

cover hub index hole write-protect notch

disk inside cover opening for read-write head

cartridge disk

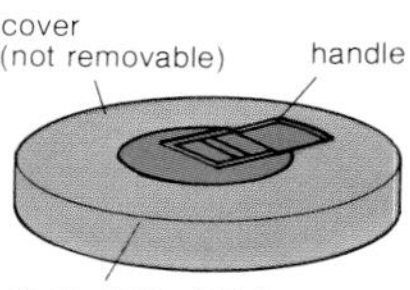

removable disk a disk pack (↑) which can be taken off the disk drive (↑) and stored separately or placed on another disk drive.

fixed disk a disk pack (↑) which cannot be taken off the disk drive (↑). It is usually larger and faster than a removable disk (↑).

hard disk a disk (↑). The term is generally used to mean that it is not a floppy disk (↑).

floppy disk a small disk (↑) which consists of a single platter (p. 68) which is not fixed to a spindle (p. 68). It has a small hole in the centre which can be used to turn the platter when it is placed in a suitable disk drive (↑). The platter is in a card cover with a space for the read-write head (p. 202) to access the surface of the platter. Data can be recorded on one surface of the platter, and sometimes on both. The capacity is usually 250,000 bytes (p. 17) to 2 megabytes (p. 43). It is slower than a normal disk and commonly used only on micro and mini-computers (p. 9).

floppy (*n*) = floppy disk (↑).

diskette (*n*) = floppy disk (↑).

Winchester disk (1) a special disk pack (↑) which has a cover that is not removed when it is placed on a disk drive (↑). There may be several platters (p. 68) and the pack may have its own read-write heads (p. 202) which touch the recording surface; (2) a hard disk (↑) suitable for smaller computers.

cartridge disk a disk pack (↑) which can be placed on a disk drive (↑) without taking its cover off. It usually has one platter (p. 68) with two recording surfaces.

direct access[2] of a piece of data which can be read, or written, without the need to read or write any other data which is stored on the same device. It usually means that data is on a disk storage (↑) device but is also used for access to memory.

random access[2] = direct access (↑).

direct access device a device, usually a disk (↑), which allows a particular piece of data to be read or written without accessing any other data.

random access device = direct access device (↑).

direct access storage device = a direct access device (p. 67). It is sometimes used to mean that it is a device such as a disk (p. 66) or a drum (p. 87) and does not include memory.
DASD = direct access storage device (↑).
spindle (*n*) (1) the part in the centre of a disk pack (p. 66) to which the platters (↓) are fixed and which is turned round by the disk drive (p. 66); (2) = a disk unit.
platter (*n*) one of the flat circular parts of a disk (p. 66). Data is usually recorded on both sides but sometimes data is not stored on the outer surface of the top and bottom platters. On large disk packs one surface is used, not for data, but as a means of making sure that the read-write heads (p. 202) are in the correct position.

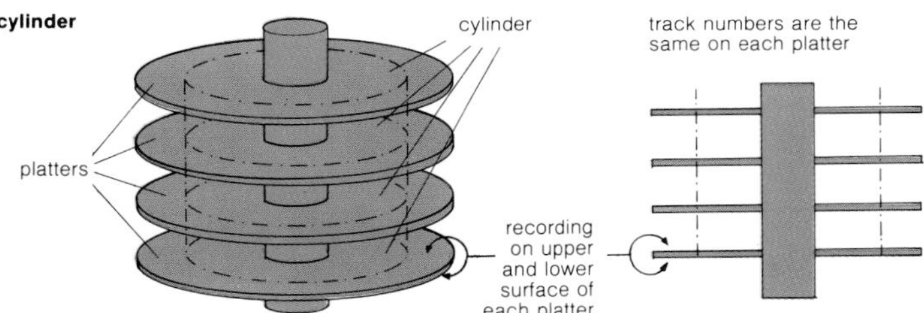

cylinder (*n*) the tracks (↓) of a disk pack (p. 66) which are directly above one another and at the same distance from the centre of the disk. Thus, without moving, an access arm (p. 70) with a read-write head (p. 202) for each surface is able to access any of the tracks which make up the cylinder.
track[1] (*n*) a part of a surface of a disk (p. 66) on which data is recorded. It is circular in shape and usually divided into several parts called sectors (↓). A surface will have between 200 and 1000 tracks depending on the size of the disk pack (p. 66).
index-point (*n*) a point on a track (↑) on a disk pack (p. 66) which the control unit (p. 27) can recognise. It is used to let the control unit know where the track starts.

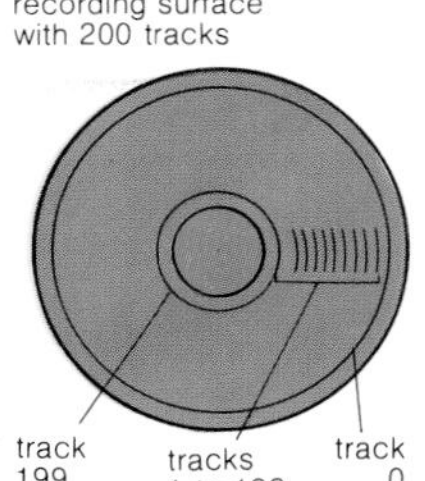

sector
track with 8 equal sectors
sector addresses
4 3 5 2 6 1 7 0
sectors — record data
index-point marks start of track

disk address

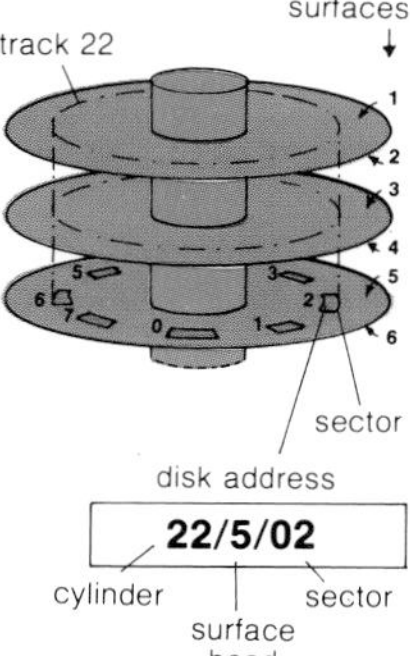

sector (*n*) a part of a track (↑) on which data is held. It is the smallest part of a disk pack (p. 66) that can be read or written to, and the whole of it has to be read, or written, at one time. A track usually has a number of sectors but they may hold the same or different amounts of data depending on the length of the sector. On some disks (p. 66) it is possible to have sectors of different lengths, on others all sectors must be of the same length.

disk space the number of sectors (↑) available for a particular purpose, or for a particular user.

soft sectored of a disk pack (p. 66) in which the size of a sector (↑) can be fixed or changed by a special program.

hard sectored of a disk pack (p. 66) in which the size of a sector (↑) is fixed when it is made and cannot be changed.

disk address the address which is needed to find a particular part of the disk pack (p. 66) so that data can be read or written. The address usually consists of the number of the cylinder (↑), the number of the surface and the number of the sector (↑).

count, key and data ckd. A way of holding data on a disk (p. 66) so that the length of the data and the key (p. 156) to the data are held in a group in front of the data. This allows the key to be found before the data and so the data is read only if the key is the one which the program is looking for.

address track a track (↑) on a disk pack (p. 66) which holds the addresses of data held on other tracks.

access time (1) the time taken from the start of an instruction to transfer data to when the data begins to be transferred. In this form the access time is considered to be separate from the data transfer time. This tends to be the way the term is used when using direct access devices (p. 67); (2) the total time taken by a complete access from the point when the instruction is started until the data has been read or written. In this form the access time includes the data transfer time.

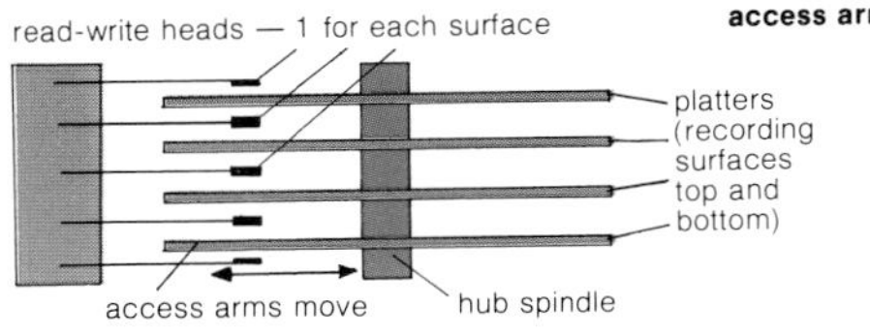

access arm

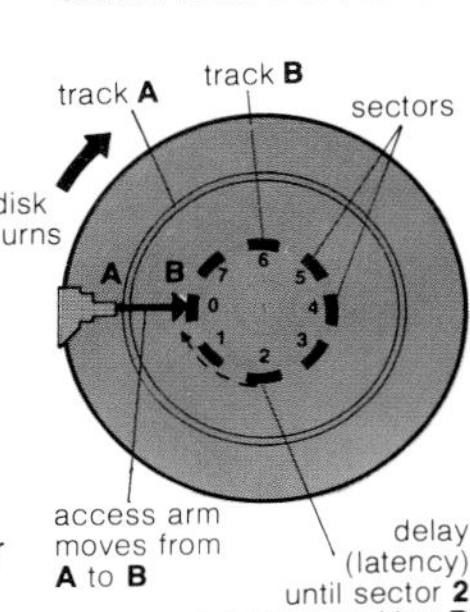

access sector **2** of track **B**

access arm the part of a disk (p. 66) which holds the read-write heads (p. 202) and which can usually be moved across the disk.

seek (*n*) a movement of the access arm (↑) across the disk (p. 66) surface from one cylinder (p. 68) to another. **seek** (*v*).

latency (*n*) after an access arm (↑) has been moved to a new cylinder (p. 68), data transfer cannot start until the pack (p. 66) has turned and brought the required sector (p. 69) beneath the read-write head (p. 202). The time this takes is called the latency. On average it is about half the time it takes for the pack to turn through a complete circle.

rotational delay = latency (↑).

head crash an event where the read-write head (p. 202) on an access arm (↑) has accidentally touched the surface of a disk pack (p. 66). This usually damages both the head and the pack. The data on the damaged part will be lost.

contention (*n*) an event where two or more users or programs are trying to use the same device at the same time but the device can handle only one of them. Commonly used when two programs are trying to use the same disk (p. 66) or the same transmission line (p. 76).

key-to-disk (*n*) a small computer with VDU's (p. 83), a disk drive (p. 66) and a tape drive (↓). The computer is used only for entering source data (p. 183). The data is held on the disk until it is needed for processing. It is then usually transferred on to a tape reel (↓) which is then read into a mainframe (p. 8) computer.

VTOC Volume Table of Contents. A file (p. 153) held on a special part of a disk pack (p. 66) which holds the names and the disk address (p. 69) of all other files stored on the disk pack.

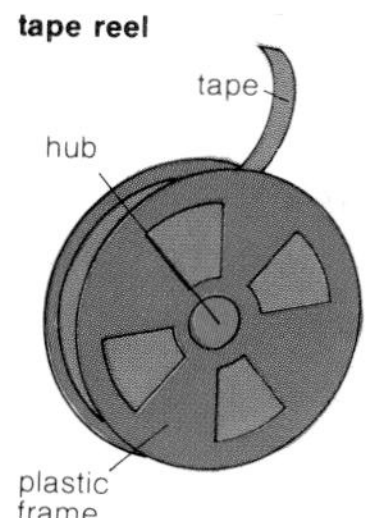

tape (*n*) (1) a long thin film of plastic which is covered on one side with magnetic material on which data can be recorded; (2) = a tape unit (↓).

magnetic tape = tape (↑).

tape unit a device which will read or write data from a tape (↑). The unit is connected to a control unit (p. 27) which is connected to the CPU (p. 31).

tape drive = tape unit (↑).

tape deck = tape unit (↑).

cartridge tape drive a tape (↑) held in a small plastic case, about 10 cm by 15 cm. The tape can hold 40 to 70 megabytes (p. 43). The tape is used for dumping (p. 125) of disks (p. 66) not for normal processing.

reel (*n* (1) a light plastic frame which can hold tape (↑). The usual lengths of tape are from 200 feet to 2400 feet; (2) a tape and reel together.

tape reel = reel (↑).

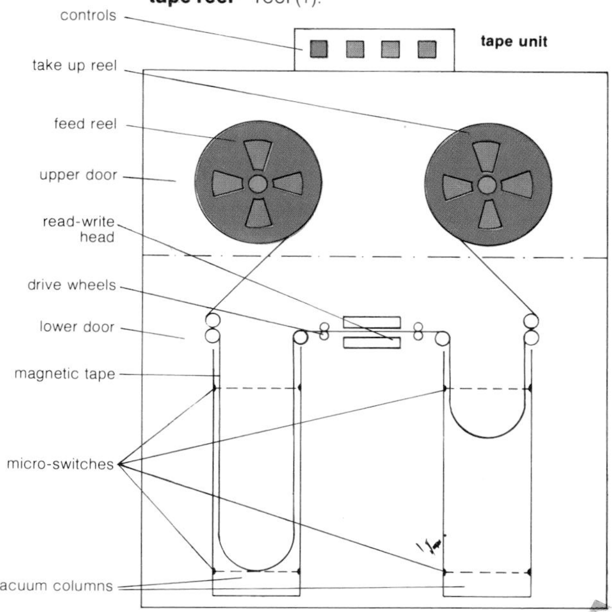

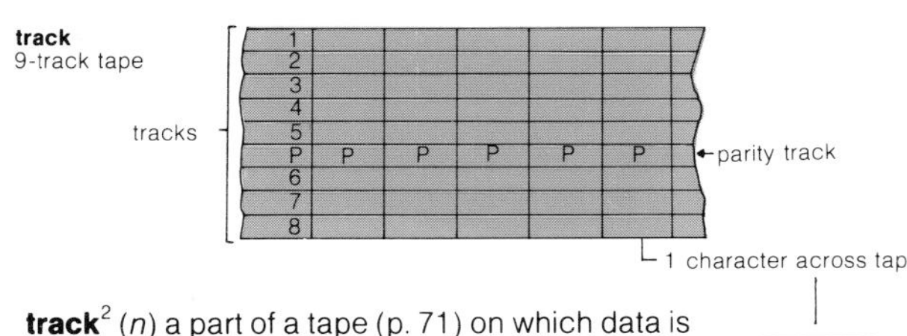

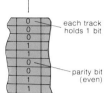

track[2] (*n*) a part of a tape (p. 71) on which data is recorded, and which holds a bit (p. 17). The tracks lie along the tape and not across it. Older tapes had 7 tracks, but 9 tracks are now the most common. There is a track for each of the eight bits in a byte (p. 17) and one for a parity bit (p. 29).

scratch tape a tape (p. 71) which can always be over-written. It is used to hold data for short amounts of time. It is usually written by one program and then read by another soon afterwards.

scratch (*v*) to mark the data on a tape (p. 71) as no longer needed, and the tape as available for new data. The usual way is not to erase (p. 74) the whole of the data but to write a new header label (p. 154) which will tell the operating system (p. 130) that the data on the tape is not needed. This will have the same effect and can be done for any tape, not just for scratch tapes (↑). **scratch** (*adj*).

work tape a scratch tape (↑), especially one which is used by a sort (p. 169) program.

cassette tape a small tape (p. 71), 6 mm wide, used to record small amounts of data for micro- or mini-computers (p. 9). The data is recorded as sound and changed into digital (p. 22) input when it is read. It is very much slower than the larger magnetic tape (p. 71).

write ring a plastic ring which fits into the back of a tape reel (p. 71). It allows data to be written on to the tape (p. 71). If it is removed then the tape can only be read.

take-up drive a hub (↓) on to which an empty tape reel (p. 71) is placed. Tape (p. 71) is wound on to this as records (p. 154) on the tape are read or written.

re-wind (*v*) to move a tape (p. 71) back from the take-up drive (↑) to its original reel (p. 71). This happens when reading or writing has been completed. It leaves the tape in its original starting position ready to be read or written again from the beginning. If no further reading or writing is to be done the tape has to be unloaded (↓). **re-wind** (*n*).

unload (*v*) to take a tape reel (p. 71) off a tape unit (p. 71). The unit must first re-wind (↑) the tape (p. 71), including any that is in the vacuum columns (↓), then raise the read-write head (p. 202), before an operator can take the reel off.

vacuum column a space on a tape unit (p. 71) into which tape (p. 71) is moved by air pressure when the tape is starting or stopping. By allowing the tape to move in this way it avoids stretching it and prevents damage.

capstan (*n*) a small wheel on a tape unit (p. 71). The tape (p. 71) passes over it. It is used to help in moving the tape along for reading and writing.

pinch roller a small wheel on a tape unit (p. 71) which presses against a capstan (↑). The tape (p. 71) passes between them. The pinch roller is driven around and this causes the tape to move.

hub (*n*) a circular piece of metal on a tape unit (p. 71) onto which a tape reel (p. 71) is placed. The hub is driven around and this allows the tape (p. 71) to be wound on or off the reel. This takes up or feeds the tape into the vacuum columns (↑). It does not usually move the tape across the read-write heads (p. 202); this is done by the pinch roller (↑) and the capstan (↑).

load point the part of the tape (p. 71) after which data can be recorded (p. 203). It is marked by a reflective spot (↓).

reflective spot a piece of very thin shiny metal film, about three centimetres long, which is stuck on to a tape (p. 71) about 10 metres from the front end to mark the part after which data can be recorded (p. 203). The control unit (p. 27) searches for the spot when a tape is placed on the tape unit (p. 71) for reading or writing.

reflective spot

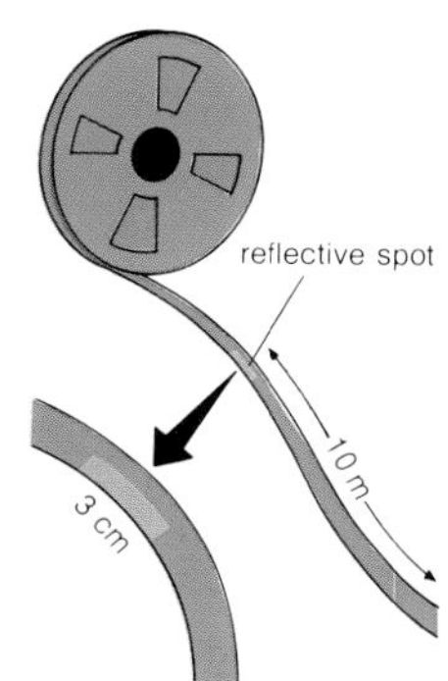

backspace[2] (*v*) to move a tape reel (p. 71) backwards one block (p. 159), usually so that it can be read or written again. **backspace** (*n*).

erase (*v*) to write over a bad part of a tape (p. 71) so that no data is recorded on it, or to remove any data that is on the tape. **erasure** (*n*).

erase head a head on a tape unit (p. 71) which removes all data from a tape (p. 71).

longitudinal check a parity check (p. 30) which is made on the number of bits (p. 17) in each track (p. 72) of a block (p. 159) on a tape (p. 71). It is used to detect and correct errors in reading or writing the tape.

longitudinal check

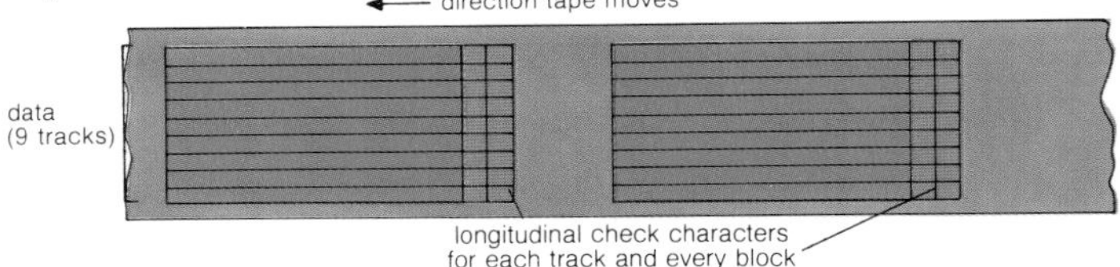

mylar (*n*) a thin plastic film on which magnetic material is placed. The name actually belongs to a particular company but is used generally to mean similar materials made by others.

recording density the number of bytes (p. 17) which can be stored on an inch of tape (p. 71). It can be between 800 and 6250 depending both on the quality of the tape being used and on the tape unit (p. 71). The usual value is 1600 bytes an inch.

NRZI non return to zero inverted recording. A way of recording (p. 203) data on tape (p. 71) which uses changes in the magnetic signals (p. 22) to store binary digits (p. 16).

phase encoding a way of recording (p. 203) data on tape (p. 71) which uses the order in which signals (p. 22) appear to store binary digits (p. 16).

creep (*n*) when tape reels (p. 71) are stored for a long time without being used, the tape tends to move slightly and may damage its smooth surface. This is called creep. Data on the tape may then be difficult to read. **creep** (*v*).

creep

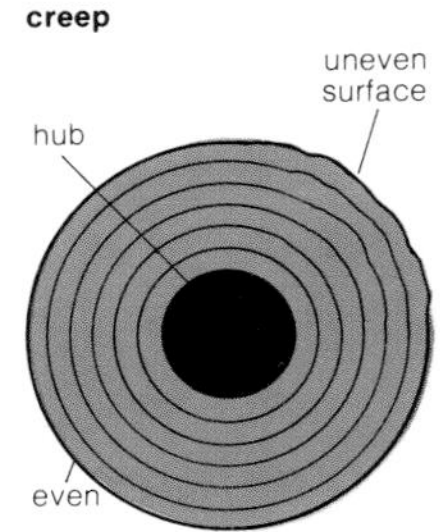

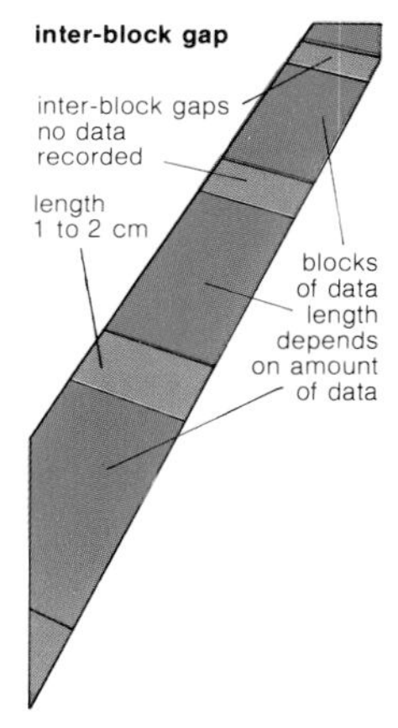

inter-block gap IBG. Space between blocks (p. 159) of data on a tape. Data is not recorded in this area. The tape has to be stopped and started between data blocks and the gaps happen because data is not transferred during this time. The gap is usually about 1 to 2 centimetres.

inter-record gap IRG = inter-block gap (↑).

start-stop time the time taken to start a tape (p. 71) which is not moving, get it up to the proper speed to transfer data, and then stop the tape. The usual length of time is 5 to 20 milliseconds.

read-while-write (*v*) to read from one device, normally a tape (p. 71), while writing to another. Because an update (p. 202) using tapes needs to read from one tape and write to another, a program can be speeded up if it is possible to overlap (p. 19) the reading and writing. It requires special circuits in the tape control unit (p. 27) and usually two channels (p. 27) between the control unit and the CPU (p. 31).

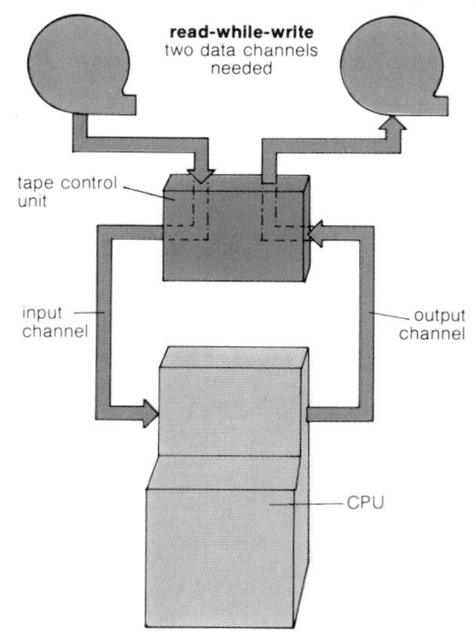

transmission (*n*) the sending of data using electric signals (p. 22). **transmit** (*v*).

reception (*n*) the receiving of data sent using electric signals (p. 22). **receive** (*v*).

data transmission the transfer of data over a communications link (↓) as opposed to the transfer of data between parts of a computer.

communications (*n*) the transfer or transmission (↑) of data from one point to another. It may be within a computer but the term is more commonly used only where the data is moved over a longer distance. The distance may be quite short, e.g. a few metres from a terminal (p. 79) to a CPU (p. 31), but is usually much longer, e.g. from a few miles upwards. **communication** (*adj*), **communicate** (*v*).

communications link a path along which data can be moved from one point to another. It can be quite short, e.g. from a nearby terminal (p. 79) to a CPU (p. 31), but it usually means the transfer over a longer distance when the transmission (↑) may be by land line or radio.

data link = communications link (↑).

transmission line = communications link (↑).

telecommunications (*n*) communications (↑) over a distance. It does not necessarily mean that computers are being used.

network (*n*) a group of nodes (↓) connected by data transmission lines (↑) along which data or programs can be moved. Usually terminals (p. 79) or computers, with peripheral devices (p. 12), are placed at the nodes. The networks can be any size from a few nodes inside one building, to a large number spread around e.g. a university, to one which covers a complete country. With suitable permission a user of one of the terminals can be connected to any of the others, either to enter data or programs or to make use of special programs or very large computers. **net** (*abbr*).

node[1] (*n*) a part of a network (↑) attached to one of the links (↓). The equipment at a node may be a printer, a terminal (p. 79) or a computer but it must have the ability to transmit (↑) or receive data. Usually it can do both.

data transmission

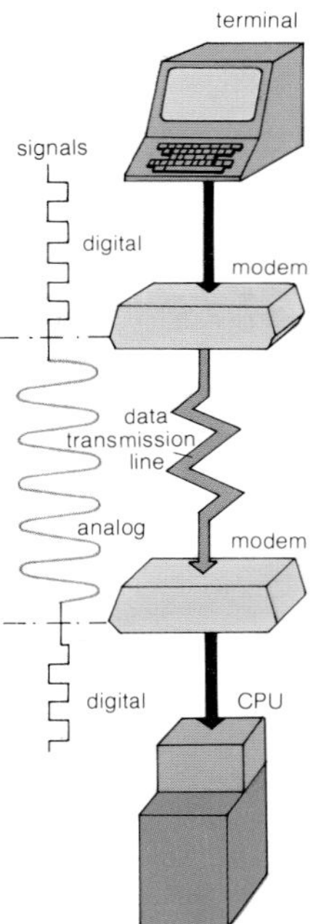

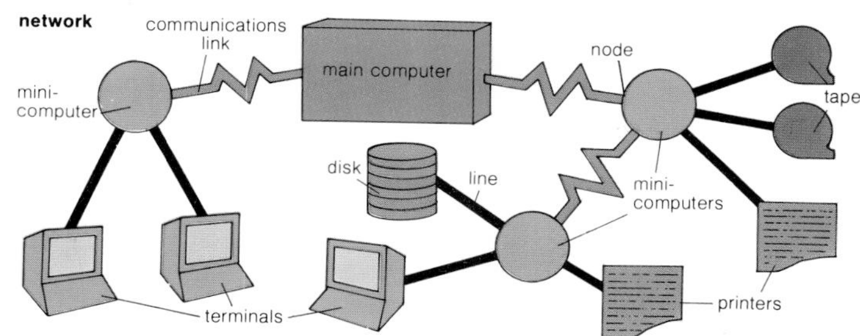

line (*n*) a wire which connects one node (↑) in a network (↑) to another node. It can also be the path for any method of transmission (↑).

link[1] (*n*) a connection between any two nodes (↑) in a network (↑) along which data can be transmitted (↑).

information theory the study of the transmission (↑) and coding of data. It covers such matters as the minimum number of bits (p. 17) required, error detection (p. 13) and error correction (p. 13).

bit rate the number of bits (p. 17) transferred each second.

baud (*n*) the number of signal (p. 22) changes each second. Where only two signal levels exist this is the same as the bit rate (↑); on high speed transmission (↑) there are usually more than two signal levels and so the bit rate is higher.

modulator (*n*) a device used in data transmission (↑) which changes digital (p. 22) data into a continuous signal (p. 22) in a form suitable for transmission (↑) along a communications link (↑). **modulate** (*v*).

demodulator (*n*) a device which receives transmitted (↑) data and changes a continuous signal (p. 22) from a form used in the communications link (↑) into digital (p. 22) form. **demodulate** (*v*).

modem (*n*) a device used in data transmission (↑) and reception which will modulate (↑) data being sent and demodulate (↑) data which is received.

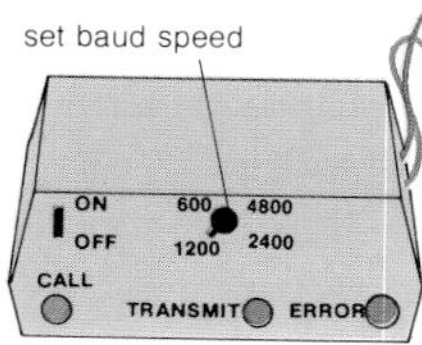

duplex, half duplex and simplex

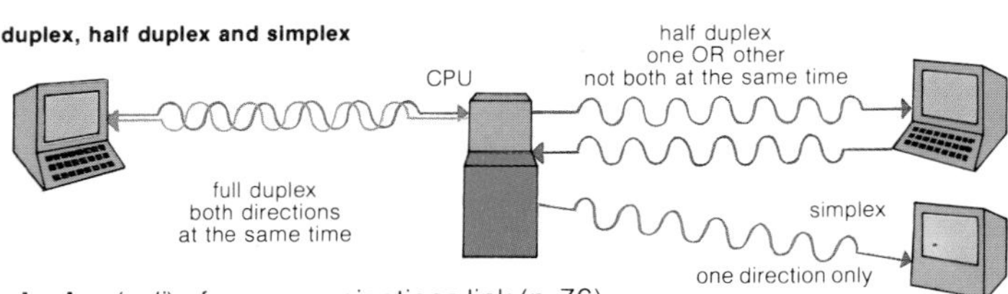

duplex (*adj*) of a communications link (p. 76) which allows data to be sent and received at the same time.

full duplex = duplex (↑).

half duplex of a communications link (p. 76) which allows data to be sent or received but not both at the same time.

simplex (*adj*) of a communications link (p. 76) which allows transmission (p. 76) in one direction only, i.e. it can be used either for sending data or for receiving data.

tie-line (*n*) a line (p. 77) which is hired by a user and which other people are not allowed to use. Normally a line is used just like a telephone line, i.e. a user will transmit (p. 76) data along it and then allow someone else to use it.

message (*n*) a group of characters which is sent from one point to another, usually in some form of network (p. 76).

message switching a method of moving messages (↑) from one point of a network (p. 76) to another. It can be done either by the main computer in the network or by a special computer which is used only for this work.

packet (*n*) a group of characters, often about 128 bytes (p. 17) long, sent along a transmission line (p. 76). The packet contains the address of the node (p. 76) to which it is being sent and the address of the sender, as well as the data.

packet switching a form of message switching (↑) in which the packets (↑) are used to send data. The links (p. 77) used are not for any particular user, instead the packets are sent along any of the available links and each node (p. 76) looks for data addressed to it. The links can therefore transmit (p. 76) packets for different users at the same time.

front end processor (1) a small computer which is placed between larger computers or devices at the nodes (p. 76) of a network (p. 76). It is used to handle the work of communications (p. 76) and allow the larger computers to do other work. It may be programmable or may have a fixed method of operation to match that of the larger computer; (2) a computer which collects input data, passes it at high speed to a larger computer for processing, and then takes the output for printing etc. It allows the larger machine to avoid dealing with slow input-output units (p. 203). The computers are not necessarily a part of a network. **fep** (*abbr*).

terminal (*n*) (1) any point in a network (p. 76) where a person can enter or receive data; (2) a device at the point where data can be entered or received. By itself the word terminal usually means a VDU (p. 83) or a teletype (p. 82) but can be a printer, a tape unit (p. 71), a telephone or another computer, (3) a point in a circuit where a connecting wire can be fixed.

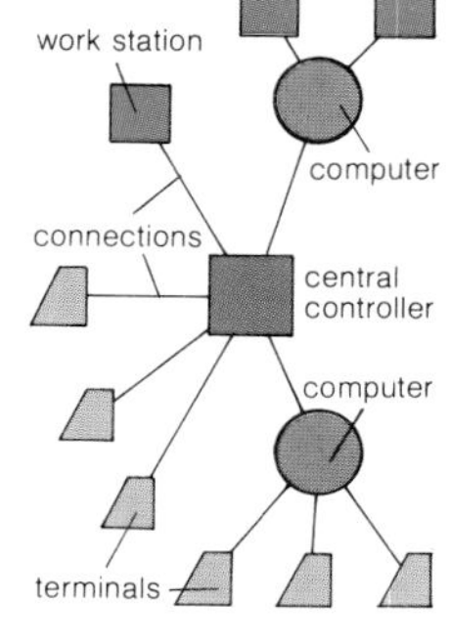

star network a way of arranging the nodes (p. 76) in a network (p. 76) so that all transmissions (p. 76) pass through a central controlling device.

ring network a way of arranging the nodes (p. 76) in a network (p. 76) so that transmissions (p. 76) move around a ring until they reach the node to which they are being sent. Quite often there are empty and full packets (↑) moving around a ring and the nodes place their data into any passing empty packet.

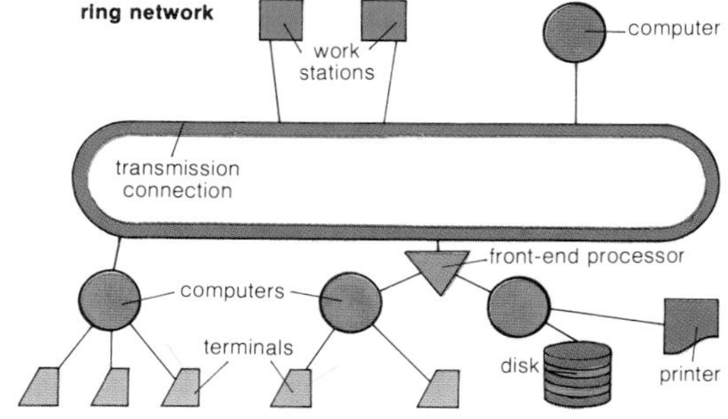

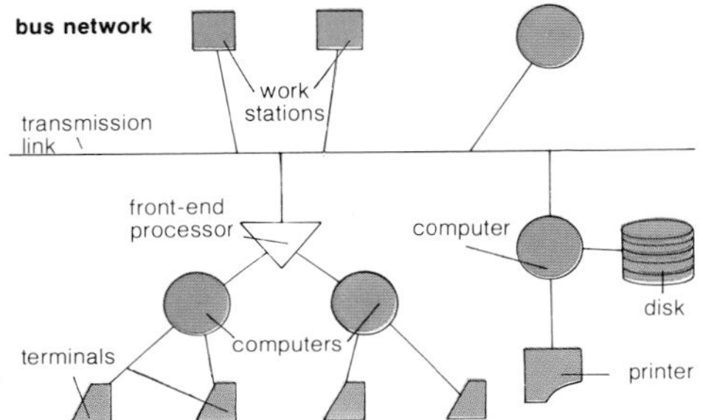

bus network a form of local area network (↓) in which all the devices are attached as separate nodes (p. 76) to a single link (p. 77). There is no central unit. A device which wants to transmit (p. 76) checks that the line is not in use before starting to send any data.

hub network a form of local area network (↓) in which connections are made from a node (p. 76) to a sub-hub which then transmits (p. 76) to a central hub. The central hub transmits to all the nodes in the network (p. 76).

tree network = hub network (↑).

local area network a network (p. 76) which operates in a small area, such as a building or a university campus. The devices at the nodes (p. 76) can usually transmit (p. 76) data to any other node. The transmission speeds are usually in the range 1200 to 48,000 baud (p. 77) but can be much higher.

LAN = local area network (↑).

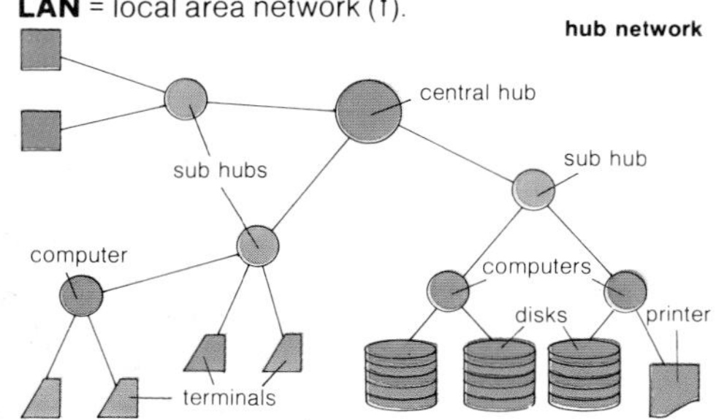

ethernet (*n*) a form of local area network (↑). The data is transmitted (p. 76) in variable length packets (p. 78) and each device on the network (p. 76) selects just the packets being sent to it.

Cambridge ring a form of local area network (↑) developed at Cambridge University. It uses a ring network (p. 79) and transmits (p. 76) 38-bit fixed-length packets (p. 78) which contain data, the address and control information.

X25 an international standard which defines the methods to be used in network (p. 76) transmission (p. 76) and data links (p. 76). It is intended for transmission of data over public communications links (p. 76).

protocol (*n*) a set of rules which state how data, addresses and control information are to be transmitted (p. 76) over a network (p. 76). The rules often have different levels, called layers, and the upper layers do not deal with the actual form of transmission; the rules for the method of transmission being given in the lower layers.

gateway (*n*) a link (p. 77) between networks (p. 76). The networks may be of different types or use different protocols (↑).

poll (*v*) to send a signal (p. 22) to a terminal (p. 79) in a network (p. 76) or one connected to a computer to see if the terminal wants to send or receive any data or run a program.

polling list a list of the terminals (p. 79) in the order in which they will be polled (↑).

polling loop a routine (p. 111) in a program which continuously polls (↑) terminals (p. 79) connected to a computer.

protocol layers

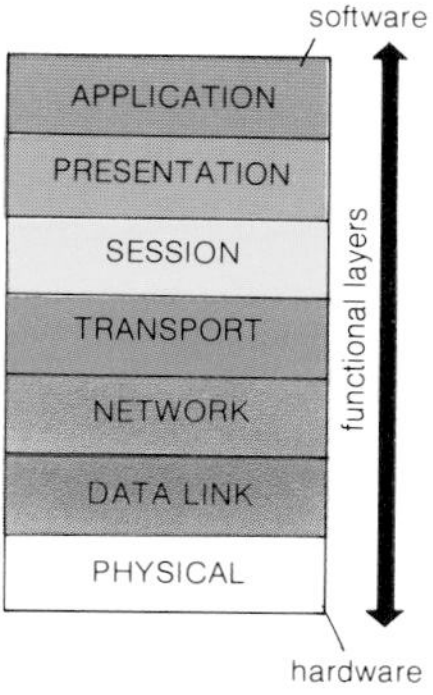

software

APPLICATION

PRESENTATION

SESSION

TRANSPORT

NETWORK

DATA LINK

PHYSICAL

functional layers

hardware

polling list

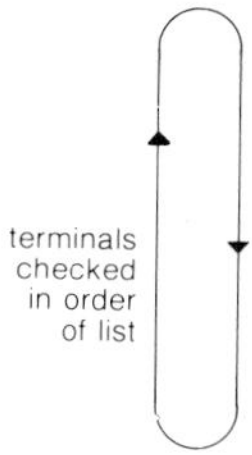

terminals checked in order of list

terminal address	type	state	trans-mitting	needs attention
TT01	VDU	ON	YES	—
TT12	VDU	OFF	—	—
TT14	VDU	ON	NO	YES
TT17	VDU	OFF	—	—
TT45	PRINTER	ON	YES	—
TT47	PRINTER	ON	NO	—

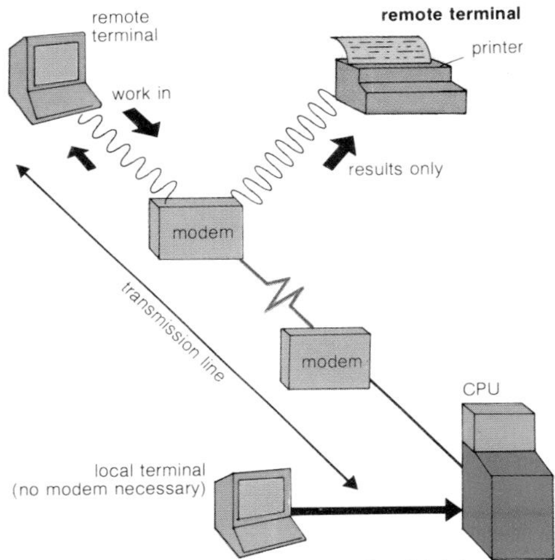

remote terminal a terminal (p. 79) which is not near enough to a computer to be directly connected to it. It has to use some form of communications link (p. 76). Data is transmitted (p. 76) using special signals (p. 22) which normally require the use of a modem (p. 77) at each end of the link (p. 77); one for the terminal and one for the computer.

remote access to access a computer using a remote terminal (↑).

remote enquiry the ability to access the files (p. 153) of a computer from a remote terminal (↑). It usually means that work cannot be entered from the terminal (p. 79).

remote job entry RJE. The entry of data and job control statements (p. 133) at a remote terminal (↑) so that a user's programs can be run on the computer to which the terminal (p. 79) is connected.

teleprocessing (*n*) the processing of data using remote terminals (↑) connected to a central computer. **TP** (*abbr*).

teletype (*n*) a terminal (p. 79) with a keyboard and a slow character printer (p. 58).

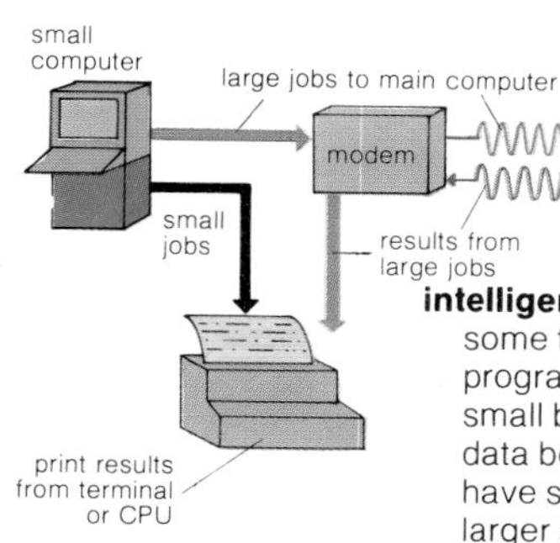

intelligent terminal

intelligent terminal a terminal (p. 79) which has some form of computer and can therefore be programmed. The computer is usually quite small but allows a user to prepare and check data before transmission (p. 76). They can also have small disks (p. 66) to allow them to store larger amounts of data.

input station a terminal (p. 79) which is mainly used for entering transactions into a computer which is in a different place.

work station (1) a terminal (p. 79) which can be used by a person to enter work for a computer to do, and to receive the results. It may be able to do quite large amounts of computing itself; (2) a powerful micro (p. 9) or mini (p. 9) which can stand alone or be attached to a network (p. 76).

response time

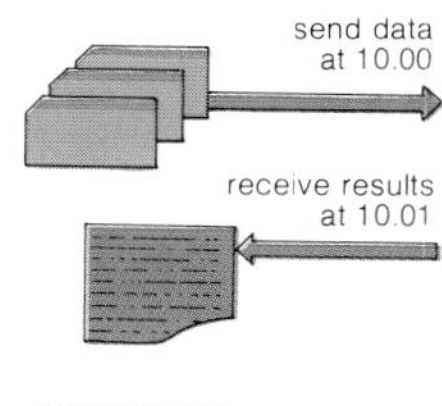

response time
= 10.01
 - 10.00
 1 minute

response time the amount of time between a user sending work or an enquiry from a terminal (p. 79) and getting information back. It is a common method of deciding how busy a network (p. 76) or a computer is; the more users there are the longer the response time is.

password (*n*) a word which has to be keyed into a machine or a terminal (p. 79) by a user before access is allowed to any data or programs. The word is known only to the user and it helps to prevent anyone else getting access to the user's files (p. 153) or programs.

VDU visual display unit. A terminal (p. 79) which has two main parts, a screen (p. 84) rather like a small television and a keyboard. By using the keyboard a user can ask for programs to be run or compiled (p. 105), enter data etc. The computer usually displays whatever is entered through the keyboard. Results or messages from the computer are also shown on the screen.

cathode ray tube the part of a VDU (p. 83) on which data can be displayed. It works in the same way as a television screen. Some can show items only in a single colour, others can show them in a range of colours. **CRT** (*abbr*).

screen (*n*) a part of a VDU (p. 83) on which data can be displayed. Very similar to a small television. The screen is usually a cathode ray tube (↑) but there are other types. Sometimes used to mean a VDU. **screen** (*v*).

cursor (*n*) a small light which flashes on a screen (↑). It shows the position on the screen where data can be entered, deleted or changed. Control keys on a keyboard can be used to move the cursor up, down, or across the screen.

scroll (*v*) to move the data on a screen (↑) up or down so that, if there is too much to fit on to the screen at one time, the user can look at any part of it.

reverse video a feature of a VDU (p. 83) which allows the display colours to be changed so that, for example, instead of showing green characters on a black screen it can show black characters on a green screen. This can be done on all or part of the screen.

flashing character one or more characters, or the cursor (↑), which can be made to change colours quickly, or to appear and then disappear. It is used to attract the user's attention.

resolution (*n*) a measure of how sharp or clear a picture is on a screen (↑). The higher the resolution the better the quality of the screen's picture.

pixel (*n*) a picture element, i.e. the smallest amount of the screen (↑) which can have its light changed, either simply on or off, or from one level of brightness to another. The more pixels the better the quality of the picture.

hard copy a print-out (p. 19) as opposed to a display on a screen (↑). Often used to mean a small printer connected to a VDU (p. 83) which will print whatever is displayed on the screen, either characters or graphics (p. 87).

cathode ray tube

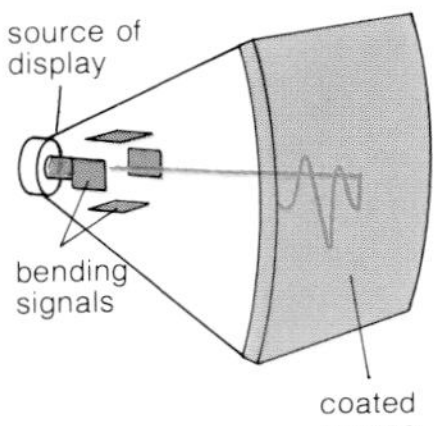

console
computer operating/testing console panel

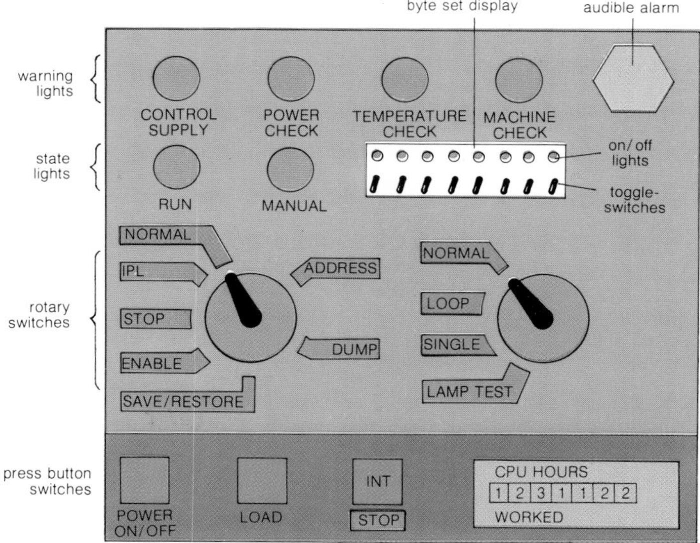

console (*n*) a part of a computer, or other machine, which usually has toggle switches (p. 86), rotary switches (p. 86) and lights. It is used by a person to set the machine in a certain way especially when the machine is being tested. It may be possible to enter data, usually addresses, into the computer but this is hardly ever done except when the computer is being started or tested.

console display a part of a console (↑) which has lights so that a user can see how the computer is set. It is quite often used when the computer is being tested.

console switch a switch (p. 24), usually a toggle switch (p. 86) or a rotary switch (p. 86), on a console (↑) which allows the user to alter the way the computer is to work. It is often used to test whether the computer is working correctly.

toggle-switch (*n*) a small arm on the outside of a machine which operates in a similar way to an electric light switch and can be turned on or off by the user. It will cause a circuit to be used or not depending on the setting. It is the same as a sense-switch (↓) but its use is often to allow special circuits to be used for testing parts of a computer or trying to find the cause if a computer fails to work. *See also* diagram on p. 85.

rotary switch a switch (p. 24) which can have more than two possible settings. There is usually a small circular handle with a metal pointer which can be turned round to show the position that is wanted. It is used in the same way as a toggle-switch (↑).

sense-switch (*n*) a toggle-switch (↑) fitted to the outside of a computer, usually on a console (p. 85), and which an operator (p. 190) can set to on or off. The switch (p. 24) can be used to control the way the program in the computer will work. It is not often used on modern computers.

LED light emitting diode. A circuit which will light up when a current (p. 24) passes through it. It is used to provide lights on a console display (p. 85) and it is also used in place of a screen (p. 84) in some small micro-computers (p. 9).

console typewriter a small character printer (p. 58) which is used with a console (p. 85) to allow the user to enter or receive small amounts of data. The data usually consists of messages to the operator (p. 190) telling what the computer is doing, e.g. it would say when a particular program finished. The operator would use it to tell the computer which programs to run, enter the date, etc.

data cell a device which contains separate sections of magnetic storage, each of which can be randomly accessed (p. 67). It holds a large amount of data but the data cannot be found as quickly as it can be on a disk (p. 66).

cell (*n*) = data cell (↑).

toggle-switch

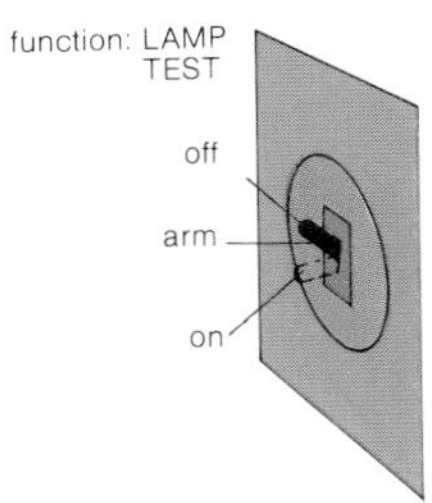

rotary switch

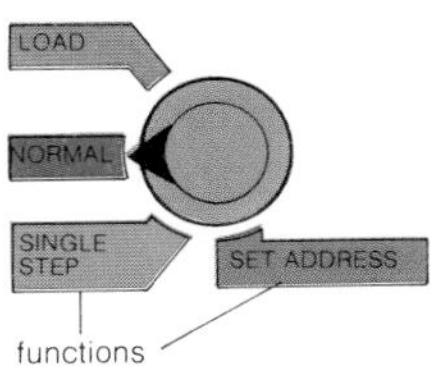

drum

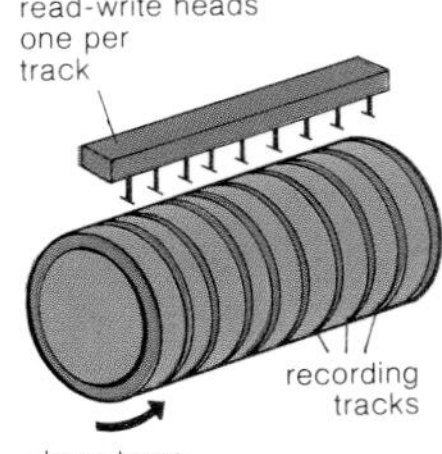

data plotter

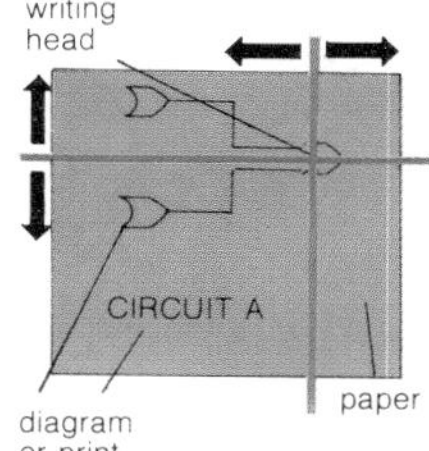

drum (*n*) a storage device in the shape of a hollow roller. The outside surface is covered with magnetic material and can store data. It turns around and read-write heads (p. 202), which are fixed above the surface, can access any part. The access is quicker than on disk (p. 66) but it usually cannot hold as much data.

data plotter a machine which is used to print or draw results in the form of diagrams or graphs (↓). Most plotters can also print letters or numbers to describe parts of the diagrams. The machines vary in size from small machines which will give a hard copy (p. 84) of a screen (p. 84), to those that can draw diagrams which measure 1 metre by 1 metre.

graph plotter a machine which will draw graphs (↓) on paper instead of printing letters and numbers.

flat bed plotter = graph plotter (↑).

plotter (*n*) = graph plotter (↑).

incremental plotter a machine which draws diagrams. It can also do some printing.

graphics display

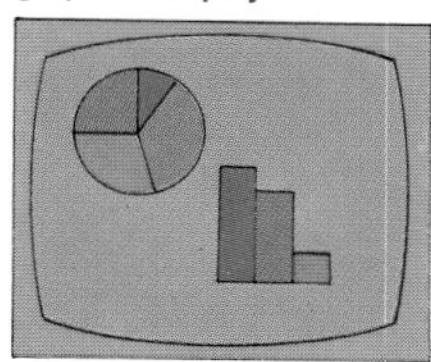

graph (*n*) a diagram which shows results in the form of curved lines and shapes rather than numbers or letters. It can be displayed on a suitable screen (p. 84) or printed on paper on a plotter (↑).

graphics (*n*) the showing of data by means of graphs (↑), diagrams or pictures instead of using letters or numbers. **graphics** (*adj*).

graphics display a VDU (p. 83) which can be used to show results in the form of graphs (↑) or diagrams.

mouse (*n*) a small box with buttons which is attached to a computer. By moving the box and operating the buttons it is possible to move data or diagrams around on the screen (p. 84).

MICR magnetic ink character recognition or reader. A way of, or machine for, recognising printed characters: the ink used contains very small pieces of magnetic material which allows the characters to be read. This is a very common way of reading data when there are small amounts of it on printed forms, e.g. numbers on bank cheques.

magnetic ink character reader a machine which will read characters printed with magnetic ink. It can be on-line (p. 11) to a computer or may be off-line (p. 11) with its own tape unit (p. 71) and simply transfer the data on to tape (p. 71).

light pen a piece of equipment about the size of a pen used mainly in graphics (p. 87) work. It is connected to a VDU (p. 83) and if pointed at the screen (p. 84) can be used to choose what is being displayed on part of the screen, or can cause shapes on the screen to be moved from one part to another to help in drawing diagrams.

E13B a special type of font (p. 59) which is used for magnetic ink character readers (↑).

E-13B
font characters

digits 0 1 2 3

amount symbol

transit symbol

OCR document

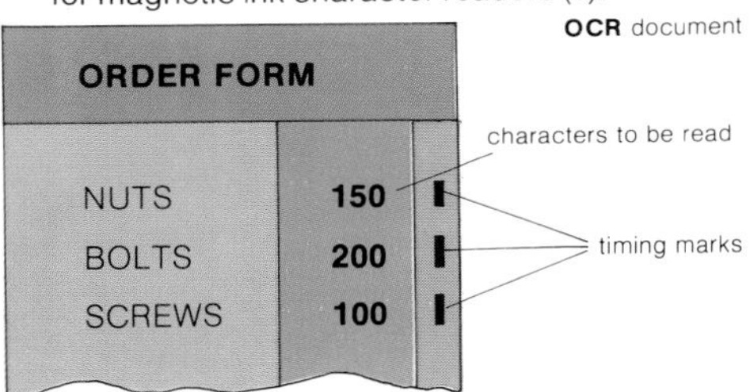

OCR optical character recognition or reader. A way of, or a machine for, recognising characters, usually on paper, by their shape. The shapes are slightly different from the usual printed ones, quite often consisting only of straight lines. They are used to allow small amounts of printed data to be read from forms but they can also read correctly shaped letters and numbers written by a person. It can be on-line (p. 11) to a computer or may be off-line (p. 11) with its own tape unit (p. 71) and simply transfer the data on to the tape (p. 71).

logging device a machine, usually with a magnetic tape (p. 71) or paper tape (p. 64), which will record data measurements. It is connected to another machine whose performance is to be measured. It records a series of measurements with the same amount of time between each measurement.

point-of-sale (*adj*) of a machine that is used to record data when a person buys something. The data recorded is usually what has been bought, and the cost.

word processor a micro-computer (p. 9) with a VDU (p. 83) and a character printer (p. 58) which is used for preparing written material, e.g. letters or reports (p. 185). It stores the data needed to print the reports and has special programs to allow them to be easily changed and re-printed. Sometimes the computer is not used for any other form of computing. (Also describes the programs used).

bar code

badge reader a device which is used for data capture (p. 183). It can read either special forms of punch card (p. 52) or, more usually, plastic cards with a magnetic strip which contains data, e.g. a person's account number. They sometimes also allow extra data to be entered by the user.

bar code a code (p. 45) which is formed of small magnetic lines with gaps between the lines. The lines can be read by a special machine, usually called a bar code scanner, which works like a light pen (↑). It is used where small amounts of data such as point-of-sale (↑) information need to be recorded.

magnetic card a card which has a magnetic strip along one side or edge to record information. The card is not usually a punched (p. 52) card but stiff paper or a plastic card. One type of card can be used to input small amounts of data into a computer, e.g. a customer account number. Another, larger type, is used, not in computers, but in accounting machines which have a small amount of computing ability.

assembly language

assembler instructions to add X to Y and place result in Z		
instruction		comment
L	R1, X	load X into register
A	R1, Y	add Y to register
ST	R1, Z	store register in Z

assembler (*n*) (1) a translator (p. 105) whose purpose is to take source language (p. 103) programs written in assembly language (↓) and produce the object program (p. 104); (2) = an assembly language. **assemble** (*v*).

assembly language a low-level language (p. 104) whose statements (p. 102) are in a similar form to the machine language (p. 104) of a computer. Because different computers have different machine languages each one needs its own assembly language which is different from those for other computers. The differences may be quite small in the case of computers made by the same manufacturer but quite large otherwise. Because of this each assembly language can be used only for writing programs for a particular type or class of computers.

autocoder (*n*) an IBM assembly language (↑) used on its early computers.

mnemonic (*n*) an abbreviation which is used to help a person remember something. They are used in assembly languages (↑) especially for the op-codes (p. 15) of an instruction, e.g. LR would mean Load Register. The names chosen by a programmer for labels (p. 96) and identifiers (p. 97) are also often mnemonic, e.g. TOTSUM would mean total sum.

mnemonics examples in assembler

mnemonic	meaning
L	LOAD
A	ADD
AP	ADD PACKED DECIMALS
BE	BRANCH IF EQUAL
BL	BRANCH IF LOW
STH	STORE HALF WORD
CVB	CONVERT TO BINARY

C (*n*) a program language (p. 103) which combines high-level (p. 104) features with detailed control of the machine in almost the same way as is possible with assembly language (↑). It is particularly useful for writing systems programs (p. 127).

C++ (*n*) an extended form of C (↑).

COBOL Common Business Oriented Language. A program language (p. 103) first used in the 1960s. It is particularly suited to business computing, and it is the most commonly used computer language.

parts of COBOL program

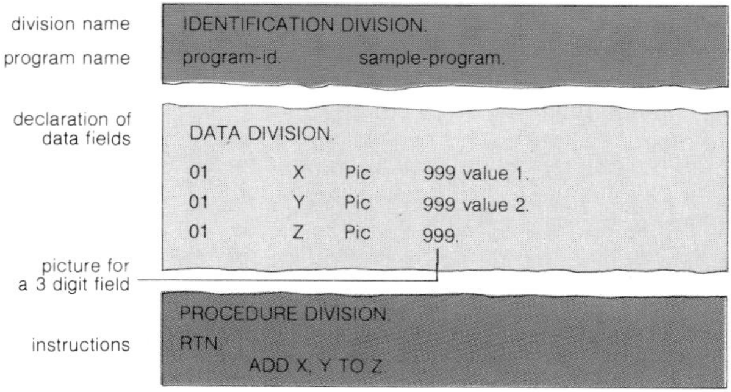

division name
program name

```
IDENTIFICATION DIVISION.
program-id.          sample-program.
```

declaration of data fields

```
DATA DIVISION.
01        X    Pic      999 value 1.
01        Y    Pic      999 value 2.
01        Z    Pic      999.
```

picture for a 3 digit field

instructions

```
PROCEDURE DIVISION.
RTN.
        ADD X, Y TO Z.
```

identification division the part of a COBOL (↑) program which gives the name of the program and, usually, its purpose.

environment division the part of a COBOL (↑) program which gives information about the computer to be used by the program.

data division the part of a COBOL (↑) program where the files (p. 153), variables (p. 119) and constants (p. 119) to be used in the program are defined.

procedure division the part of a COBOL (↑) program in which the statements (p. 102) which are to be executed are placed.

picture clause the part of a statement (p. 102) in a COBOL (↑) data division (↑) which gives the length and type (p. 99) of an identifier (p. 97).

sample of PL/1 program

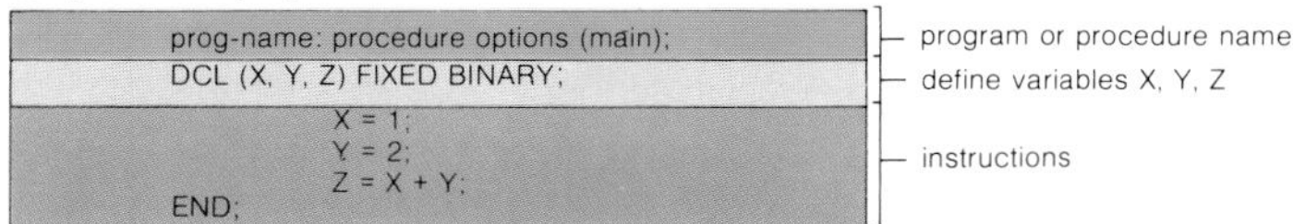

PL/1 a program language (p. 103) which can handle both scientific and business problems. It is a very large language and contains parts that are similar to both COBOL (p. 91) and Fortran (↓).

FORTH a program language (p. 103) designed (p. 121) for small computers; it uses postfix notation, i.e. one where operands (p. 15) precede an operator, and new reserved words (p. 97) can be included.

LOGO a program language (p. 103) specially designed (p. 121) to allow young children to program using a device known as a turtle.

APL *A Programming Language*. A language designed (p. 121) for mathematical applications especially those which use arrays (p. 145) including arrays of characters.

RPG *Report Program Generator*. A program language (p. 103) which is particularly suited for programs which produce printed reports (p. 185). The later versions (p. 129) of the language, called RPG II and RPG III are quite powerful and can be used for a wide range of business programming. It is quite widely used on smaller to medium-sized computers. It uses a fixed cycle, i.e. one where the sequence input-process-output is used for each record (p. 154) processed but variations are allowed. It can also do matching (p. 116).

Pascal (*n*) a program language (p. 103) which was produced in the 1970s largely for the purpose of teaching good methods of structured programming (p. 122). It is now much used as the first language for beginners. The actual language is not very large but there have been a number of additions to make it more useful in practice. It is based on Algol (↓) but is named after the 17th-century French mathematician, Blaise Pascal.

sample of Pascal program

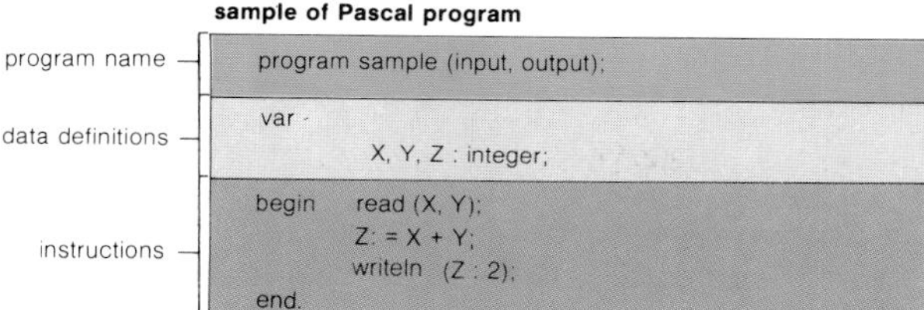

program name
data definitions
instructions
program sample (input, output);
var
X, Y, Z : integer;
begin read (X, Y);
Z: = X + Y;
writeln (Z : 2);
end.

Algol (*n*) a program language (p. 103) used in the 1960s and 1970s largely for scientific problems. The name is from the word algorithm (p. 122). It is still used but is being replaced by other languages.

Algol-68 (*n*) a program language (p. 103) which is a newer and much larger form of Algol (↑). It is rather difficult to use and is not widely used.

algorithmic language a program language (p. 103) which is used to handle problems which can be put into mathematical form. The commonest one is Fortran (↓).

Modula-2 (*n*) a program language (p. 103) which is similar to Pascal (↑) but much larger and able to handle more difficult problems. It is an algorithmic language (↑) which can also be used for writing concurrent (p. 140) programs.

sample of Fortran program

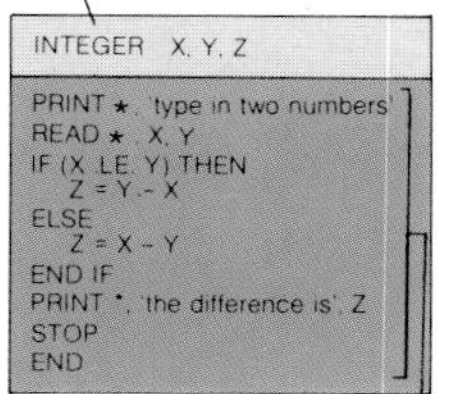

data definition
INTEGER X, Y, Z
PRINT ★, 'type in two numbers'
READ ★, X, Y
IF (X .LE. Y) THEN
Z = Y - X
ELSE
Z = X - Y
END IF
PRINT ★, 'the difference is', Z
STOP
END
instructions

Fortran (*n*) a program language (p. 103) which is very widely used for scientific work. The name comes from the two words 'formula translating'. Since it was introduced in the 1950s there have been several new versions (p. 129) of the language, e.g. Fortran-II, Fortran-IV and Fortran-77.

OCCAM a program language (p. 103) designed (p. 121) for writing programs which handle parallel processing (p. 140).

BASIC *B*eginners *A*ll-purpose *S*ymbolic *I*nstruction *C*ode. A program language (p. 103) designed (p. 121) in the 1960s for fairly simple programming. There are now many versions (p. 129) of the language, many of them not completely compatible (p. 10). Very popular with home users of micro-computers (p. 9) but not really a suitable language for large programs.

Ada (*n*) a program language (p. 103) designed in the 1980s for the American Defence Department. It is particularly intended for use as a real-time (↓) language and it employs up-to-date ideas on how programming languages should be designed (p. 121).

list processing the process of handling data which is held in the form of lists.

LISP (*n*) a program language (p. 103) for handling data in the form of linked lists (p. 146).

pattern matching the process of searching through a text (p. 102) to find groups of characters which have similar arrangements, e.g. brackets containing letters such as (*n*), (*v*), (*adj*), etc.

SNOBOL string oriented symbolic language. A program language (p. 103) which is designed (p. 121) to handle strings (p. 46) and do pattern matching (↑).

PROLOG a program language (p. 103) which is specially designed (p. 121) to handle logical operations (p. 34) on groups of data. It is a fairly new language and is used in artificial intelligence (p. 197) and expert systems (p. 197).

real-time (*adj*) of a program which gives results quickly enough for the user to decide what the next action will be. For example, a program for booking aeroplane flights must let a person know immediately whether seats are available so that a decision can be made about which flight to take. Also used in systems controlling the operation of machinery. **real-time** (*n*).

real-time operation work that must be done in real-time (↑).

real-time language a program language (p. 103) which is specially designed (p. 121) for writing real-time (↑) programs.

interactive program a program where the output is produced, usually on a VDU (p. 83), and the user then decides what to input next. The process continues with the input and output following one another.

conversational mode a method of working where the input and output of a program is interactive (↑).

pattern matching

find all words beginning comput e.g.

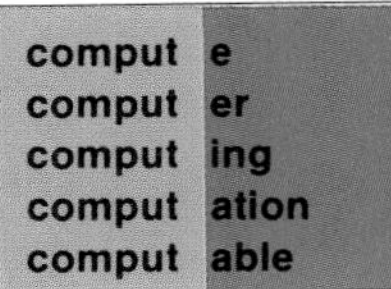

conversational mode

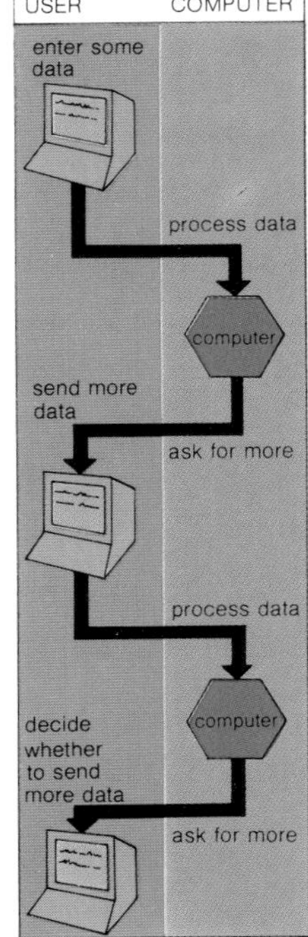

statements in assembler

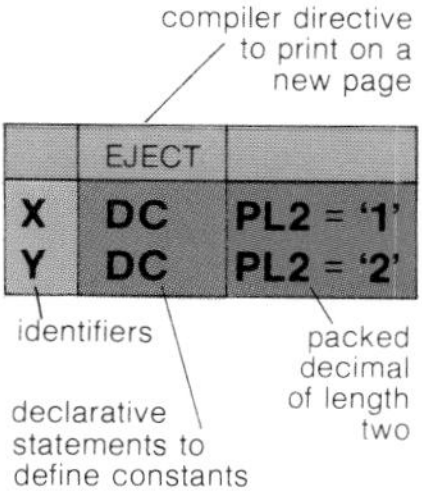

compiler directive to print on a new page

	EJECT	
X	**DC**	**PL2 = '1'**
Y	**DC**	**PL2 = '2'**

identifiers

declarative statements to define constants

packed decimal of length two

comment (*n*) a note which is included in a source program (p. 103) to explain some point in the program. It is not part of the program and is not compiled (p. 105) into instructions.

compiler directive a statement (p. 102) in a source program (p. 103) which tells the compiler (p. 105) to do something, e.g. print more information than usual, skip (p. 61) to the top of a new page, etc. The statements are not part of the program and are not compiled into instructions.

control statement (1) = compiler directive (↑); (2) a statement (p. 102) in a source program (p. 103) which usually tests the value of one or more switches (p. 24) or variables (p. 119) in order to decide which part of the program to do next.

declarative statement a statement (p. 102) in a source program (p. 103) which tells the compiler (p. 105) how variables (p. 119), constants (p. 119) etc, are going to be used or represented (p. 45). It is usual in most languages to say whether a variable will be used to hold numeric (p. 15) or alphabetic (p. 45) data but in some languages the variables have to be defined with more detail, e.g. the range of values that they are allowed to hold, whether numbers are integers (p. 209), etc. **declaration** (*n*), **declare** (*v*).

pseudo-instruction (*n*) (1) = compiler directive (↑); (2) = declarative statement (↑).

conditional statement (1) a statement (p. 102) in a source program (p. 103) which usually has several parts. The first part controls whether some or any of the other parts will be executed when the program is run. For example, the statement 'If A = 1 print message' will generate (p. 10) several instructions in the object program (p. 104). The first one will always be executed and will test the value of A, but the execution of the other instructions will depend on the result of the test. (2) a statement, quite often one in a macro (p. 101), which may or may not be compiled (p. 105) depending on the value of a parameter (p. 112).

label (*n*) a word or number which names or refers to a statement (p. 102) in a source program (p. 103). It is placed in front of the statement but does not form part of the instruction generated (p. 10) from the statement. However, any other statements can use the label to refer to the first statement, and in these statements the label will form part of the instruction and will be replaced by the address of the first statement when the program is compiled (p. 105).

dummy instruction data which is set out like an instruction but not actually executed. It is used in assembly languages (p. 90) to make sure that data or other instructions are placed correctly in memory.

location counter a counter (p. 15) in a compiler (p. 105) which keeps a count of how much memory has so far been used by the program which is being compiled.

free format of a statement (p. 102) of a source language (p. 103) which does not have to be in a specific position. In some languages, e.g. RPG (p. 92), the statements must be written in the exact form needed by the compiler (p. 105). Other languages will accept any extra blank spaces between parts of the statement and do not mind where a statement begins or ends.

label of instruction

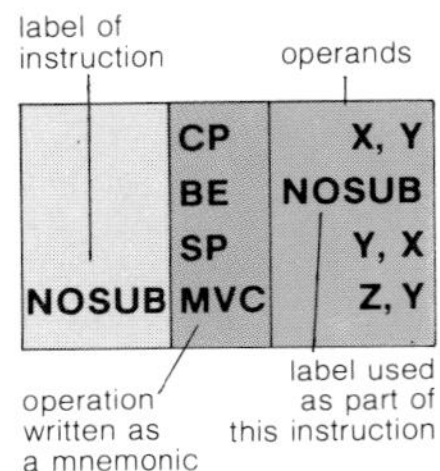

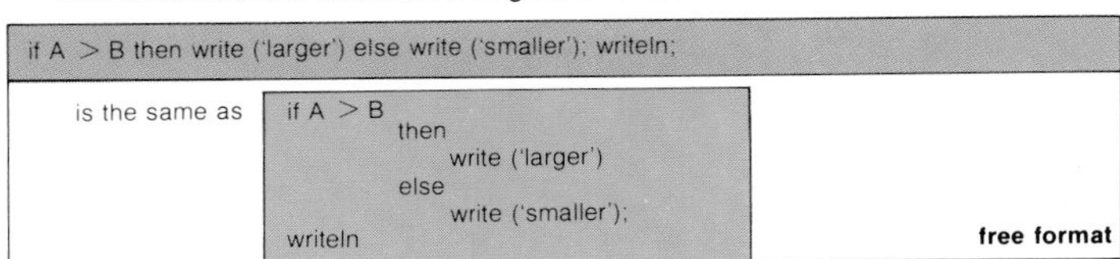

free format

reference listing a print-out (p. 19) from a compiler (p. 105) showing the source program (p. 103) statements (p. 102) and giving information about the object program (p. 104). The amount of information differs according to the compiler, those for high-level languages (p. 104) usually give less than those for low-level languages (p. 104). The amount of information printed can also be changed by compiler directives (p. 95).

identifier (*n*) a name used in a program to refer to data, either variables (p. 111) or constants (p. 119), or to names of procedures (p. 111) and functions (p. 18). It can refer to a single item of data or groups of items. It can also refer to labels (↑), and in some program languages (p. 103) to key words (↓).

key word

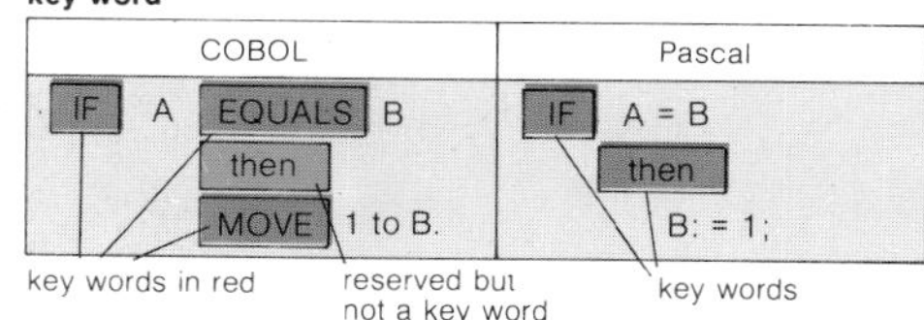

reserved word a word which is used by the program language (p. 103) and which must not be used by the programmer as a label (↑) or identifier (↑) in any statement (p. 102), e.g. the words 'if', 'for', 'print', etc.

key word[2] In some languages reserved words (↑) may be used to make the program more readable but they are not necessary. For example, in the COBOL (p. 91) statement (p. 102) 'On Size Error' the word 'On' is a reserved word but it may be omitted. The words 'Size Error', however, are key words and must be included.

literal (*n*) a piece of data used in a program which is defined, or appears, in a declarative statement (p. 95), or in the source language (p. 103) statement (p. 102) that uses it. The literal cannot have an identifier (↑), or name, and the programmer cannot refer to it in other statements, but it can be used to give a value to a variable (p. 119) or constant (p. 119) which does have an identifier.

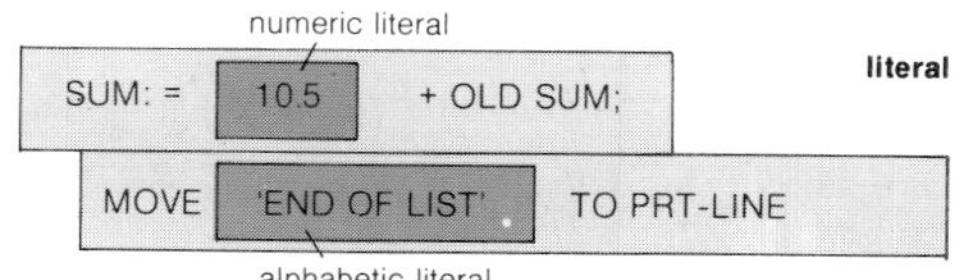

literal

delimiter (*n*) one or more characters which mark the end of a string (p. 46), a statement (p. 102) or even a part of a statement. In program languages (p. 103) they can be words such as 'begin' or 'end', single characters e.g. '.' or ';', or even operators such as '+' or '-'. **delimit** (*v*).

separator (*n*) (1) a character or characters which separate the parts of a statement (p. 102) rather than mark the end of it, e.g. in written English blanks separate one word from the next but a full stop marks, i.e. delimits (↑), the end of a sentence; (2) = a delimiter.

implementation (*n*) the way a compiler (p. 105) is actually programmed for a particular computer. Languages have general rules on how they are to work but the manner in which a particular compiler will carry out these rules will differ from one computer to another.

interpreter[2] (*n*) a form of compiler (p. 105) which translates (p. 105) source language (p. 103) statements (p. 102) into a special code (p. 102) which is then compiled and executed. It may do this for the program as a whole, or statement by statement. It compiles more quickly than normal compilers but does not produce an object program (p. 104). The resulting programs usually execute more slowly but the use of an interpreter can speed up the writing and testing of a program. **interpret** (*v*).

symbol (*n*) the name actually used for a label (p. 96) or identifier (p. 97).

symbol table a table (p. 144) produced by a compiler (p. 105) which includes all the symbols (↑) used in a source program (p. 103) and the relative address (p. 114) which each symbol has been given.

token (*n*) the name given to each different part of a statement (p. 102) when it is parsed (↓). Tokens are produced by the lexical analyser (↓). Also known as **lexical element.**

lexical analyser the part of a compiler (p. 105) which takes the source program (p. 103) and removes any unwanted parts of the text (p. 102), e.g. blank spaces, and produces tokens (↑) which can be handled by the syntax analyser (↓).

lexical analyser

tokens

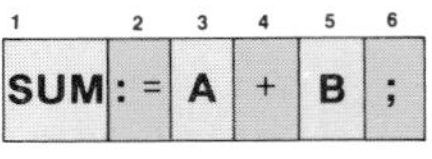

token table

no.	token	type
1	SUM	2
2	: =	1
3	A	2
4	+	1
5	B	2
6	;	1

type 1 — symbols with a fixed meaning in the language

type 2 — names or identifiers with meaning only in this program

syntax error

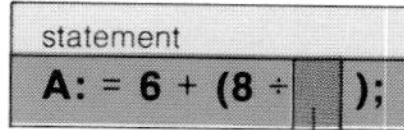

missing number
or name of divisor

semantic error

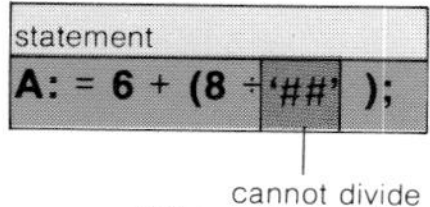

grammar (*n*) the rules for a program language (p. 103) saying what sort of statements (p. 102) can be used and the format in which they have to be written.

syntax (*n*) the rules for a program language (p. 103) which say how a statement (p. 102) in a language can be written. The meaning of words and characters in a statement is not considered, only the order in which they are allowed to be written. The sentences 'the boy ate an apple' and 'an apple ate the boy' are both syntactically correct English, although the second one does not make sense. The sentence 'an the ate boy apple' has the same words as the first two sentences but is not syntactically correct. **syntactic** (*adj*).

syntax analyser the part of a compiler (p. 105) which checks that the syntax (↑) is correct. Also known as **syntactic analyser**.

parse (*v*) to examine a statement (p. 102) to decide whether its syntax (↑) is correct. **parser** (*n*).

semantics (*n*) the rules which decide whether a statement (p. 102) in a program language (p. 103) has an acceptable meaning. The English sentence 'an apple ate the boy' is syntactically (↑) correct but is semantically unacceptable.

code generation the action of that part of a compiler (p. 105) which produces the actual machine language (p. 104) instructions of the object program (p. 104). **generate** (*v*).

garbage collection a process in the execution of a program where the data which is still needed is arranged, usually into one area of memory. The space taken by data which is no longer needed and any spare memory is made available for the next part of the program.

type (*n*) a particular class of data. For example, characters, as a group, form a type which itself consists of several other types, e.g. the letters a-z, the numbers 0,1,2, etc and special characters (p. 46). A type may also limit the operations which can be carried out, e.g. if variables (p. 119) are described as characters, it is not usually possible to add or subtract them.

bind (*v*) to give an actual value to a symbol (p. 98) or variable (p. 119). The symbol may be a label (p. 96), an identifier (p. 97) or a parameter (p. 112).

binding time the actual point when a value is given to a symbol (p. 98) or variable (p. 119). It can happen during compilation (p. 105), or when a program is being loaded (p. 106), or during execution. For example, the actual address (p. 113) of a variable might be fixed when a program was loaded but the variable might not have a value until some point during the execution of the program.

meta-language (*n*) a special type of language, not a program language (p. 103), whose purpose is to allow other languages, especially program languages, to be specified (p. 203).

Backus-Naur form BNF. A meta-language (↑), named after Backus and Naur, which is often used to describe the syntax (p. 99) of program languages (p. 103).

Backus normal form = Backus-Naur form (↑).

Backus-Naur form meta-language

means a digit is a '0' or a '1' or a '2' etc

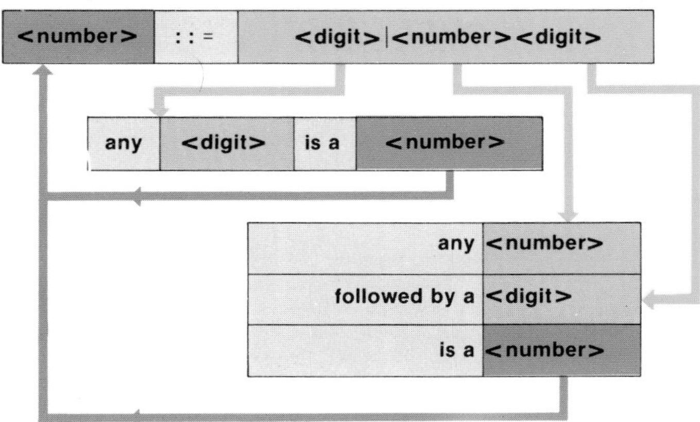

macro definition

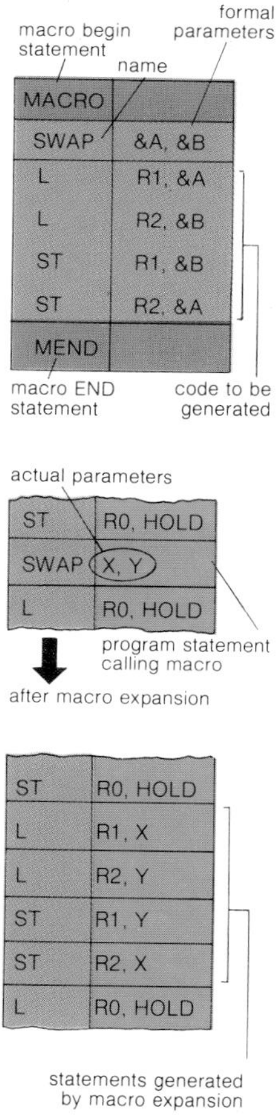

macro begin statement — name — formal parameters

MACRO	
SWAP	&A, &B
L	R1, &A
L	R2, &B
ST	R1, &B
ST	R2, &A
MEND	

macro END statement — code to be generated

actual parameters

ST	R0, HOLD
SWAP	X, Y
L	R0, HOLD

program statement calling macro

after macro expansion

ST	R0, HOLD
L	R1, X
L	R2, Y
ST	R1, Y
ST	R2, X
L	R0, HOLD

statements generated by macro expansion

Chomsky grammar one of the grammars (p. 99) described and defined by Chomsky, whose ideas are commonly used in the definition of program languages (p. 103).

macro (*n*) a single statement (p. 102) in a source program (p. 103) that produces a number of source language (p. 103) instructions which are then compiled (p. 105) into the actual object program (p. 104). A macro usually does something which is often needed by programmers and so the use of a macro saves time and avoids errors. Macros can have parameters (p. 112) to allow slightly different instructions to be produced which do exactly what is wanted by a particular program.

macro expansion (1) the set of instructions produced by a macro (↑); (2) the process in a compilation (p. 105) where a macro is replaced by source program (p. 103) instructions.

macro definition the statements (p. 102) which make up a macro (↑). They contain formal parameters (p. 113) which have to be replaced by actual parameters (p. 113) when the macro is used.

macro generator the part of a compiler (p. 105) which changes macros (↑) into source language (p. 103) instructions.

compiler compiler a program which will take the rules for a language and produce a compiler (p. 105) for the language.

cross compiler a compiler (p. 105) which runs on one computer but produces object programs (p. 104) for a different computer. Often a cross compiler is used on a large machine to produce object programs for micro-computers (p. 9) for which there is no compiler available, or which are too small to do the compilation themselves.

cross-reference listing a printed list which shows all the identifiers (p. 97) used in a program. The list is usually in alphabetical (p. 45) sequence and gives the name, the address, and type (p. 99) of each identifier, the number of the statement (p. 102) where it is defined and also the numbers of all the statements where it is used.

code part of assembler program listing showing object code and source code

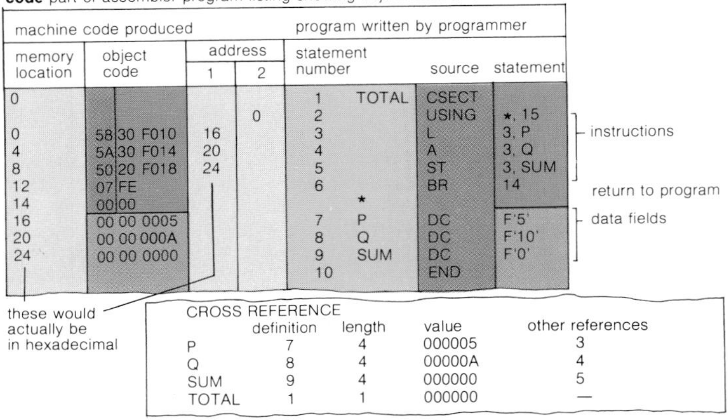

machine code produced				program written by programmer				
memory location	object code	address 1	address 2	statement number		source	statement	
0				1	TOTAL	CSECT		
			0	2		USING	*, 15	
0	58 30 F010	16		3		L	3, P	instructions
4	5A 30 F014	20		4		A	3, Q	
8	50 20 F018	24		5		ST	3, SUM	
12	07 FE			6		BR	14	return to program
14	00 00				*			
16	00 00 0005			7	P	DC	F'5'	data fields
20	00 00 000A			8	Q	DC	F'10'	
24	00 00 0000			9	SUM	DC	F'0'	
				10		END		

these would actually be in hexadecimal

CROSS REFERENCE

	definition	length	value	other references
P	7	4	000005	3
Q	8	4	00000A	4
SUM	9	4	000000	5
TOTAL	1	1	000000	—

code[3] (*v*) to write a program or part of a program. **coder** (*n*).

code[1] (*n*) the set of instructions, or a listing of them, which make up a program or a module (p. 106). Can mean either the source program (↓) or the object program (p. 104).

coding sheet a sheet of paper on which a programmer writes source language statements (↓). The paper is usually ruled to help the programmer.

text (*n*) (1) = source code (↓); (2) the listing or contents of any file (p. 153) but particularly one which contains ordinary written English.

statement (*n*) a single complete instruction in a source language (↓) or a job control language (p. 132). The instruction in the source language may produce more than one machine language (p. 104) instruction.

programmer (*n*) a person who writes programs. As well as writing the statements (↑) the programmer usually decides how the program will be set out and the order in which it will deal with the data.

coder (*n*) a programmer, especially one who writes programs whose general arrangement has been prepared by someone else.

program language the language used to write a program. There are hundreds of such languages. Some are for general use and can be used for a wide range of work, e.g. COBOL (p. 91) and Fortran (p. 93); others are used only for special purposes, e.g. LISP (p. 94) and SNOBOL (p. 94).

language (*n*) (1) = a program language (↑); (2) = a machine language (p. 104).

sub-set (*n*) a part of a language which has enough instructions to write programs but does not contain all the instructions which are available in the complete language. Some languages are very large and the full set of instructions can be used only with large computers; smaller computers have to use sub-set.

source language the actual language that a programmer uses to write a program. It is fairly easy for humans to understand but it is not in the form that a computer can use directly. It needs to be translated (p. 105) into the machine language (p. 104) that the computer uses.

source program a program written in a source language (↑).

source code = source program (↑).

source computer a computer on which a source program (↑) is compiled. It might not be the same as the one on which the object program (p. 104) will be run.

source program

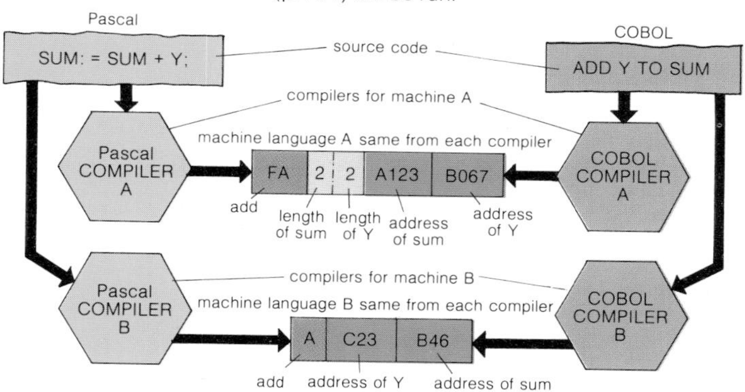

machine language the only form of language that a computer can actually understand and use directly. It consists of instructions in the exact format used by the computer. Each make of computer has its own machine language. Programs for one computer will not run on another if it has a different machine language.
object program a program produced by translating (↓) a source program (p. 103). It is in the machine language (↑) of the computer which is going to be used for running the program.
object code = object program (↑).
object deck a set of punch cards (p. 52) which contains an object program (↑).
object computer a computer on which a program is going to be run. It does not have to be the same as the computer used to translate (↓) the source program (p. 103), but the object program (↑) must be in the correct machine language (↑) for the computer which is to run the program.
target computer = object computer (↑).
low-level language a program language (p. 103) in which the statements (p. 102) are similar to the actual instructions a computer uses. A single statement usually produces a single computer instruction. It is possible with a low-level language to control the computer very closely and produce programs which will work very quickly, but it is usually a language which is difficult to use. The source programs (p. 103) take longer to write and test.
high-level language a program language (p. 103) in which the statements (p. 102) are not very similar to actual computer instructions. A single statement will usually produce more than one computer instruction. The programs produced are not as quick as those written in low-level languages (↑) but the source programs (p. 103) are much easier to write and to understand and easier to move from one computer to another.
problem-oriented language a program language (p. 103) which is used for a special class of problem. For example, a language such as SNOBOL (p. 94) handles strings (p. 46) of characters but can only handle this class of work.

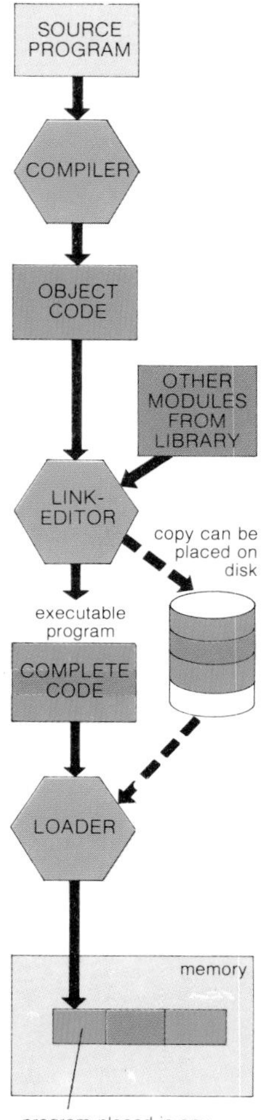

procedure-oriented language a program language (p. 103) which handles general problems. The programmer writes a sequence of procedures (p. 111) which will do the work wanted. These languages differ in the sort of problems they will handle, e.g. Fortran (p. 93) is intended for scientific problems, COBOL (p. 91) is intended for general business work.

translate (*v*) to take a source program (p. 103) as input to a compiler (↓) and output an object program (↑). **translation** (*n*).

compiler (*n*) a program whose purpose is to change a source program (p. 103) into an object program (↑). Each source language (p. 103) needs its own particular compiler, for example, a program written in Fortran (p. 93) can be compiled only by a Fortran compiler. Compiler is the word always used when the source language is not in assembly language (p. 90), and is sometimes used when it is in assembly language. **compile** (*v*), **compilation** (*n*).

translator (*n*) = compiler (↑).

compile time the time when a source program (p. 103) is being compiled (↑). Any errors found because the source program is not using the program language (p. 103) correctly are called compile time errors. If there are errors the compiler will usually not be able to produce an object program (↑).

relocation (*n*) the process of making the necessary changes to an object program (↑), mainly to memory addresses, so that it can be placed in any part of memory. **relocate** (*v*), **relocatable** (*adj*).

relocatable program a program which can be loaded (p. 106) into any part of the memory of a computer. Early compilers (↑) produced object programs (↑) which had to go into a particular part of memory, decided by the programmer. Modern compilers usually produce programs which have to be relocated (↑) before they can be used but this allows them to be loaded into any part of memory which is available when they need to be run.

module compiling and linking separate modules

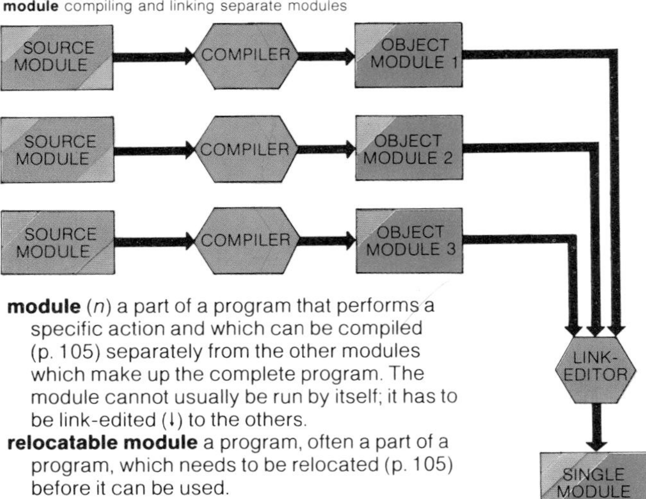

module (*n*) a part of a program that performs a specific action and which can be compiled (p. 105) separately from the other modules which make up the complete program. The module cannot usually be run by itself; it has to be link-edited (↓) to the others.

relocatable module a program, often a part of a program, which needs to be relocated (p. 105) before it can be used.

load (*v*) to take a program from the place where it is stored, usually a disk (p. 66), and place it in memory so that it can be run. The program is usually stored as a relocatable module (↑) and is relocated (p. 105) by the loading program.

loader (*n*) a special program whose purpose is to load (↑) other programs or modules (↑) into memory.

link-editor (*n*) a special program whose purpose is to join together a number of relocatable modules (↑) which have been loaded (↑) into memory. Also known as **linker**. **link-edit** (*v*), **link** (*v*).

link-loader (*n*) a program which will both link-edit (↑) and load (↑) program modules (↑). **link-load** (*v*).

compile-and-go (*n*) a compilation (p. 105) which produces an object program (p. 104) in memory for immediate execution but does not store a copy on disk (p. 66). The program may need to be link-edited (↑) but it does not need to be loaded (↑).

load-and-go (*n*) = compile-and-go (↑).

re-run (*v*) to run a program again, usually because something was not right with a previous run.

run-time (*n*) (1) the time when an object program (p. 104) is running on a computer. Any errors which are found are because the program does not do exactly what was intended or because the data it is using is wrong, i.e. different from what was expected; (2) the actual time taken for a program to execute.

execution time = run-time (↑).

directory (*n*) (1) a list of the files (p. 153) contained on a disk pack (p. 66). The files may be data, computer programs, or just routines (p. 111). The list often holds details such as disk address (p. 69), size, type (p. 99), date written etc. The directory may be one of the files; (2) = library (↓).

library (*n*) a collection of programs, routines (p. 111), or files (p. 153) usually held on a disk pack (p. 66). It may have a directory (↑) giving the name and the disk address (p. 69) of each file.

program library a collection of programs, either source programs (p. 103) or object programs (p. 104). The library is usually held on a disk pack (p. 66).

catalogue (*v*) to place a file (p. 153) or program in a library (↑).

cataloguing a program

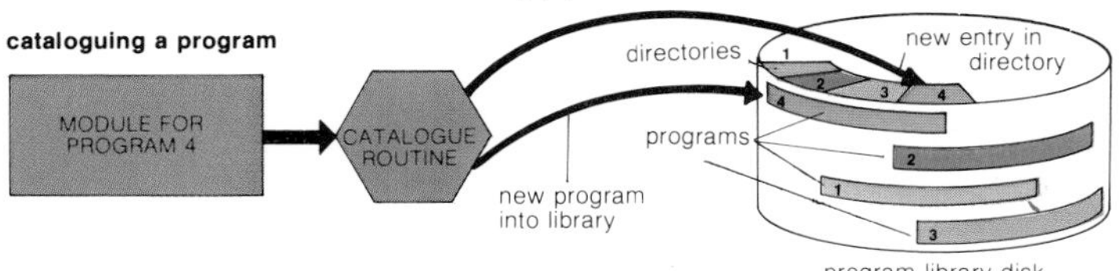

optimize (*v*) to get the best arrangement possible. It is possible to write programs either so that they run quickly or so that they take as little space in memory as they can and programmers may try to do one or the other. Some compilers (p. 105), known as optimizing compilers, can be set to provide either the quickest or the smallest program. **optimization** (*n*).

transparent (*adj*) of something which performs a necessary action but of which a program is not aware, or need not concern itself; the action has no effect on the working of the program. The word can refer to a routine (p. 111), a program or a device.

re-entrant program a program, or routine (p. 111), that has been written in a way that allows it to be used by two or more users at the same time. It avoids the need to have a copy of the same program in memory for each user. **re-entrant** (*adj*).

one program for 3 users

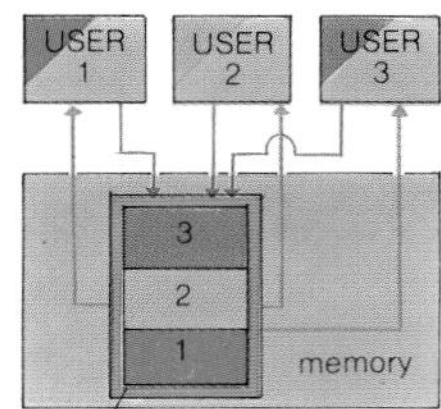

1 copy of program

re-entrant program

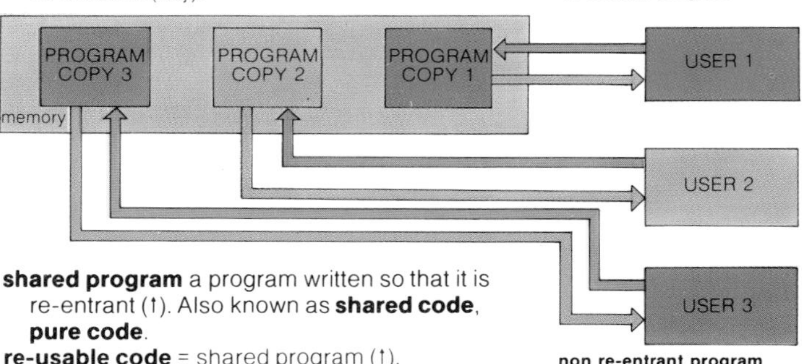

non re-entrant program

3 copies for 3 users

shared program a program written so that it is re-entrant (↑). Also known as **shared code**, **pure code**.

re-usable code = shared program (↑).

emulation (*n*) a means of running programs written for one computer on another computer. The second computer has special circuits whose purpose is to allow it to handle programs and data just as if they were running on the computer for which they were written. It avoids changing the data and programs to the form needed by the second computer. **emulate** (*v*), **emulator** (*n*).

simulation[1] (*n*) (1) a form of emulation (↑), but instead of using special circuits extra programs are written for one computer which will take data and programs written for another computer and run them just as if they were on the computer for which they were written; (2) the use of a specially written program to carry out the same kind of actions that happen in daily life to see what the effects of changes would be. **simulate** (*v*), **simulator** (*n*).

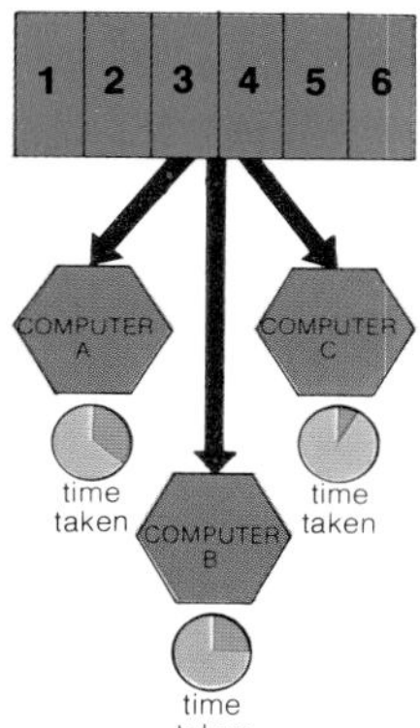

transformation (*n*) the process of changing, usually data, from one arrangement to another. Quite often items of data entered into a computer are arranged in the way in which it is easiest for persons to enter them, but this may not be the most suitable for the computer to use so the items are re-arranged. **transform** (*v*).

benchmark (*n*) a set of programs and files (p. 153) which are run on different computers to see how quickly each computer performs the work. The programs and data may be specially written or they may be chosen from a user's application programs (p. 128). **benchmark** (*v*).

information hiding a method which limits information to just those procedures (p. 111) which need it.

portable (*adj*) of a program which can be taken from one computer and used on another with no change or with only small changes. Object programs (p. 104), which are in machine language (p. 104), are usually not portable unless the computers are very similar. Source programs (p. 103) written in a high-level language (p. 104) are usually portable. For example, a program written in Fortran (p. 93) for one computer could be taken to another computer and the Fortran compiler (p. 105) on the second machine will probably be able to compile it so that is can run. Source programs written in low-level languages (p. 104), especially those in assembly language (p. 90), are not usually portable. **portability** (*n*), **port** (*v*).

machine independent of a program which does not depend in any way on the particular computer which is being used to run the program. It is similar to the idea of portability (↑). It can also mean that some part of the program is not dependent on the use of a particular computer, thus a statement (p. 102) in a high-level language (p. 104) to add two numbers is likely to be machine independent but the number of digits (p. 16) that can be handled may well depend on the size of the particular computer being used.

in-line code (1) a sequence of instructions which either does not contain a branch instruction (p. 37) or does not contain an instruction which causes the program to branch (p. 116) outside the sequence; (2) the main-line code (↓) of a program. **in-line** (*n*).

main-line code the main part of a program which either carries out the work needed or branches (p. 116) to sub-routines (↓) which handle pieces of work not dealt with in-line (↑).

main program the main part or module (p. 106) of a program. It contains the main-line code (↑) and controls the work of the program largely by calling other routines (↓) to do various parts of the work as the need arises. The term may also have a special meaning in a particular program language. For example, a main program in Fortran (p. 93) cannot contain sub-routines (↓).

sub-routine (*n*) a group of instructions which do a particular piece of work that usually needs to be done several times but at different places in the program. It can be placed in-line (↑) in which case the instructions are repeated each time they are needed. More often it is not in-line, i.e. it appears just once in the program, and so whenever it is needed the main-line code (↑) will branch (p. 116) to the sub-routine. Special arrangements are made so that after the sub-routine has been completed it returns to the main-line code at the place where it was called from.

open sub-routine a sub-routine (↑) which is in-line (↑), i.e. the code (p. 102) is repeated whenever it is used.

in-line sub-routine = open sub-routine (↑).

closed sub-routine a sub-routine (↑) which is not in-line (↑). It is branched (p. 116) to from the main-line code (↑) and must go back there when it has completed its work.

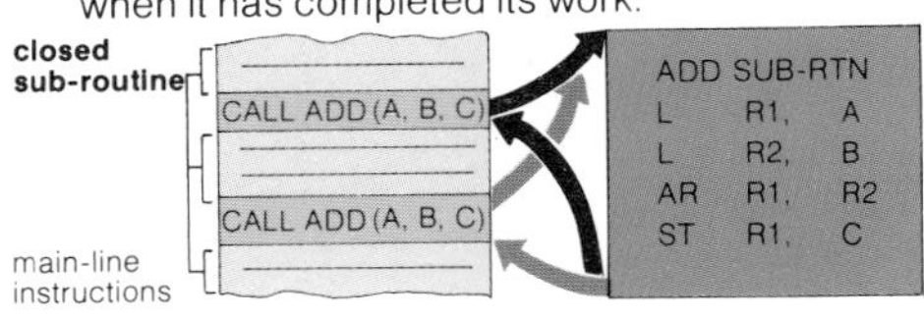

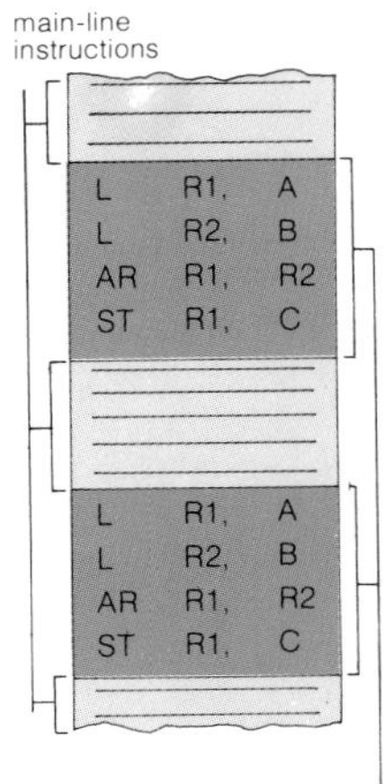

procedure (*n*) (1) a closed sub-routine (↑) in high-level languages (p. 104) which has parameters (p. 112), local (p. 119) variables (p. 119), and constants (p. 119). It can sometimes be compiled (p. 105) separately; (2) a sequence of commands to an operating system (p. 130) which says which programs are to be run and which files (p. 153) to be used.

routine (*n*) a sub-routine (↑) which performs more general work and so is made available to a range of programs. For example, the instructions to deal with file (p. 153) input or output might be handled by a separate routine which could be included in a number of different programs.

calling procedure (1) a procedure (↑) which is calling (↓) another procedure or sub-routine (↑); (2) = a calling sequence (↓).

calling routine = calling procedure (↑).

calling sequence a group of instructions which needs to be executed before branching (p. 116) to a sub-routine (↑) or a procedure (↑). The instructions may do a number of things such as set up and pass parameters (p. 112) correctly, set values for program switches (p. 120), and provide the return address (p. 112).

call (*n*) a statement which causes a transfer to a sub-routine (↑) or procedure (↑). Some languages e.g. Pascal (p. 92) use just the name of the procedure, others e.g. PL/1 (p. 92) precede the name by the word CALL. **call** (*v*).

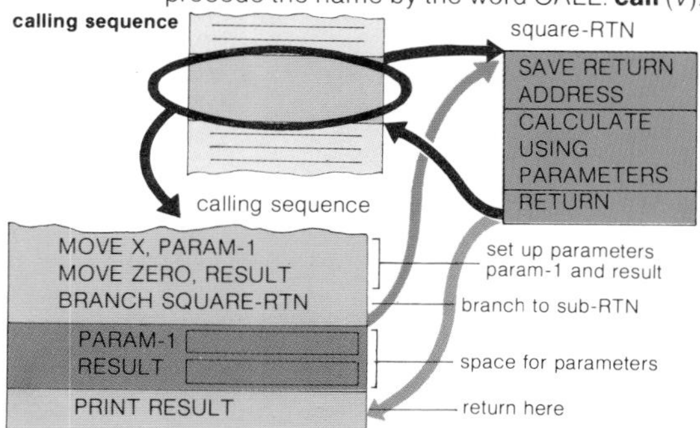

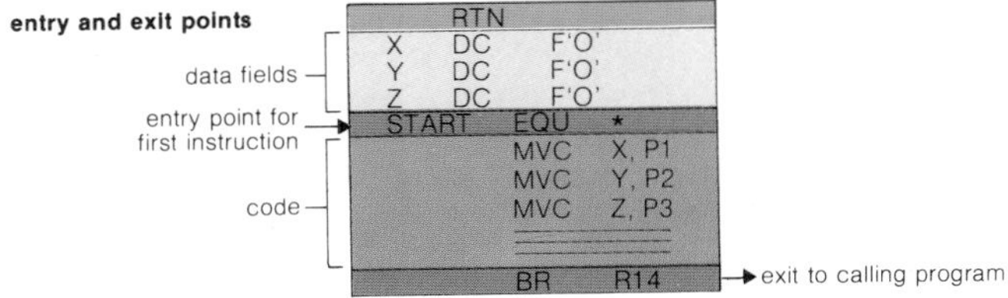

entry point the instruction in a program or sub-routine (p. 110) at which execution can begin. There may be one or more such points depending on the work which is to be done.

exit (*v*) to leave a program or, more commonly, a sub-routine (p. 110). It is usually an instruction which branches (p. 116) to the return address (↓). **exit** (*n*).

return address the address of the point in the main program (p. 110) or calling routine (p. 111) where a sub-routine (p. 110) is to return on completion. The address is usually that of the instruction after the one that branched (p. 116) to the sub-routine.

parameter (*n*) the name or address of a variable (p. 119) or a constant (p. 119) which is passed to a sub-routine (p. 110) in order for the sub-routine to carry out its work. For example, if the sub-routine has to add any two numbers and give the result, then the numbers, or the addresses of the numbers would be supplied as parameters. The name or address of the variable which was to receive the result might also be a parameter. **parameterize** (*v*).

call by value a call (p. 111) which copies a parameter (↑) to a sub-routine (p. 110) or procedure (p. 111). The original value cannot be altered by this call.

call by reference a call (p. 111) which passes the address of the parameter (↑) to a sub-routine (p. 110) or procedure (p. 111); it allows the original value to be altered.

call by name = call by reference (↑).

value parameter a parameter (↑) which contains the actual value to be used or returned by the sub-routine (p. 110).

actual and formal parameters

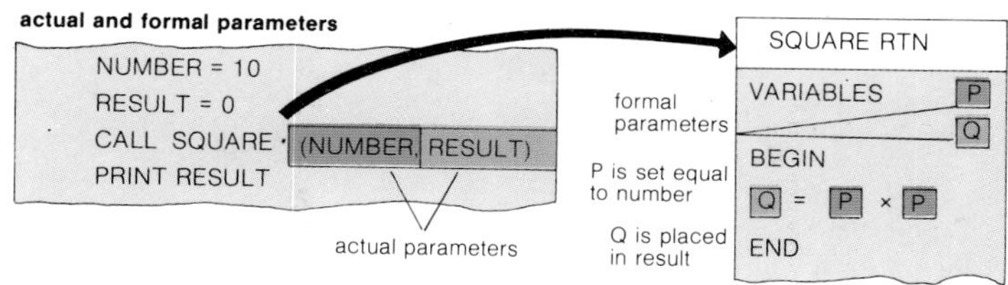

address format

different ways of writing SUM = X + SUM

machine A

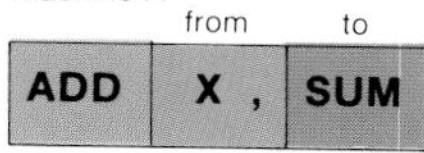

machine B

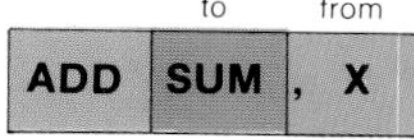

absolute address

instruction with absolute addresses

add contents of 111 to contents of 112

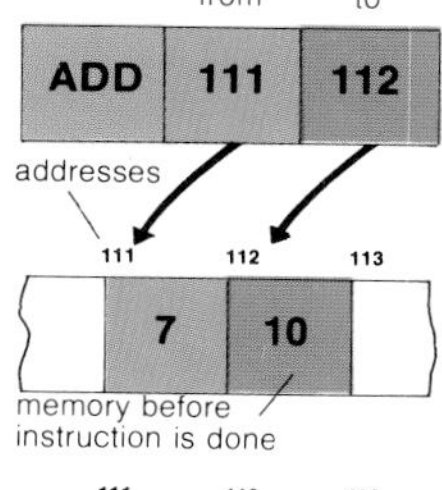

memory before instruction is done

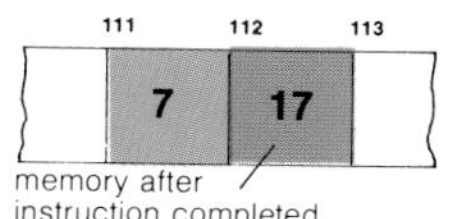

memory after instruction completed

actual parameter a parameter (↑) supplied by the part of the program which calls (p. 111) a sub-routine (p. 110).

formal parameter the name of a variable (p. 119) or constant (p. 119) in the sub-routine (p. 110) which is to be used to hold the actual parameter (↑).

variable parameter a parameter (↑) whose value, which is stored in the main program (p. 110), can be altered by a sub-routine (p. 110) so that the new value then becomes the one used by the main program.

address format the way an address is set out in an instruction. For example, it may show that an address consists of two parts, the number of a register (p. 14) and another number. The computer would add the second number to the register and use the result as the actual address (↓).

from-address (*n*) the place where an instruction is to get its data. Most instructions have two addresses saying where the data is to be taken from and where it is to be placed but the order in which they appear in an instruction differs from one computer to another.

to-address (*n*) the place where an instruction is to send data.

absolute address the actual number of a memory location. Most addresses in a program are not in this form since the use of absolute addresses would prevent the program from being relocatable (p. 105). Certain special memory locations however hold data such as the date, which any program may wish to use. This would be in a fixed memory location and would be accessed by using its absolute address.

actual address = absolute address (↑).

generated address an address found by calculation when a program is being run.

direct address the address part of an instruction which is to be used as the address. It is not the same as an absolute address (p. 113). It will usually consist of a number which has to be added to the contents of register (p. 14) to find the absolute address.

indirect address the address part of an instruction that points to another memory location which does not hold the data to be used but contains the address which points to the data.

immediate address an address in an instruction which does not point to a memory location but is the actual data to be used by the instruction.

base register a register (p. 14) which is being used for addressing. It will contain a value, which is usually the start of an area of memory. The absolute address (p. 113) is found by adding the displacement (↓) to the base register.

base address the address in a base register (↑). It is the address of the start of an area of memory.

displacement (*n*) the number of positions from a fixed starting point such as the start of an area of memory or the beginning of a record (p. 154).

reference address = displacement (↑).

relative address (1) = displacement (↑); (2) the address of a record (p. 154) in a relative file (p. 166).

relative code a code (p. 102) in which the addresses are given as a displacement (↑) from the actual start position of the program or sub-routine (p. 110).

address modification the process of changing an address. The change is usually made by changing the value in a base register (↑) or an index register (p. 145). It is a very common way of making one instruction refer to different memory locations.

overlay (*n*) a method of using less memory to run a program. The program is in segments (↓) and when a new segment is needed it is placed in the same part of memory previously used by another segment which is now no longer needed.

indirect address
instruction with indirect addressing

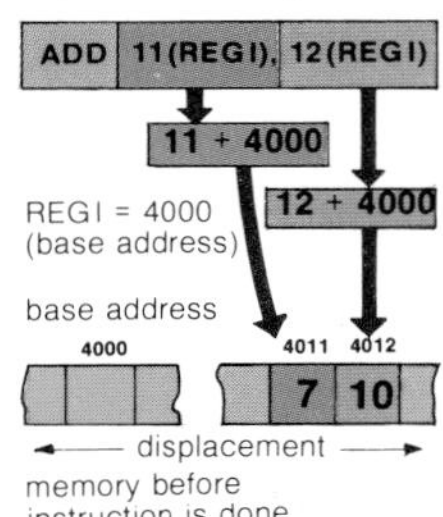

memory after instruction completed

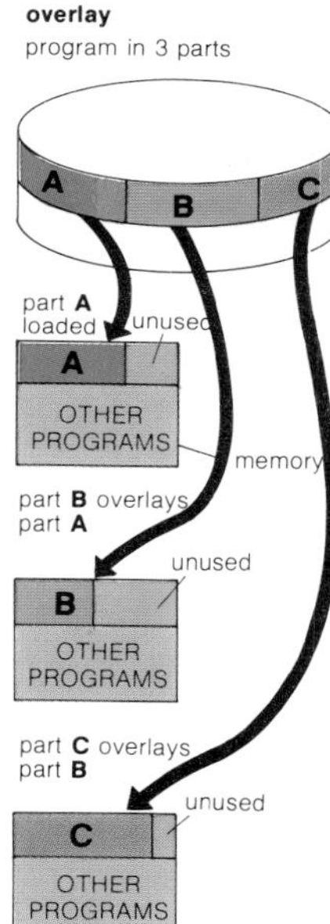

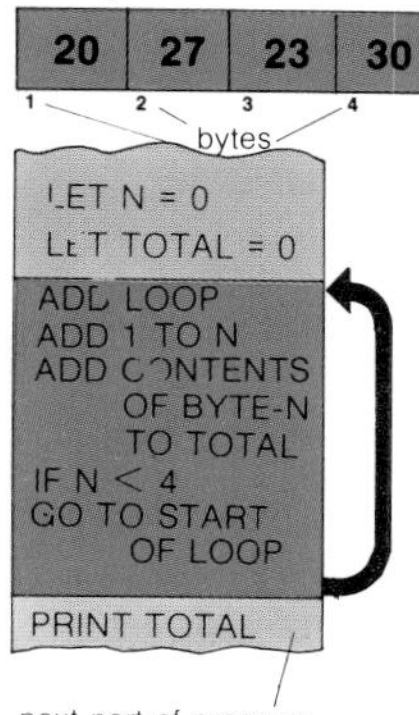

segment (*n*) a part of a program which can be executed without the rest of the program being in memory at the same time.

initialization (*n*) the work done at the start of a program, or before entering a loop (↓) or subroutine (p. 110), to make sure that all variables (p. 119) and switches (p. 120) have the correct value. For example, it might make sure that all accumulators (p. 15) were empty. **initialize** (*v*).

housekeeping (*n*) the work of the part of a program which sets things up at the beginning of a program or clears them at the end, but is not connected with the actual work of the program. When the program starts it may check that devices are ready, open (p. 161) files (p. 153), clear (↓) memory to the values needed by the program etc. When it is finished it may close (p. 161) files, print control totals (p. 182), etc.

clear (*v*) (1) to set a variable (p. 119) or switch (p. 120) back to the value it had at an earlier part of a program; (2) to over-write an area of memory with spaces or a special character (p. 46), to delete the data.

loop (*v*) to repeat a group of instructions. For example, a program which adds up all the numbers in a list will contain a loop which repeats the add instruction for every number in the list. The loop may be done for a fixed number of times which is set when the program is written or it may be done for a varying (p. 119) number of times which is calculated during the execution of the program. It is a very common operation in programming. There are four main kinds of loop: (1) *while loop* where the condition controlling the execution is tested before each pass; the loop is thus done zero or more times; (2) *for loop* which operates in a similar manner to a while loop; (3) *repeat loop* where the condition controlling its execution is tested after each pass; the loop must always be executed at least once; (4) *do loop* which is usually the same as a for loop but in some languages it is identical to a repeat loop. **loop** (*n*).

nest (*v*) to place one group of instructions inside another group. The inside group is executed one or more times every time the outside group is done once. There can be more than two groups; group C could be inside group B which is inside group A. **nesting** (*n*).

level (*n*) (1) the depth of a group of instructions in a set which is nested (↑); (2) = modification level (p. 129); (3) = index (p. 164) level.

branch (*n*) a point where it is possible to go in two or more directions. The word can be used of a place in a program where it can either carry on with instructions in sequence, or go to another group or routine (p. 111), depending on some condition. It is also used to describe trees (p. 149) where nodes (p. 149) have several paths which can be followed. **branch** (*v*), **branch** (*adj*).

conditional branch a branch instruction (p. 37) where some condition is tested first and depending on the result of the test the program either does or does not branch (↑). For example, an instruction might test whether the contents of a register (p. 14) were greater than 0 and branch if they were; when the register contents were equal to 0 no branch would be taken and the program would carry on with the next instruction in sequence.

unconditional branch a branch instruction (p. 37) which always causes a branch (↑).

unconditional jump = unconditional branch (↑).

go to a statement (p. 102) in a high-level language (p. 104) which causes an unconditional branch (↑). Also known as **goto**.

matching (*n*) the process of looking at the keys (p. 156) or the control field (p. 155) of two or more files (p. 153) to make sure the records (p. 154) are taken in the correct order from the files. **match** (*v*).

control break the condition when the key (p. 156) of a record (p. 154) differs in whole or in part from the previous record, i.e. there is a change in the value of one of the control fields (p. 155). A program processing records in sequence will often print out sub-totals at such a point.

branching

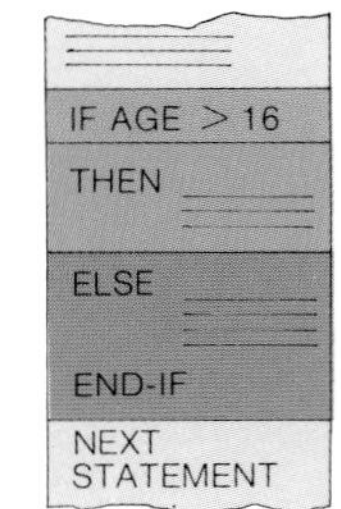

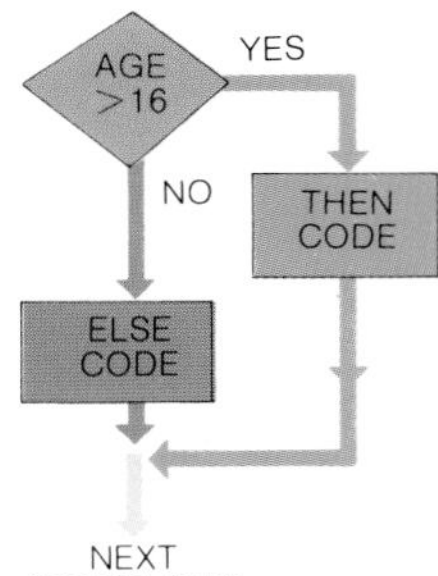

matching records in two files

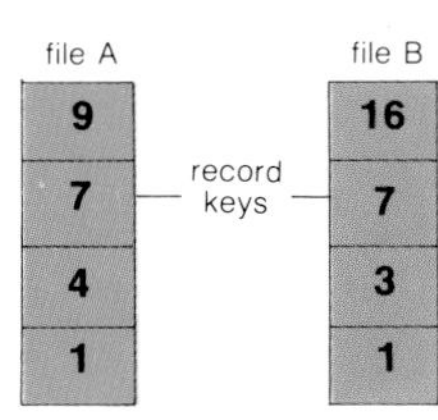

only keys 1 and 7 match

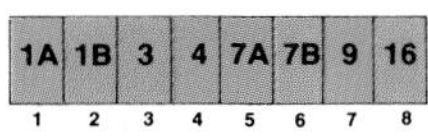

order of processing

increment and decrement

LOOP 10 TIMES	
SET LOOP COUNTER TO 10	SET LOOP COUNTER TO 0
LOOP	LOOP
SUBTRACT 1 FROM LOOP COUNTER	ADD 1 TO LOOP COUNTER
decrement counter	increment counter

increment (*v*) to add something. Usually used when a program is adding an amount, quite often a fixed amount, to an accumulator (p. 15) or a register (p. 14). **increment** (*n*).

decrement (*v*) to subtract something. Usually used when a program is subtracting an amount, quite often a fixed amount, from an accumulator (p. 15) or a register (p. 14). **decrement** (*n*).

select[1] (*v*) to choose between two or more paths through a program as the result of comparing (p. 37) data or switches (p. 120). **selection** (*n*).

wait (*n*) an instruction or group of instructions which cause a program to do nothing until some operation is complete. Usually happens when a program wants to read or write a record (p. 154) but cannot do so because the peripheral device (p. 12) is busy (p. 40).

checkpoint (*v*) to take a copy of enough information so that if a program has to be stopped for some reason then it will be possible to re-start it from the same place. Programs which run for a long time often take checkpoint regularly; if something goes wrong with the computer before the run is finished then the program does not have to be re-run (p. 107) from the beginning. **checkpoint** (*n*).

edit word an item of data in a program which is used to change other data, usually numbers, so that they are printed the way the user wants. Edit words can cause zero suppression (p. 118), floating dollar signs (p. 118), insertion of decimal points (p. 16), etc.

zero suppression a process in which numbers are printed with any zeros at the left hand of the number end replaced by blanks. For example, 00123 would print as 123 with two spaces to the left of the number.

floating dollar sign a dollar sign which is printed immediately before an amount. Any zeros at the left hand are replaced by spaces, but 00123 dollars would print as $123, not as $00123. The $ sign is said to float down to the figures. It is also possible to float + and - signs. **float** (*v*).

asterisk protection zero suppression (↑) in which the zeros are replaced with asterisks. For example, 00123 would print as **123. It is very commonly used for printing amounts on cheques to prevent them being changed.

menu (*n*) a list of actions a program can do. They are displayed on a VDU (p. 83) so the user can choose which one the program is to do.

map (*v*) to have two sets of data so that the first set either points to, or represents (p. 45), the state of the second set. For example, the first could be a set of bits (p. 17) and the second a set of records (p. 154) on disk (p. 66). A bit would be 0 if the record was empty, 1 if it was full. The first set would be much smaller and could be examined much more quickly. This idea is often used in computing. **mapping** (*n*).

backtracking (*n*) the process of going back through a list, a tree (p. 149) or a part of a program, i.e. the opposite of the usual way. A program may reach a point where there are several possible paths; it may have to try each path to find the best one. If the first path chosen is not satisfactory it will go back along it and then try another. **backtrack** (*v*).

error message (1) a message from a program to tell an operator (p. 190) that something unusual or unexpected has happened, e.g. the data given to the program is not correct; (2) a message given by an operating system (p. 130) because a program either has an error or cannot find the files (p. 153) or peripherals (p. 12) it needs to run.

zero supression

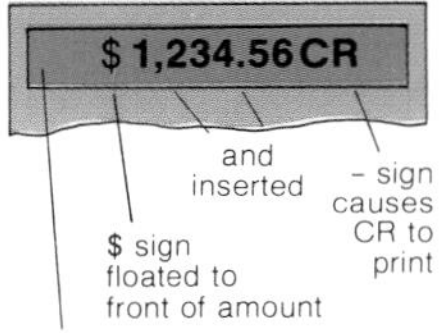

menu

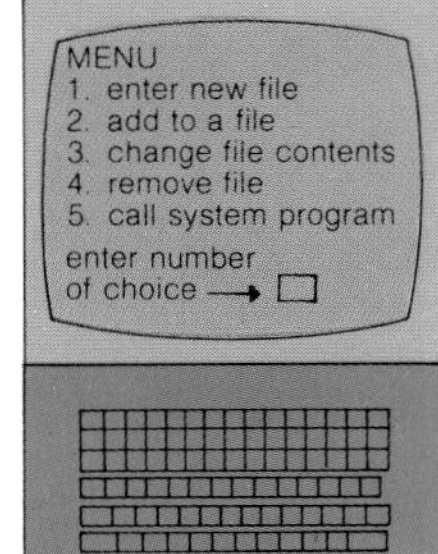

variables and constants

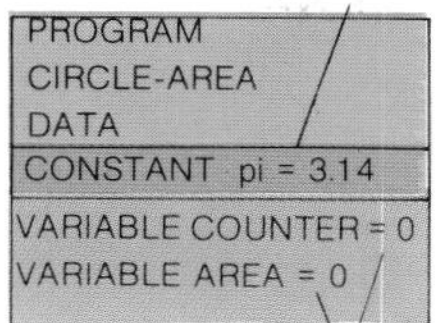

variable[2] (*n*) (1) a part of a program which holds data, i.e. it is not an instruction. It has a name and holds a value which can be changed during program execution, e.g. an accumulator (p. 15) which would be added to at different parts of the program.

variable[1] (*adj*) of something which can be changed. **vary** (*v*).

constant (*n*) a part of a program holding some data which is not changed during program execution, e.g. the heading on every page.

global (*adj*) of a variable (↑) or constant (↑) which can be used anywhere in the program.

local (*adj*) of a variable (↑) or constant (↑) which can be used only in the procedure (p. 111) or module (p. 106) where it is defined, or sometimes in a procedure called (p. 111) by the defining procedure.

scope (*n*) the area or part of a source program (p. 103) where a variable (↑) or constant (↑) can be used. A variable which is defined in one part or in a module (p. 106) may or may not be available for use in other parts. In some languages, e.g. COBOL (p. 91), a variable, once defined, can be used anywhere. Other languages, e.g. Pascal (p. 92), can have either global (↑) variables which can be used anywhere, or local (↑) variables which can be used only in the procedure (p. 111) or module in which they are defined.

global and local scope

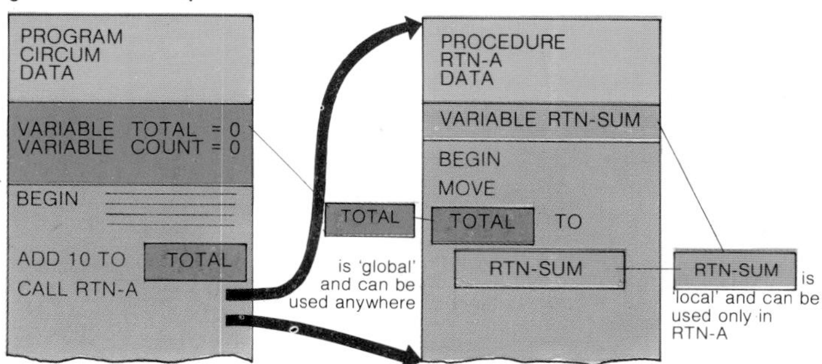

assignment (*n*) (1) a statement (p. 102) in a source language (p. 103) which will cause a change to the contents of a variable (p. 119). The variable is on one side of the assignment statement and it takes the value of whatever is on the other side; (2) the process of saying which devices are to be used for the files (p. 153) that a program needs. The files are usually on tapes (p. 71) or disks (p. 66) and since there is often more than one such device the operating system (p. 130) has to know which ones are to be used for a program. **assign** (*v*).

overflow indicator (1) a switch (↓), usually in the CPU (p. 31), which is set on when an arithmetic result is too large for a register to hold; (2) a switch which is set on to indicate that data being printed is more than will fit on a single page.

argument (*n*) a variable (p. 119), or its value, which is used to search a list or a table (p. 144).

switch[2] (*n*) a variable (p. 119) which does not hold data for processing but stores the result of the comparison (p. 37) of two or more items of data. The switch usually has two conditions, on or off, and instructions examine the switch to decide whether to branch (p. 116) or continue with the next instruction. Also known as **Boolean** or **program switch**. **switch** (*v*).

flag (*n*) (1) a switch (↑); (2) a character which is used to show that part of the data in a record (p. 154) is not correct, or has an unusual value; thus the flag may not be tested in the program that finds the error. It is placed with the record and used by a later program. **flag** (*v*).

indicator (*n*) = flag (↑).

sentinel (*n*) (1) a special flag (↑) which is used to mark the end of data in a list or table (p. 144); (2) = switch (↑); (3) = flag.

drop-through switch a group of instructions, the first of which is a conditional branch (p. 116). The first time the instructions are executed the branch is not taken and so the following instructions are executed. These change the first instruction to an unconditional branch (p. 116) and so the second instruction and those following are done only once.

assignment
statement in Pascal

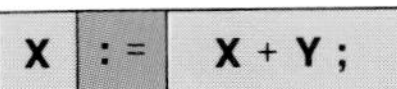

X takes the value of (**X** + **Y**)

switch
setting and testing

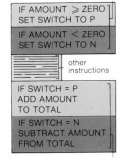

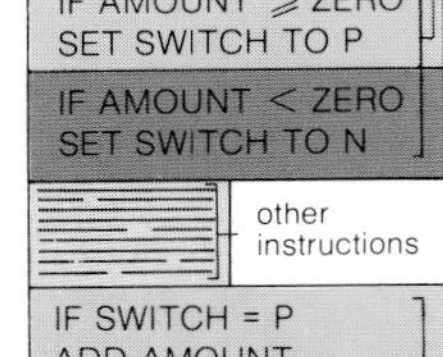

documentation (*n*) a collection of listings of programs, written explanations of how to use programs, how they work, copies of tests of the program, flowcharts (↓), etc. These are kept together so that persons other than the one who wrote it can understand what a program or group of programs is meant to do and how it is done. **document** (*v*), **document** (*n*).

program specification a document (↑) which defines what a program is to do, i.e. what input it will accept and the results it should produce. It is usually prepared before a program is written.

design (*v*) to examine the possible ways in which a problem or a program can be done, choose one of these ways, and work out how each part is to be handled. **design** (*n*).

flowchart symbols small shapes, e.g. circles, squares, etc. which are connected by lines with arrows on them. They are used to show the flow of data in a system (p. 181) or to show how a program is meant to work.

flowchart (*n*) a diagram which uses flowchart symbols (↑) to show the way in which a system (p. 181), or a program works. **flowchart** (*v*).

flowchart with various symbols

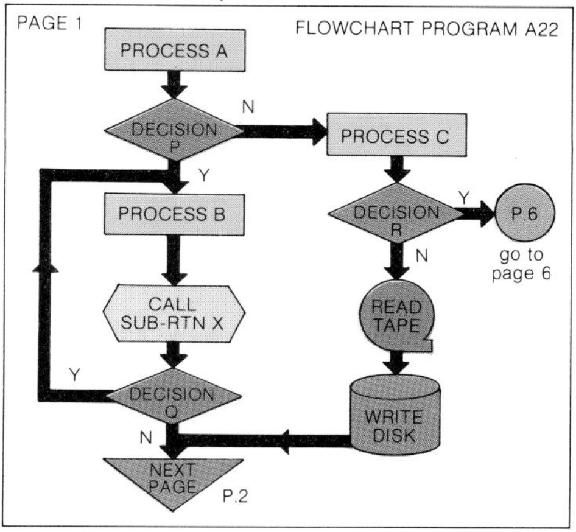

block diagram a diagram which uses flowchart symbols (p. 121) to show how a system (p. 181) or a program is meant to work. It is similar to a flowchart (p. 121) but tends to have fewer symbols and show less detail. For example, it might use a single box to show a routine (p. 111) while a flowchart would give details of the parts of the routine.

algorithm (*n*) a plan setting out the actions which must be done in order to produce the answer to a problem. It is usually written in English and a programmer will use it to produce the source language (p. 103) statements (p. 102).

pseudo-code (*n*) a form of written English for writing a program; the program cannot be compiled (p. 105) directly but can be understood by a person without much knowledge of computing. Used by programmers to set out how programs are to work before they are coded (p. 102) in a source language (p. 103).

structured programming a method of programming that makes the programs easier to write, test and maintain. The general aim is to have procedures (p. 111) or routines (p. 111) which can call (p. 111) others below them but any routine always returns to the one which called it. Modern languages, e.g. Pascal (p. 92) tend not to allow programs to be written any other way; older languages, e.g. Fortran (p. 93) are not very suitable for this method.

modular programming a method of writing programs. They are written as a collection of modules (p. 106) each doing some particular part of the work. The aim is to avoid a large single piece of programming which is difficult to understand and to change.

block diagram

modular programming

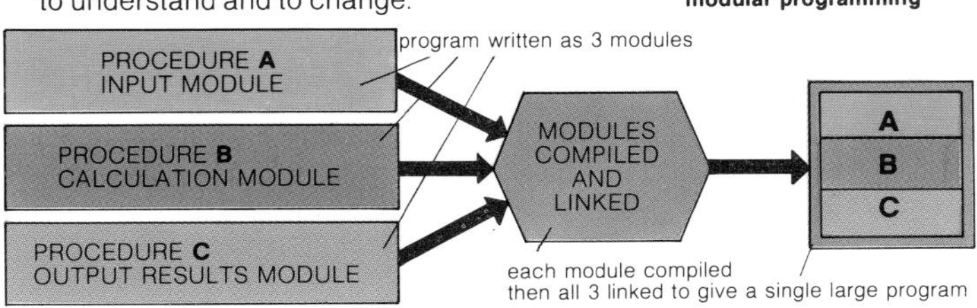

top down of a way of dealing with a problem or a program by first designing (p. 121) or coding (p. 102) or testing the main procedure (p. 111) and then the procedures called (p. 111) by the main one. The smaller, less important procedures, are left until the end.

bottom up of a way of dealing with a problem or a program where the smaller procedures (p. 111), which do simple parts of the work, are designed (p. 121), coded (p. 102) or tested first. Those procedures which use these simple procedures are done next and so on until the complete program has been produced.

step-wise refinement a method of handling a problem or a program by first producing a general design (p. 121) then improving on it and repeating this until a complete design is produced. Used in deciding the best way to set out a program.

decision table

conditions		possible values			
1	age > 18	Y	Y	N	N
2	studied maths	Y	N	Y	N
actions		1	2	3	4
1	admit to college	Y	Y	N	N
2	admit to computing	Y	N	N	N
3	refer to tutor	N	N	Y	N

decision table a method of setting out a list of things which can have different values and the action to be taken on each value. It is used as an aid in writing programs to make sure that every possibility has been considered.

stub (*n*) a procedure (p. 111) in a program which is only partly coded (p. 102). Quite often it contains only a few of the instructions that it will contain when it is completed. It is included in the program to allow other procedures, which have been fully coded, to be tested.

desk checking the process of working through a program with pencil and paper to see whether it will produce the results that it should. Usually done before a program is actually tested.

dry run = desk checking (↑).

program test

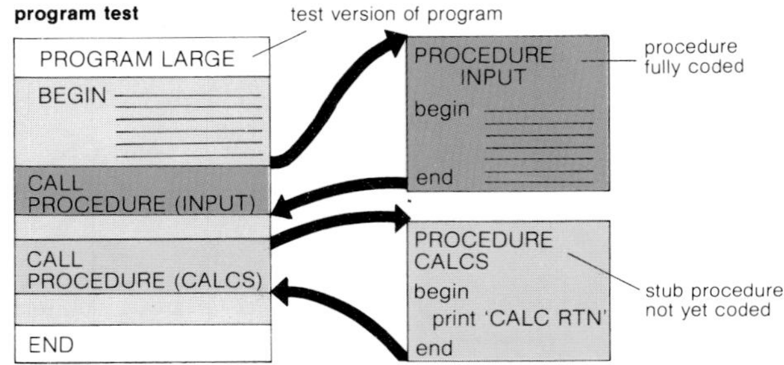

program test to run a program to see whether it works correctly. Except with small programs it is not common to test all the parts of a program at one time and so there are likely to be a number of tests before it is correct. **test** (*n*).

test data data which is specially made up to test one or more parts of a program.

test pack a set of data which is used to test a program or a system (p. 181). The amount of data is not large but it is designed (p. 121) to check for as many error conditions as possible. It can be used in testing a program before it goes into use and also when a program is changed.

test harness a collection of special programs and test data (↑) which is used to test whether a group of programs is correct. It is usually only used if there is either a large number of programs to be tested, or the programs are difficult ones which will need a lot of tests.

cross check to find results by two different methods and check to see if they are the same.

program check a fault in a program which causes it to stop running.

program check

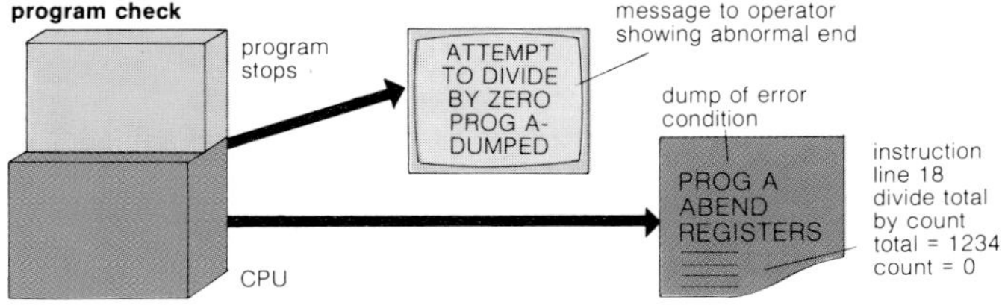

bug (*n*) a fault in a program which either prevents it from working or causes it to produce the wrong results.

de-bug (*v*) to examine a program which has errors and try to find and correct them.

abend (*n*) abnormal end, i.e. a program or its data has gone wrong and it has been stopped.

dump (*n*) a condition in which there is an error in a program and it has stopped. The contents of memory and registers (p. 14) are usually printed to find the cause of the error. **dump** (*v*).

core dump a print of the contents of memory and other data, e.g. register (p. 14) contents, usually as a result of a program dumping (↑).

memory dump = core dump (↑).

selective dump a dump (↑) of a particular part of memory so that a possible or actual error in a program can be examined.

post-mortem dump a core dump (↑) taken at the end of a program which is being tested.

snapshot (*n*) a print of a particular part of memory, registers (p. 14) and other data at some point during the execution of a program. It is usually used to try to find what is causing a program fault. The program does not stop and there may be several snapshots taken on one run.

dynamic dump a print of the contents of part of memory during the execution of program. The program does not stop.

trace (*n*) a list which shows the actions of a program. It may give the numbers of the instructions executed, variables (p. 119) which have been used, values in those variables, etc. Its purpose is to help in finding the cause of errors in programs. **trace** (*v*).

trace prints instruction line and values of selected fields whenever they are changed

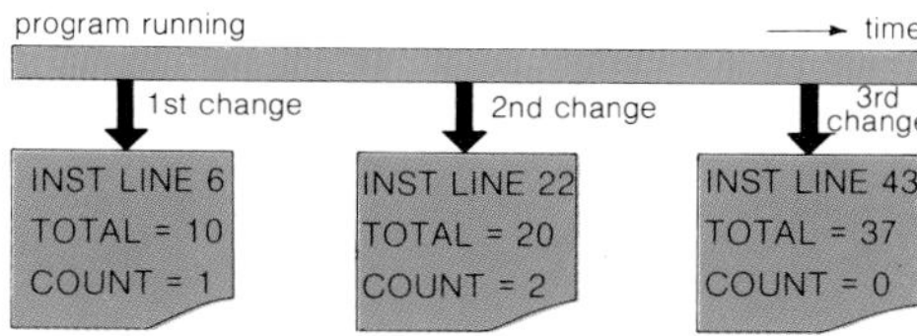

trace program a special version (p. 129) of a program which contains extra instructions whose purpose is to follow what happens when the normal instructions of the program are executed. It may show the changes in value of a variable (p. 119) or register (p. 14); it may show when and how often a variable or instruction is used; it may allow the data in the program to be displayed or changed. It is used as an aid in finding the cause of errors in programs.

debugger (*n*) = trace program (↑).

error codes for a disk read

VALUES IN STATUS BYTE AFTER DISK READ PROCEDURE	
VALUE	MEANING
00	READ SUCCESSFUL
01	DISK NOT ON-LINE
02	SEEK FAILED
03	WRONG LENGTH RECORD
04	ERROR IN DATA TRANSFER
05	FILE ACCESS PROTECTED
06	

error code (1) a value returned by a procedure (p. 111) which shows that something is wrong, e.g. it may be that data is not correct or that a file (p. 153) which should be available cannot be found; (2) a letter or number printed which shows that an error has been found in the data which is being examined. The data in error is usually printed as well.

patch (*v*) to make a change to a machine language (p. 104) program so that the program can be re-run (p. 107) without the need to compile (p. 105) it again. **patch** (*n*).

remote testing testing a program which is entered at a work station (p 83) at one place and run on a computer which is somewhere else.

system program a program whose purpose is to arrange the work of a computer or help the computer to carry out its work. Examples are programs to arrange files (p. 153) on a disk pack (p. 66), to take copies of files for safety, or to control where programs are loaded (p. 106) in memory. Some system programs may provide a service to a user, e.g. a sort (p. 169) program, but they are mostly used by the computer itself or by the operators (p. 190).

systems software a collection of system programs (↑) usually provided by the manufacturer of the computer. The software (p. 14) generally consists of an operating system (p. 130), compilers (p. 105) for different program languages (p. 103), and service programs (↓).

systems disk

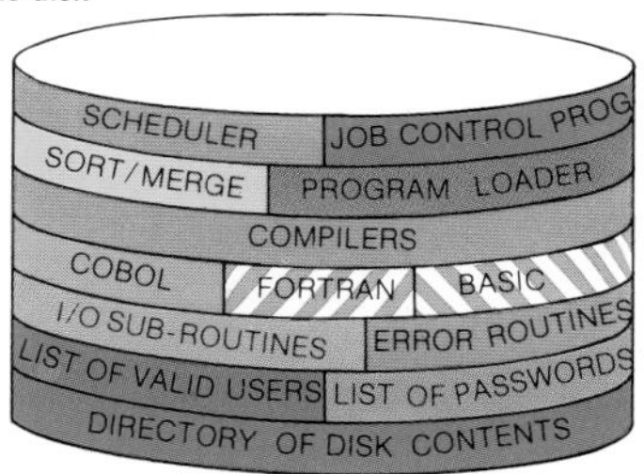

systems disk a disk pack (p. 66) which holds only system programs (↑), their data, and space for the operating system (p. 130) to use.

systems programmer a programmer who specializes in writing or maintaining system programs (↑).

utility program a program which is available for all the users of a computer and does things that are generally needed by a user from time to time, e.g. a program which prints the contents of a file (p. 153).

service program = utility program (↑).

editor (*n*) a special utility program (↑) which allows users to enter text (p. 102) into a file (p. 153) and makes it easy to change and correct the text. **edit** (*v*).

line editor an editor (p. 127) which allows only a single line of text (p. 102) to be corrected at a time, i.e. the cursor (p. 84) can be moved along a line but not from one line to another.
screen editor an editor (p. 127) which allows the correction of the text (p. 102) of any line which is on the screen (p. 84), i.e. it is possible to move directly from any part of one line to any part of another by moving the cursor (p. 84).

applications program

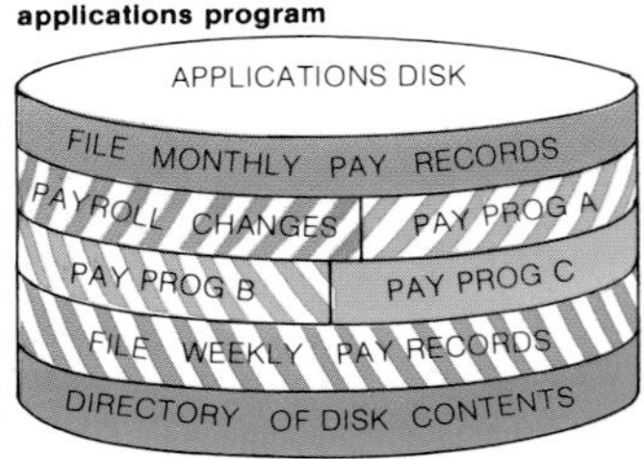

screen editor

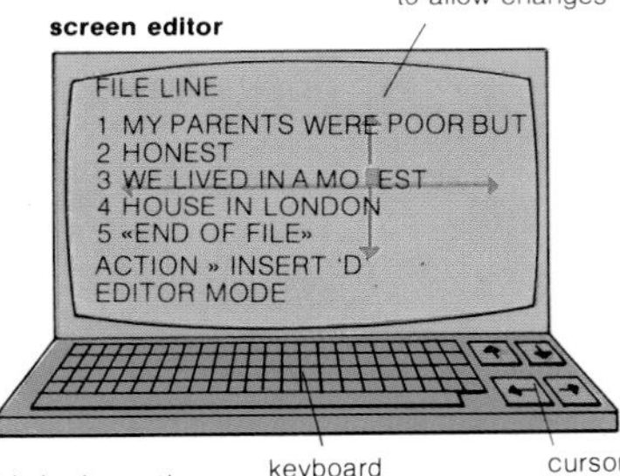

applications program a program which does the work for some particular computer user. It is written specially for that user and is not likely to be of use to someone else.
user program = applications program (↑).
applications programmer a programmer who specializes in writing applications programs (↑).
package (*n*) a group of programs and documentation which performs a specialized piece of work and which is useful to a number of users. The package is quite often written not by a manufacturer but by a software house (p. 181) and sold to people who want to use it.
modify (*v*) (1) to change a program either because it is wrong or because the work it was intended to do has changed; (2) to change an address particularly as in address modification (p. 114). **modification** (*n*).
maintenance[1] (*n*) the work done in changing programs which are not working correctly or, more commonly, because the work they were intended to do has been changed. **maintain** (*v*).
software maintenance = maintenance (↑).
program maintenance = maintenance (↑).

maintenance programmer a programmer who specializes in the maintenance of programs, not in writing new ones.

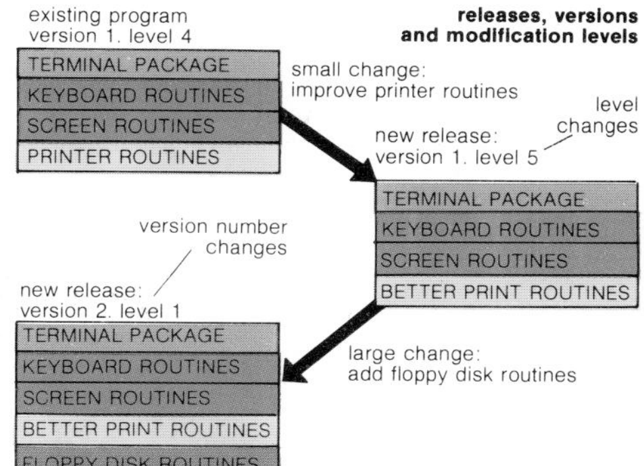

releases, versions and modification levels

modification level an updated (p. 202) system program (p. 127) or package (↑) which has had small changes made to it, usually to correct errors, and is only slightly different from the previous program.

version (*n*) (1) a different form of something. It can be the same thing presented in a different way, e.g. the binary number (p. 49) 1111 is the same as the decimal number (p. 16) 15. It can also be something which is similar but not exactly the same. For example, when a file (p. 153) is updated (p. 202) some, but not all, of the information will be changed and the updated file is said to be the new version of the file. (2) a program, usually a system program (p. 127) or package (↑), to which large changes have been made, i.e. it may do extra things such as allow the use of variable length (p. 156) records (p. 154) which the previous version would not handle. It may also no longer do things that were previously done. The changes are much larger than for a new modification level (↑).

release (*n*) a new version (↑) or modification level (↑) of a program, especially systems software (p. 127) or a package (↑). **release** (*v*).

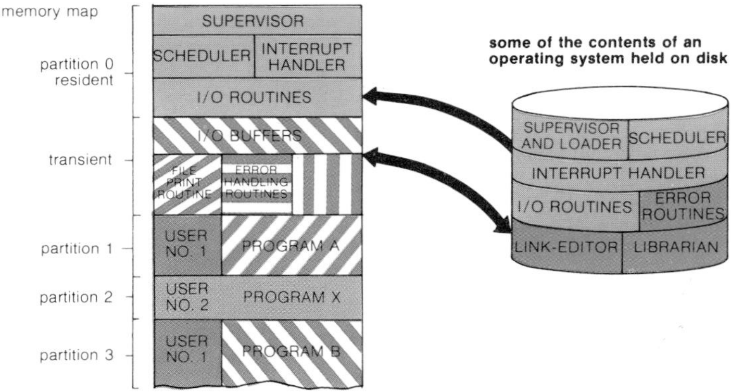

operating system a group of programs which controls how a computer works. They will maintain libraries (p. 107), load (p. 106) programs to be run, open (p. 161) and close (p. 161) files (p. 153), handle hardware (p. 14) errors etc, for the user's programs. Usually the operating system is provided by the computer manufacturer.

OS operating system. Originally the operating system (↑) provided by IBM for their larger computers; nowadays any operating system.

DOS disk operating system. An operating system (↑), especially a small one, suitable for mini-computers (p. 9).

MS/DOS a widely used operating system (↑) for micro-computers (p. 9).

UNIX (*n*) an operating system (↑) developed by Bell Telephone Laboratories in America. It has been widely used on small and mini-computers (p. 9) but is now also used on larger computers. UNIX is a trademark.

CP/M control program for micro-computers. An operating system (↑) used on micro-computers (p. 9). CP/M is a trademark.

supervisor (*n*) a program, usually part of an operating system (↑), which actually controls the running of other programs in the machine. It is resident (↓) all the time the computer is working. **supervise** (*v*).

executive (*n*) = supervisor (↑).
executive program = supervisor (↑).
monitor (*n*) = supervisor (↑).
kernel (*n*) = supervisor (↑).
supervisor call SVC. An instruction in a program which requests (p. 204) something, such as an input or output operation to be done by the operating system (↑). The program is halted and the supervisor (↑) starts to do whatever is necessary to meet the request.
system call = supervisor call (↑).
resident (*adj*) of a routine (p. 111), usually part of an operating system (↑), which remains in memory while programs are being run.
transient routine a routine (p. 111), usually part of an operating system (↑), which is not used often enough to be held in memory at all times. It is held on disk (p. 66) and brought into memory whenever it is needed. **transient** (*n*).
transient area a part of memory, usually fixed, which is set aside for storing transient routines (↑).
tpa transient program area. The term used by the CP/M (↑) operating system (↑) for the current program.
privileged instruction an instruction which can be used only by the supervisor (↑) or other parts of the operating system (↑). The instruction would be one of a group which is needed to control the way a computer works, e.g. an instruction to set memory protection (p. 43). Other programs are not permitted to use these instructions.
super-user (*n*) a person who is treated as a special user by an operating system (↑). A super-user is usually a systems programmer (p. 127) who is employed to control the use of the computer by everyone else, and who allocates (p. 134) the amount of disk space (p. 69), the priority (p. 132) and the amount of time given to normal users. The super-user can use special operating system programs to access or delete other users' programs or data, and to allow or prevent them using the computer.

priority list

USER	PARTITION NO.	PRIORITY
SUPERVISOR OPER-SYSTEM	0	16
USER-1 — PROG A	1	12
USER-2 — PROG X	2	4
USER-1 — PROG B	3	10

highest priority

low priority

same user with different priorities in different partitions

priority (*n*) the importance given to something which decides the order in which things are to be done. Usually each user's programs are given a number which shows the priority to be given to that work. If there are several programs from different users to be run then the one with the highest priority is executed first. An operating system (p. 130) needs to maintain queues (p. 134) of things to be done and uses the priority to decide the order in which to do them. The operating system keeps a note of the priority that a user has: it can be changed by a super-user (p. 131) but not by a normal user. It can also be changed by the operating system during the execution of a program. It is also quite usual to give priority to partitions (p. 134) in memory.

schedule[1] (*v*) to arrange the order in which things are to be done. **schedule** (*n*).

scheduler (*n*) a part of an operating system (p. 130) whose purpose is to schedule (↑) programs but it also usually causes them to be started and stopped as and when necessary.

priority scheduler a scheduler (↑) which uses the priority (↑) given to programs or partitions (p. 134) to decide which things to do next.

interrupt handler the part of an operating system (p. 130) which handles interrupts (p. 39).

job control language JCL. A set of statements (p. 102) which can be used to tell the operating system (p. 130) what has to be done, i.e. what program is to be run, which files (p. 153) are to be used, etc. It is not a program language (p. 103) and the statements are not compiled (p. 105), instead they are read directly by one of the operating system programs called the job control program (↓).

job control statement a statement (p. 102) in the form required by a job control language (↑). It will usually tell the operating system (p. 130) which program is wanted, the files (p. 153) to be assigned (p. 143), etc, so that a program can run.

catalogued procedure a set of procedures (p. 111), not part of a program, which consists of a group of job control statements (↑) to the operating system (p. 130) and which have been placed in a library (p. 107). Very commonly used for batch processing (p. 181).

job (*n*) a complete piece of work to be done by a computer. It includes the job control statements (↑) for the operating system (p. 130) saying which programs and devices are needed as well as the data to be used.

job step a part of a job (↑) which asks for a particular program.

job control program a part of the operating system (p. 130) which reads and processes the job control statements (↑) and takes the necessary action, e.g. it assigns (p. 143) input-output devices etc, so that a job (↑) can be run.

job stream the list of the job control statements (↑) for the jobs (↑) that a computer has to do. It is usually stored on tape (p. 71) or disk (p. 66) and as each job is finished the operating system (p. 130) will fetch (p. 33) the next one from the job stream.

EOJ end of job (↑).

job stream for compilation and test

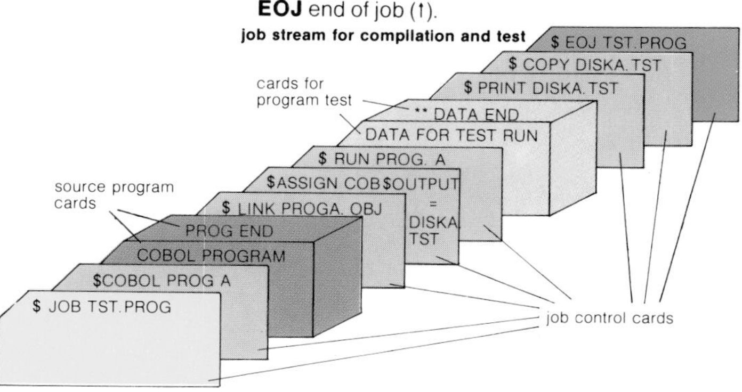

queues used by operating system

queue for printer	queue for disk	queue for CPU
OP-SYS JCL	USER-1—PROGA	USER-1— PROG A
USER-1—PROG A	USER-1—PROG B	USER-1— PROG B
USER-1— PROG B		USER-2—PROG X
USER-2—PROG X		

current use

queue[1] (*n*) a list of things to be done, held in the order in which they are to be done. The operating system (p. 130) maintains queues for several things, e.g. data waiting to be read, data waiting to be written, programs ready to use the CPU (p. 31), etc.

allocate (*v*) to share out or give a part of something, usually computer resources such as disk space (p. 69), memory or processor time, to a user or a program. **allocation** (*n*).

partition (*n*) a part of memory which is available for a program. One method of allowing memory to be used by different programs at the same time is to split it into a number of partitions each of which can be used by one program. The partitions can be fixed or they may change in size while the program is running, depending on the operating system (p. 130). Partitions can also have a different priority (p. 132). **partition** (*v*).

partition memory arranged in fixed partitions

partition number		partition priority
0	OPERATING SYSTEM SUPERVISOR AND RESIDENT ROUTINES	16 — highest
1	OPERATING SYSTEM TRANSIENT ROUTINES	14
2	SPOOLING OF INPUT-OUTPUT	10
3	FOREGROUND PARTITION (TERMINAL HANDLING)	12
4	BACKGROUND PARTITION (MAIN PROCESSING PROGRAM)	8
5	PROGRAMMERS TESTING PARTITION	4 — lowest

foreground partition the partition (↑) in memory which has the highest priority (p. 132).

foreground program a program in a foreground partition (↑). On many computers it is not the main program; it is usually one which works in real-time (p. 94) or handles teleprocessing (p. 82) and so whenever the program is needed it has to be made available immediately.

background partition the partition (↑) in memory which has lowest priority (p. 132).

background program a program in a background partition (↑). It is usually an important and large program which takes a long time to run and it can be halted every now and again to allow the foreground program (↑) to use the CPU (p. 31).

memory management the method of paging (↓) used by the operating system (p. 130) to control the allocation (↑) of memory between programs.

paging (*n*) a system (p. 181) in which a whole program is held on backing store (p. 12) but only parts of it are brought into memory when it is loaded (p. 106). The parts are a fixed size and are called pages. If a page is needed and it is not present in memory then it has to be fetched (p. 33) from the backing store. If there is no spare space in memory then one of the pages which is already there has to be overwritten but before this is done the page in memory will be copied on to backing store if it has been changed in any way since it was first loaded. The backing store must be on a direct access device (p. 67), almost always a disk (p. 66). The method allows large programs to be run in a small amount of memory. The paging is transparent (p. 108) to the program and to a programmer. **page** (*v*), **page** (*n*).

paging

parts of programs in pages of memory

1 A	2 C	3 B
4 B	5 page not used	6 D
7 C	8 B	9 A
10 A	11 C	12 D
13 C	14 D	15 page not used

page size the size of the page (p. 135) used by an operating system (p. 130). It is usually fixed, i.e. the operating system will only work with one size of page, usually 512, 1024, 2048 or 4096 bytes (p. 17). Some operating systems on larger computers allow the page size to be changed.

page frame an area of memory which can hold exactly one page (p. 135). An operating system (p. 130) will usually allocate (p. 134) memory in page frames. Also known as **frame**.

working set (1) the number of page frames (↑) in memory made available to a program; (2) the number of pages used by a program, usually ones which have been accessed recently.

page fault a fault caused when a program has tried to access a page (p. 135) which is not in memory. It is not an error; the program is simply halted while the operating system (p. 130) gets the necessary page from backing store (p. 12) and loads (p. 106) it into memory.

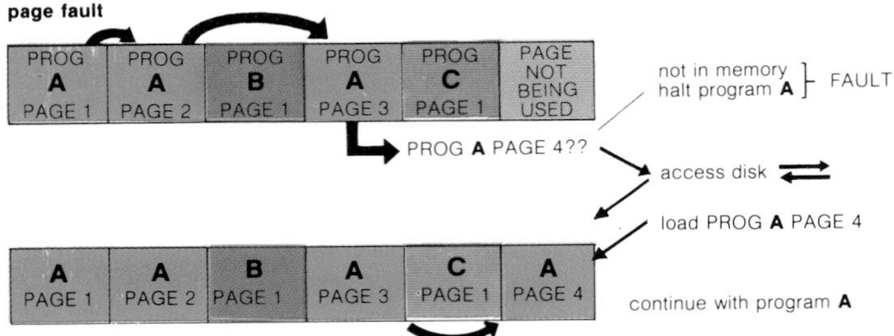

least recently used LRU. A method of paging (p. 135) where, if there is no unused frame (↑) available when a new page has to be brought into memory, the operating system (p. 130) will over-write the page already in memory which has spent the longest time unused.

last-in first-out LIFO. A method of paging (p. 135) where, if there is no unused frame (↑) available when a new page has to be brought into memory, the operating system (p. 130) will over-write the page already in memory which has been there for the shortest time.

first-in first-out FIFO. Of a method of paging (p. 135) where, if there is no unused page frame (↑) available when a new page has to be brought into memory, the operating system (p. 130) will over-write the page already in memory which has been there for the longest time, whether it has been used or not.

page replacement the process of writing pages (p. 135) from memory on to backing store (p. 12) and over-writing the memory with other pages held on backing store.

swap-out (*v*) to write from memory on to backing store (p. 12) all the pages (p. 135) belonging to a single program, so that space can be made available for another. **swap** (*n*), **swap** (*v*).

roll-out (*v*) = swap-out (↑).

swap-out, swap-in

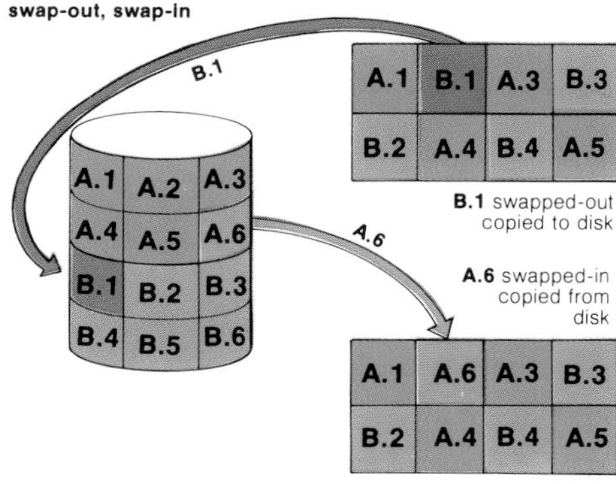

swap-in (*v*) to read pages (p. 135) belonging to a single program, from backing store (p. 12) into memory, and into the page frames (↑) of program that has been swapped-out (↑).

roll-in (*v*) = swap-in (↑).

demand paging the system of bringing pages (p. 135) belonging to a single program into memory only when they are needed.

anticipatory paging the system of bringing pages (p. 135) belonging to a single program into memory whenever there is space to do so in case they may be needed.

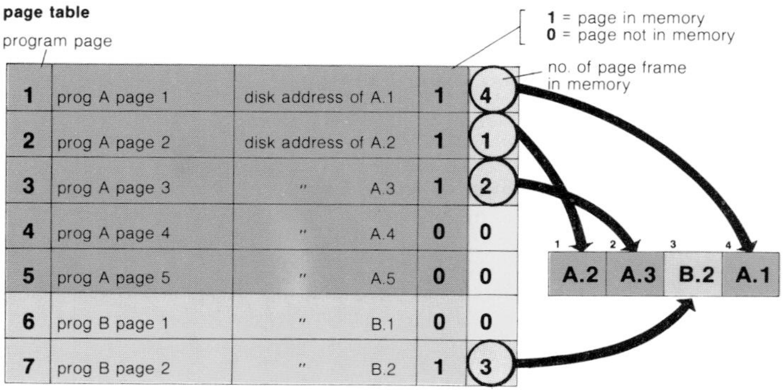

page table

program page

1 = page in memory
0 = page not in memory

no. of page frame in memory

1	prog A page 1	disk address of A.1	**1**	**4**
2	prog A page 2	disk address of A.2	**1**	**1**
3	prog A page 3	" A.3	**1**	**2**
4	prog A page 4	" A.4	**0**	**0**
5	prog A page 5	" A.5	**0**	**0**
6	prog B page 1	" B.1	**0**	**0**
7	prog B page 2	" B.2	**1**	**3**

1	2	3	4
A.2	**A.3**	**B.2**	**A.1**

page table a list kept by the operating system (p. 130), to show which pages (p. 135) of a program are actually in memory, which page frames (p. 136) they are in, and which pages are on backing store (p. 12).

clean page a page (p. 135) in memory which has not been written to since it was brought into memory. It is therefore exactly the same as the copy on backing store (p. 12) and need not be written to backing store if it has to be swapped-out (p. 137).

dirty page a page (p. 135) in memory which has been written to, and so changed, since it was brought into memory from backing store (p. 12). If the page has to be swapped-out (p. 137) then it has to be written out to backing store so that the backing store copy is up to date.

dirty bit a bit (p. 17) in the page table (↑). It is set to 0 when a clean page (↑) is brought into memory and only set to 1 if the page (p. 135) is written to, and so changed. If the page has to be swapped (p. 137) then the operating system (p. 130) examines the dirty bit to see if it is necessary to write the page to backing store (p. 12).

sticky bit a bit (p. 17) in the page table (↑). It is set to 1 when a shared program (p. 108) is in use to prevent its pages (p. 135) being replaced as long as at least one user is executing the shared program.

thrashing

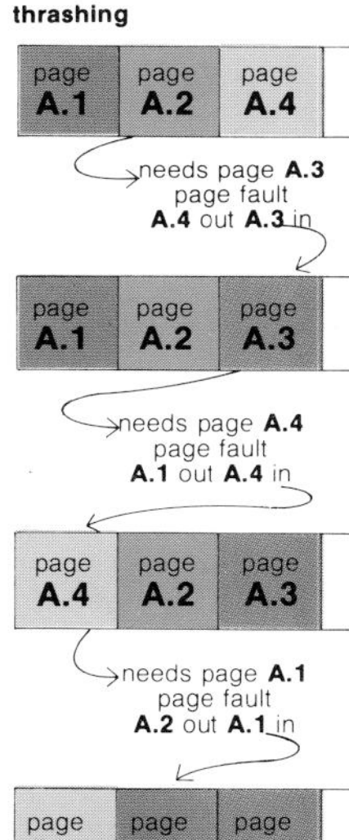

sneaky write the act of writing a dirty page (↑) to backing store (p. 12) even though it is not yet being swapped (p. 137). This has the effect of making it a clean page (↑), i.e. the page on backing store is the same as the one in memory. The writing is done only if the CPU (p. 31) happens to have spare time to do it. The aim is to keep the number of clean pages in memory as high as possible and thus avoid the re-writing of pages when the CPU is busy.

thrashing (*n*) a state in which too much paging (p. 135) is being done. It can be caused by having too many programs in memory. The programs do not get given enough page frames (p. 136) so the number of page faults (p. 136) increases to a point where the operating system (p. 130) is doing so much swapping (p. 137) that there is very little time left for the programs to do their work. It can also happen if one program is given too few page frames and so produces a very large number of page faults.

dynamic storage allocation a system in which the amount of memory allocated (p. 134) to programs is changed while the programs are running, i.e. it is not fixed when they are first loaded (p. 106). It means that high priority (p. 132) programs can be given more memory if they need it. If necessary low priority programs will be swapped-out (p. 137).

dynamic memory allocation = dynamic storage allocation (↑).

dynamic allocation a system in which the allocation (p. 134) of any of the computer parts, e.g. CPU time (p. 143), memory, can be changed while programs are running so that high priority (p. 132) programs can be given more. It is often used to mean dynamic storage allocation (↑).

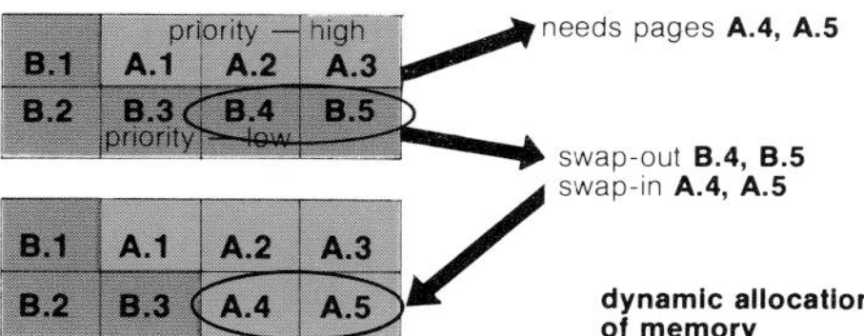

dynamic allocation of memory

concurrent process

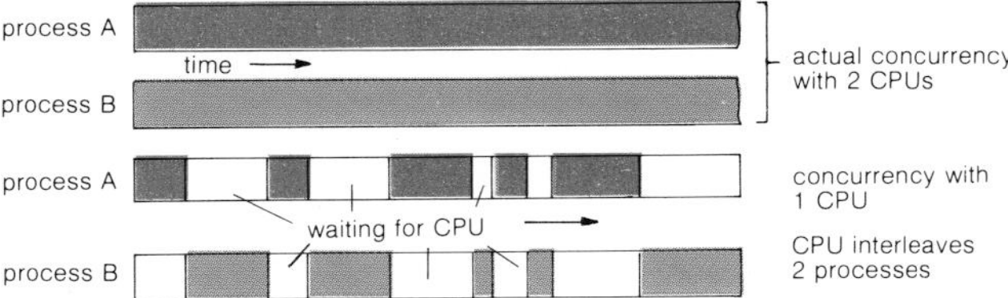

concurrent process a process which can be carried on at the same time as another one. Most computers have only a single CPU (p. 31) and so can execute only one process at a time but, by giving the CPU first to one process and then to another, they may appear to be doing several processes at the same time. A process can only be run concurrently with another if it does not need the results of the other process. There are, however, computers which do have more than one CPU and can handle more than one process at the same time. **concurrent** (*adj*), **concurrency** (*n*).

parallel process = concurrent process (↑).

simultaneous process = concurrent process (↑).

interleave[2] (*v*) to give the CPU (p. 31) to different processes, one after the other, so that each can do a certain amount of computing. The computer appears to be executing the processes at the same time. **interleaving** (*n*).

communicating process a process which needs to pass or receive results from another process so that they can both continue running.

task (*n*) (1) the name given to a program or complete routine (p. 111) which can be run concurrently (↑) with other routines; (2) = job (p. 133).

multi-tasking (*n*) the concurrent processing (↑) of two or more tasks (↑). The tasks can belong to the same program. **multi-task** (*v*).

multi-programming (*n*) the concurrent processing (↑) of two or more programs. It is not quite the same as multi-tasking (↑) since the programs are separate but the words are often used to mean the same thing. **multi-program** (*v*).

multi-processing (*n*) (1) = multi-tasking (↑); (2) = multi-programming (↑); (3) the execution of more than one instruction at the same time by a multi-processor (p. 38). **multi-process** (*v*).

multi-threading (*n*) a system in which a program can allow several paths through it so that it can be used by more than one user at the same time. Generally refers to shared programs (p. 108) which handle terminals (p. 79) and which may cause the sticky bit (p. 138) to be set.

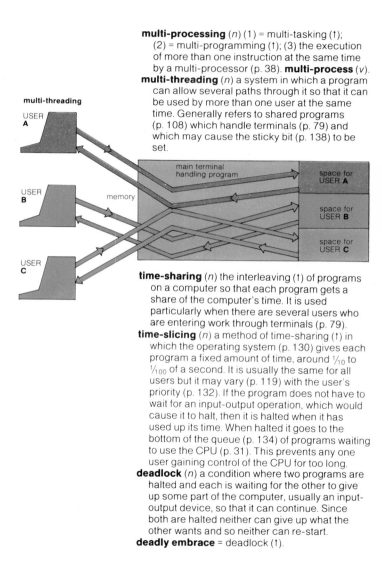

multi-threading

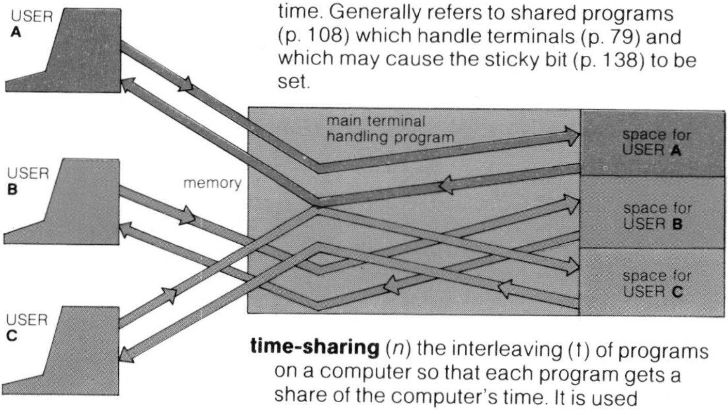

time-sharing (*n*) the interleaving (↑) of programs on a computer so that each program gets a share of the computer's time. It is used particularly when there are several users who are entering work through terminals (p. 79).

time-slicing (*n*) a method of time-sharing (↑) in which the operating system (p. 130) gives each program a fixed amount of time, around $\frac{1}{10}$ to $\frac{1}{100}$ of a second. It is usually the same for all users but it may vary (p. 119) with the user's priority (p. 132). If the program does not have to wait for an input-output operation, which would cause it to halt, then it is halted when it has used up its time. When halted it goes to the bottom of the queue (p. 134) of programs waiting to use the CPU (p. 31). This prevents any one user gaining control of the CPU for too long.

deadlock (*n*) a condition where two programs are halted and each is waiting for the other to give up some part of the computer, usually an input-output device, so that it can continue. Since both are halted neither can give up what the other wants and so neither can re-start.

deadly embrace = deadlock (↑).

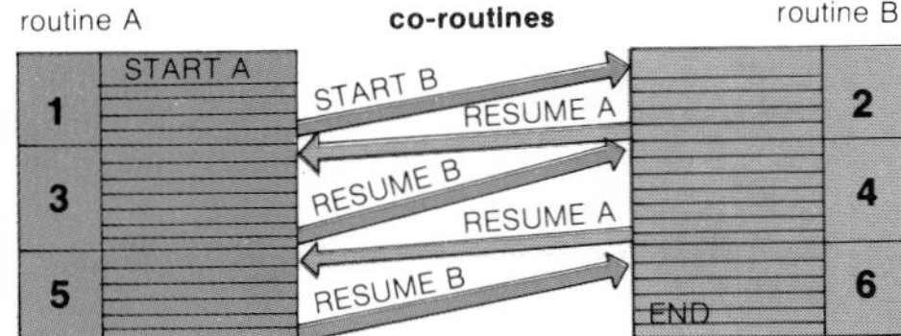

co-routines

race condition a condition where two communicating processes (p. 140), running at different speeds and passing results to one another, get out of step. Each process halts and waits for the other to continue and to pass it a result.

co-routine (*n*) a routine (p. 111) which has to work with another. It passes results to the second routine which is then given the use of the CPU (p. 31) to continue. The second routine passes its results back to the first one which then gets control of the CPU again. Neither routine is in control of the other.

sleeping process a process which is waiting for something else to happen before it does any work. It may be awaiting the result from some other task (p. 140). It may be awaiting some particular event, e.g. a process which runs at a fixed time would wait for a signal (p. 22) from the timer (p. 24).

wake-up bit a bit (p. 17) which is examined by the scheduler (p. 132) to decide whether to start up a sleeping process (↑). If the bit is 0 then the process continues sleeping until the event for which it is waiting sets the wake-up bit to 1. It is really only a satisfactory method if there are two or three processes. **wake-up** (*v*).

sleeping state of processes

partition	process	active or sleeping	send wake-up bit when
1	program A	active	–
2	program B	sleeping	timer = 10.00
3	program C	active	–
4	program D	sleeping	end of prog C
5	program E	sleeping	two tapes free

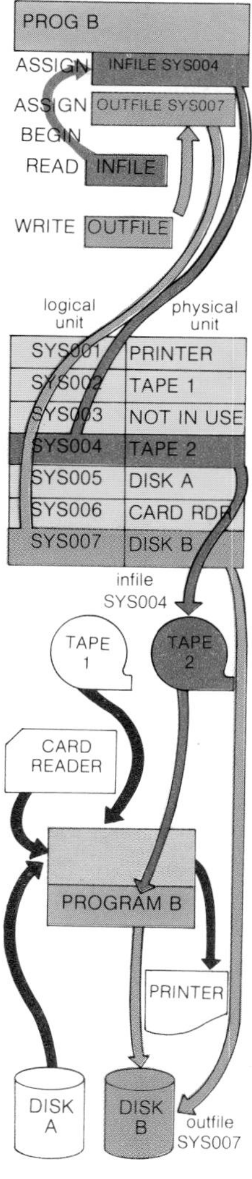

semaphore a number which is used to show how many wake-up (↑) signals (p. 22) have been sent. By using two semaphores, called 'up' and 'down', it is possible to handle more than two communicating processes (p. 140).

assign (*v*) to give a program some part of the computer to work with. A program can be given a certain amount of memory, a certain amount of space on disk (p. 66), etc. The word is particularly used to show which input-output devices a program can use (*device assignment*). **assignment** (*n*).

logical unit a device as it appears or is known to a program. Instead of using the actual address of a device the program uses a logical unit number and when the program is run the operating system (p. 130) assigns (↑) the actual device address to the logical unit. It avoids having to specify a particular peripheral device (p. 12) when a program is written.

abort (*n*) the action taken by an operating system (p. 130) to stop a program before its normal end. The action can also be taken by a user. It can be because there is a serious error in the program or its data, or it can sometimes be done if there are too many small errors. **abort** (*v*).

overhead (*n*) (1) the time taken by the operating system (p. 130) as opposed to the time taken by users' program; (2) the amount of memory, disk space (p. 69) which needs to be given to the operating system.

system overhead = overhead (↑).

elapsed time the actual time taken by a program from start to finish. On a time-sharing (p. 141) or multi-programming (p. 140) computer this will always be greater than the time the program would take to execute if it were the only program.

wall clock time = elapsed time (↑).

CPU time (1) the time a program will take to execute if it has complete control of the CPU (p. 31) and does not have to give way to other programs; (2) the time taken by the CPU to execute instructions as opposed to time spent accessing data from peripheral devices (p. 12).

data structure the way data is arranged so that parts of it can be accessed or changed quickly, or entries can be added or deleted. It may be in lists, tables (↓), or arrays (↓), where the position of an entry can be calculated. It may be in files (p. 153) with records (p. 154) in sequence. It may be in lists where each entry contains data and a pointer (↓) which points to the next entry in the list. It can be arranged into trees (p. 149), where each entry can point to two or more further entries. There are many ways to arrange data and the choice depends on what the data is to be used for. **structure** (*n*), **structure** (*v*).

linear list a list which can be accessed by starting at one end and moving from one entry to the next. The entries need not be the same length but they are usually in order by a key (p. 156). The list may be stored in sequential memory locations, with no spaces between the entries, or may be in different parts of memory with each entry containing a pointer (↓) to the next entry.

linear list items not of same length
item no:

1	2	3	4	5
CLARKE	JONES	ROSS	SMITH	WILSON

table (*n*) a list in which all the entries are similar, e.g. each entry could be the name of a school. All the entries are usually the same length so an entry can be found by calculation or by using a single subscript (↓), e.g. the table might consist of the names of a group of schools. This would be a *one-dimensional table*. If for each school we had another list giving the names of all the students this would be a *two-dimensional table*. We would need two subscripts to find a student, one for the school and one for the student's entry in that school. Entries in a table may have more than one field (p. 155), e.g. the entry for a student could also include his or her age. It is a very common way of structuring data, particularly if the size of the table is known at the time a program is being written.

table
list as a table with all items of same length

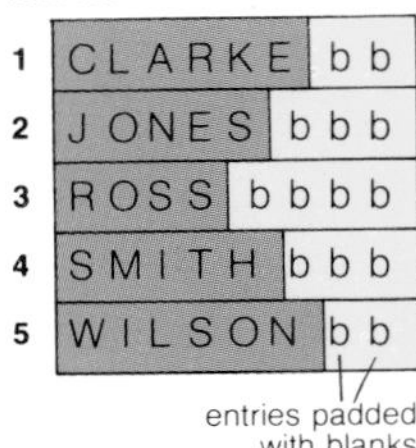

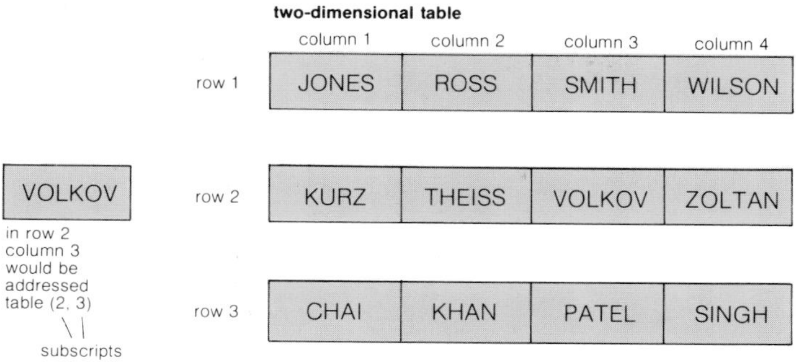

two-dimensional table

	column 1	column 2	column 3	column 4
row 1	JONES	ROSS	SMITH	WILSON
row 2	KURZ	THEISS	VOLKOV	ZOLTAN
row 3	CHAI	KHAN	PATEL	SINGH

VOLKOV

in row 2 column 3 would be addressed table (2, 3)

subscripts

array (*n*) a table (↑), especially in scientific programs where the entries are usually numbers being used in calculations.

look-up (*v*) to search a table (↑) or a list for a particular value or entry. Some languages provide a macro (p. 101) instruction to do this. **look-up** (*n*).

table look-up = look-up (↑).

subscript (*n*) a number which gives the position of an entry in a table (↑) or an array (↑). Very often the whole of a table will have a name. For example, a table of book titles might be called book-table and the name with a subscript, e.g. book-table [3], would mean the third book title in the table. **subscript** (*v*).

index[2] (1) (*n*) = subscript (↑); (2) (*v*) to set up a table (↑) of keys (p. 156) and addresses for records (p. 154) in a file (p. 153).

index register a register (p. 14) which is used to index (↑) a table (↑). The register may be a base register (p. 114) or one which is added to a base register.

pointer (*n*) a variable (p. 119) which is the address of an entry in a list or a record (p. 154) in a file (p. 153). The entries are not placed next to each other but, in addition to the data, each entry contains a pointer to show where the next entry is to be found. It is a very common way of addressing data structures (↑). **point** (*v*).

link[2] (*n*) = pointer (↑).

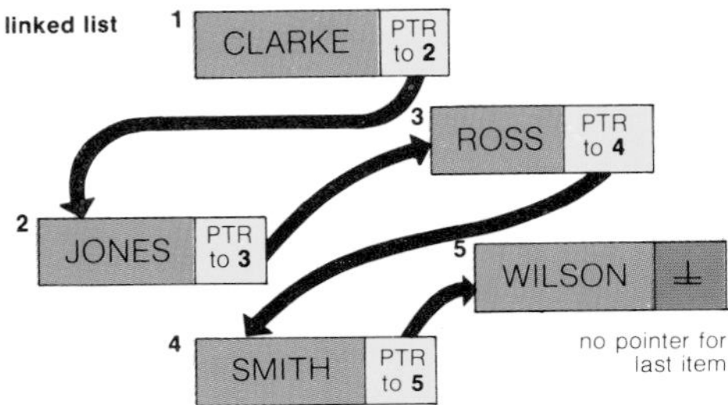

linked list a list held in memory in which each entry consists of data and a pointer (p. 145) which gives the location of the next entry in the list. The list may be in a sequential order if the pointers are followed but the entries are not in sequence by memory location. Entries can only be accessed by starting at the first entry and following the pointers. It is easy to insert or delete entries at any part of the list provided the pointers are changed.

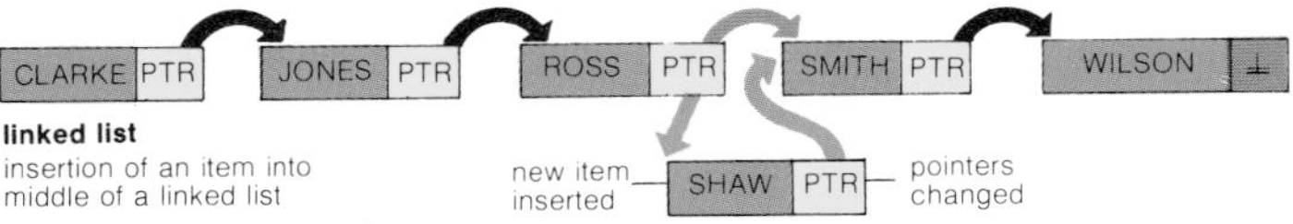

linked list
insertion of an item into middle of a linked list

doubly linked list a linked list (↑) where each entry has two pointers (p. 145), one which points to the previous entry and another to the next entry. The entries can be accessed sequentially either backwards or forwards.

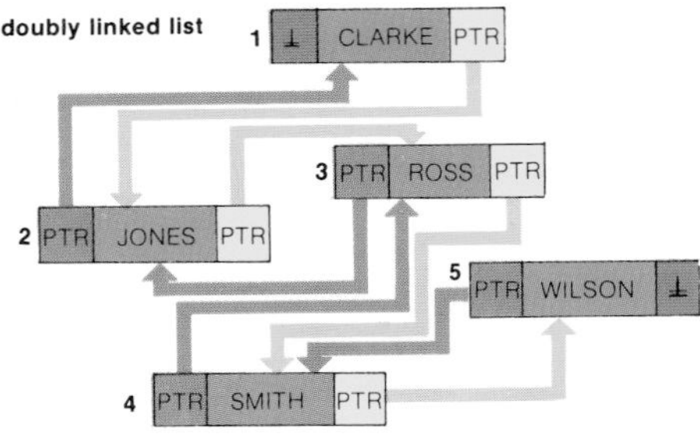

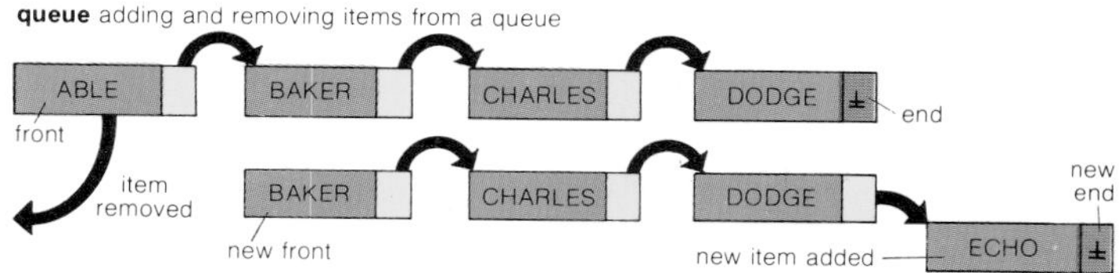

circular list

1 CLARKE
2 JONES
3 ROSS
4 SMITH
5 WILSON
pointer to head of list

queue[2] (*n*) a linear list (p. 144) where any items to be added are always placed at the tail of the list. Items can only be deleted or accessed from the front end. Items are never added to or deleted from any other part of the list. **queue** (*v*).

deque (*n*) a double ended queue (↑). A linear list (p. 144) where items can be added, deleted or accessed from either end of the list but not from any other part.

circular list a list where the last entry points to the first entry. It can also be doubly linked (↑).

circular buffer a buffer (p. 161) which is a circular list (↑). Inside the buffer there is a queue (↑) and new data is added to one end and old data is deleted from the other. Often used where the data is wanted only for a short time, e.g. data which is going to be printed is often held in memory, or a disk (p. 66), in this manner.

stack (*n*) a linear list (p. 144) in which all additions, deletions and access are to one end of the list which is considered to be the top of the stack. Also known as **heap**. **stack** (*v*).

push-down stack = stack (↑).

push-down store = stack (↑).

nesting store = stack (↑).

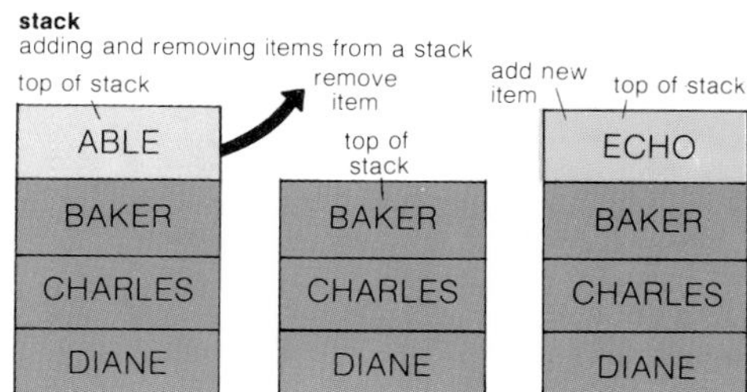

push (*v*) to place another item on the top of a stack (p. 147).

pop (*v*) to take the item from the top of a stack (p. 147).

stack pointer a pointer (p. 145) which points to the top of a stack (p. 147). Because items are added or deleted from the tops of stacks the position of the top item in memory changes. Whenever the stack is changed the stack pointer is also changed so that it always points to the top of the stack.

linear search a search of a list which starts by examining an entry at one end of the list. If this is not the entry which is being looked for then the next entry in the list is examined and so on until either the entry is found or the other end of the list is reached. The list does not have to be in sequential order.

linear search items need not be in sequential order

binary search for JILL — list must be in sequential order

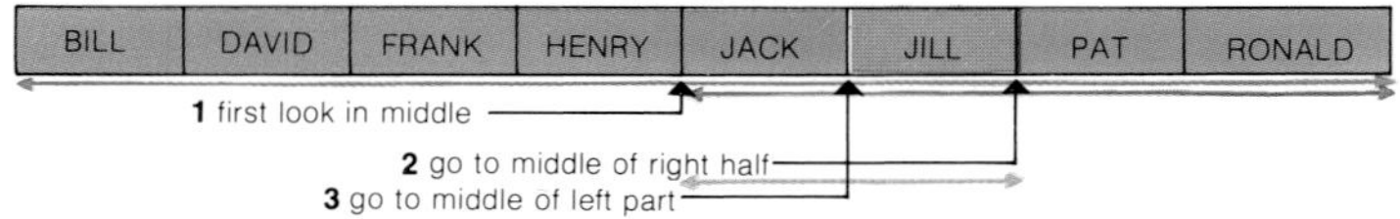

binary search a very common method of searching a sequential list. The middle entry of the list is examined to decide whether it is the entry you are looking for. If it is not then it is either larger or smaller and the program can decide which half of the list the entry must be in. A search is then made of the correct half in the same way, i.e. its middle entry is examined. Each succeeding step cuts the part of the list to be searched down by half. It is faster than a linear search (↑) but the list must be in sequence.

binary chop = binary search (↑).

search time the time taken to carry out a search, usually of a list in memory.

tree

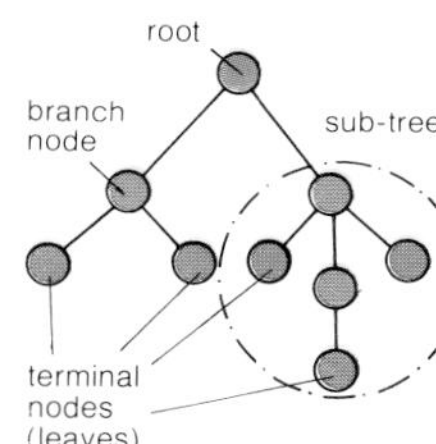

binary tree

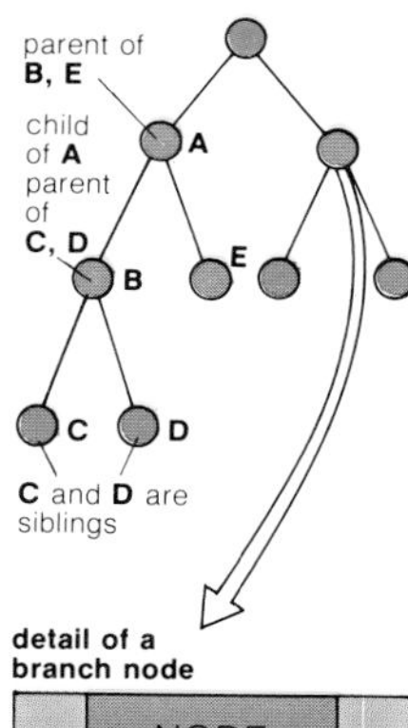

detail of a branch node

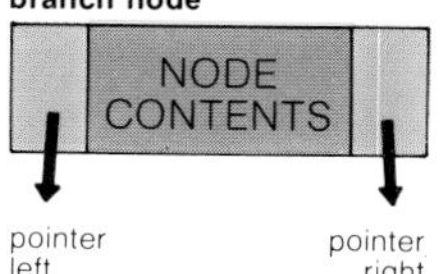

hit rate the proportion of searches which are successful i.e. the object is found.

tree (*n*) a data structure (p. 144) where each entry, called a node (↓), contains data and pointers (p. 145) to two or more other entries, each of which can also point to two or more entries and so on. There is always one entry not pointed to by any other, called the root (↓), and entries, called leaves (↓), which do not point to further entries. There is only one possible path between any two nodes. In diagrams a tree is always drawn with the root at the top and the leaves at the bottom.

root (*n*) the top or first entry in a tree (↑). It contains pointers (p. 145) to those nodes (↓) immediately below it in the tree.

root node = root (↑).

node[2] (*n*) (1) an entry in a tree (↑) which has pointers (p. 145) to those entries immediately below it, and which is pointed to by the entry immediately above it, or both, i.e. it can include both the root (↑) and a leaf (↓); (2) an entry in a tree which points to further nodes or leaves but is not a leaf itself; i.e. a leaf is not considered to be a node.

branch node a node (↑) which points (p. 145) to other nodes, i.e. it is not a leaf (↓).

leaf (*n*) an entry in a tree (↑) which does not point (p. 145) to any further entry, i.e. it is at the bottom of the tree.

terminal node = leaf (↑).

sub-tree (*n*) the part of a tree (↑) which can be accessed from a particular node (↑).

binary tree a tree (↑) where each node (↑) is either a leaf (↑) or points (p. 145) to two nodes. It is a very common way of arranging a tree.

parent-child (*adj*) of the relation between a node (↑) and the entries it points (p. 145) to. The node is the parent (↓) and the entries pointed to are the children (↓).

parent (*n*) a node (↑) in a tree (↑) which points (p. 145) to other nodes which are called its children (↓).

child (*n*) a node (↑) or leaf (↑) in a tree (↑) which is pointed (p. 145) to by a parent (↑).

sibling (*n*) a second, or another, child (p. 149) node (p. 149) or leaf (p. 149).

height (*n*) the longest path from the root (p. 149) to a leaf (p. 149), counting one for each node (p. 149) accessed. The height affects the time taken to access the entries.

balanced tree (1) a tree (p. 149) where all leaves (p. 149) are at the same height (↑) (a difference of ±1 may be allowed); (2) a tree where each parent (p. 149), save possibly one, has the same number of children (p. 149); one parent may have fewer, any new leaf would be attached to this parent. In this form the leaves need not be at the same height.

prefix walk a method of examining every entry in a tree (p. 149). Starting with the root (p. 149) as parent (p. 149) it accesses the left-most child (p. 149). It repeats this as long as the next node (p. 149) is also a parent. When it is a leaf (p. 149) it goes to the next child of the last parent.

pre-order traversal = prefix walk (↑).

suffix walk a method of examining every entry in a tree (p. 149). This gives the leaves (p. 149) from left to right, examining a parent (p. 149) only when all the children (p. 149) have been accessed. Starting at the left-most leaf, it goes to all the leaves which can be reached from the same parent. Whenever all the children of a parent have been accessed it goes to the parent. With a binary tree (p. 149) this is the same order as reverse Polish notation (p. 15).

B-tree (*n*) a tree (p. 149) where each branch node (p. 149) contains some keys (p. 156) in sequence and the number of children (p. 149) is one more than the number of keys. The number of children is not fixed, the smallest number allowed is about half the largest number. The tree is arranged so that the leaves are at the same height (↑) and the keys they contain are in sequence. Keys can be inserted or deleted from the leaves. If the number of keys in a leaf becomes too large then it is divided into two; if the number becomes too small then it is joined to the next leaf. This type of tree is commonly used to index (p. 145) large files (p. 153).

unbalanced tree

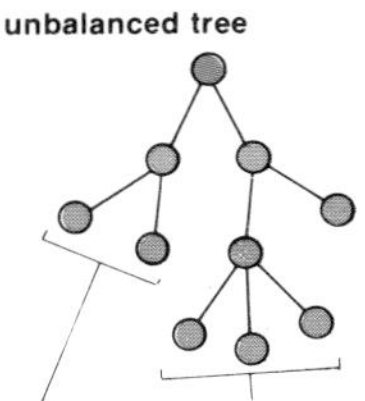

balanced tree

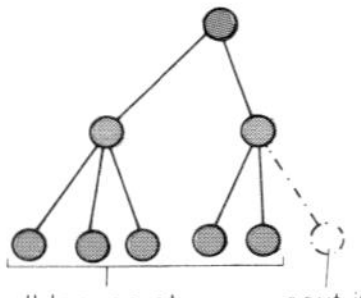

prefix walk
order in which nodes are visited **A B D E C F H I G**

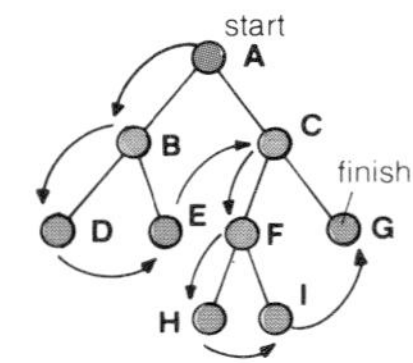

suffix walk
order in which nodes are visited **D E B H I F G C A**

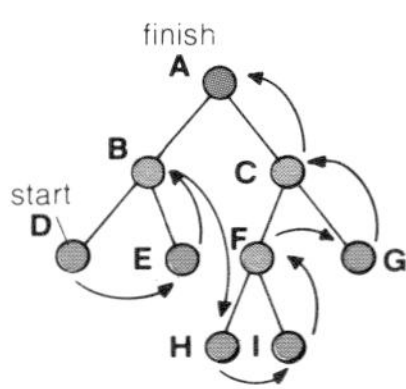

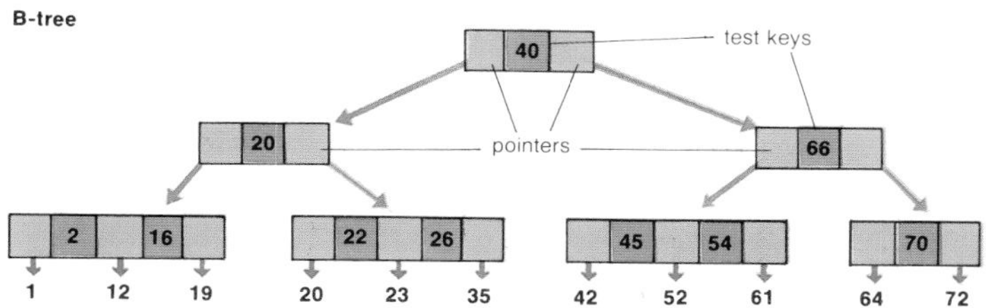

hash routine a system in which the key (p. 156) of a record (p. 154) is changed into a number. The number is then used as the address, either of a sector (p. 69) on disk (p. 66) or a memory location. The record is then placed at that address. To find the record, given its key, the same routine is used to produce the same number again and this gives the address where the record has been stored. **hashing** (*adj*), **hash** (*v*).

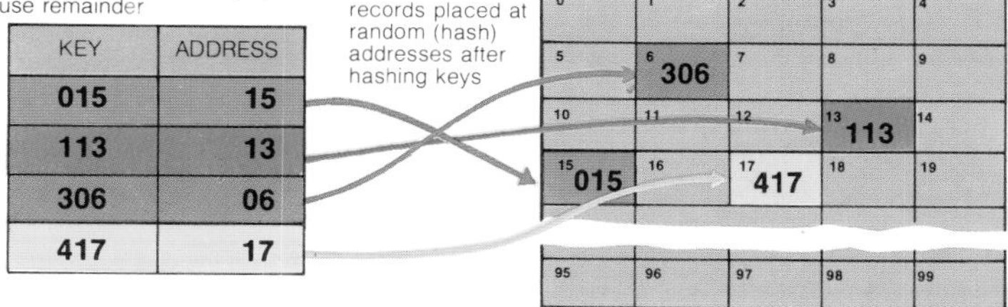

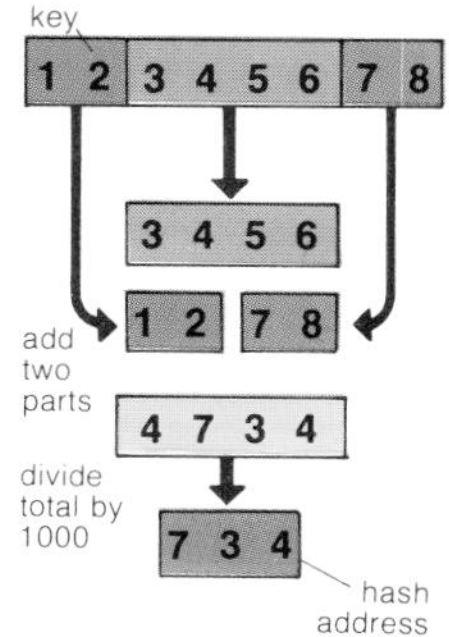

folding (*adj*) of a hash routine (↑) where the end parts of a key (p. 156) are moved to, or added to, the middle of the key before hashing takes place.

division method a method of hashing (↑) where the value of the key (p. 156) is divided by a number close to the number of available addresses, and the remainder is used as the address where the record (p. 154) is to be placed.

home record a record (p. 154) which is placed at the exact address produced by the hash routine (↑).

home address an address occupied by a home record (p. 151). For a given key (p. 156) it is the same as the address produced by the hash routine (p. 151).

collision (*n*) a collision occurs if the same key (p. 156) appears more than once or if a hash routine (p. 151) produces the same address for two or more different keys. Only one of the records (p. 154) can be placed at the home address (↑). The remaining records have to be placed at other addresses in such a way that they can be found even though their keys will produce the address of the home record and not the address where they have actually been placed.

synonym (*n*) = collision (↑).

clustering (*n*) the result of too many different keys (p. 156) hashing (p. 151) to the same or neighbouring addresses thus producing too many collisions (↑) and too few records (p. 154) actually located at their home address (↑). This causes a program to take longer to find a particular record than it otherwise would.

open insertion a method of dealing with collisions (↑) where the record (p. 154) causing a collision is placed at the next sequential address which does not already contain a record. If there is no space before the end of the file then the search continues from the beginning.

open addressing = open insertion (↑).

progressive overflow = open insertion (↑).

progressive linear overflow = open insertion (↑).

chain[2] (*n*) a method of dealing with collisions (↑). The first record (p. 154) is placed somewhere else in the file (↓) and the home record (p. 151) has a pointer (p. 145) added to it. Further collisions are handled in the same way; each record in the chain contains a pointer to the address of the next record in the chain. **chain** (*v*).

chained record a record (p. 154) in a file (↓) which has a pointer (p. 145) to another record that either has the same key (p. 156), or a different key which has hashed (p. 151) to the same home address (↑).

collision
hash by dividing key by 10

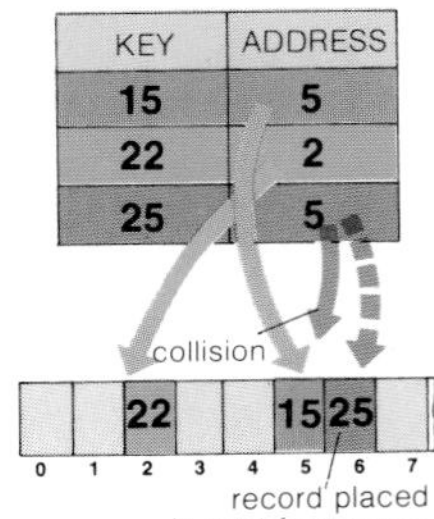

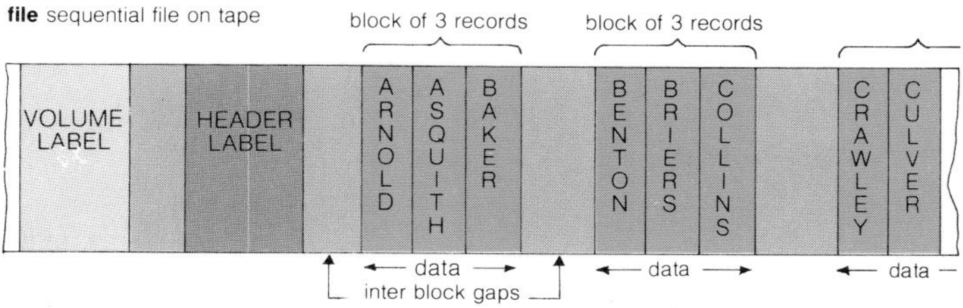

file sequential file on tape

file (*n*) a collection of records (p. 154) which all deal with the same sort of data. For example, a record might have details about one customer of a company, the file would consist of all the records for all the customers. New records can be included in a file while keeping the records in the correct order. Records can be deleted, or parts of them can be changed. This is called amending the file. Files will not normally fit into memory so programs which need to process files do so by reading in a few records at a time, sometimes just one, processing the records and then getting the next ones and so on. The records are often in a particular order and must be kept in that order if a program is to access them correctly. There are files where the records are not in any particular order but these are handled in a different way.

data set = file (↑).

file identification the process of naming a file (↑) to make certain that the correct file is being used. Each file usually has a header label (p. 154) which can be read and checked by a computer but there is usually also something handwritten which a person can read.

file name the name given to a file (↑), such as 'Monthly Pay', which is stored in a header label (p. 154) and usually checked whenever a file is read.

volume label a record (p. 154) which is placed on each separate tape reel (p. 71) or disk (p. 66). It usually contains information saying who owns it and a number. The number is usually placed on the reel or pack before it is first used in an installation (p. 10) and not usually changed.

FILE NAME	'CLASS LIST'
DATE WRITTEN	'01061986'
KEEP UNTIL	'31121986'
BLOCK — SIZE	300 BYTES
RECORD — SIZE	100 BYTES
START ADDRESS	CYL 05 TRACK 5
END ADDRESS	CYL 06 TRACK 9

header label information

name
creation date
retention date

used for disk files only

header label a record (↓) which is part of a file (p. 153) but separate from the data records. It contains information about the contents of the file, its name, its creation date (p. 157), how long it must be kept, etc. The information is checked by each program to make sure that it is processing the correct file.

file label (1) = a volume label (p. 153); (2) = a header label (↑).

trailer record a special record (↓) written after the data records of a file (p. 153) on a tape reel (p. 71). It contains information, such as the number of blocks (p. 159) written, which will be used to check that the file has been read correctly whenever it is processed.

file layout (1) the arrangement of records (↓) in a file (p. 153); (2) a written explanation of the arrangement and permitted contents of the fields (↓) in the records.

record[1] (*n*) data which consists of a collection of fields (↓) about some particular thing and which is held and moved as if it were a single piece of data. For example, a record for a student might contain a name, a course of study, and the marks given. Records are stored on backing store (p. 12) and read or written by programs as needed. It is usual to read or write a complete record, not parts of it.

sub-fields or elements of date of birth field

DAY MONTH YEAR

record contents of a particular record

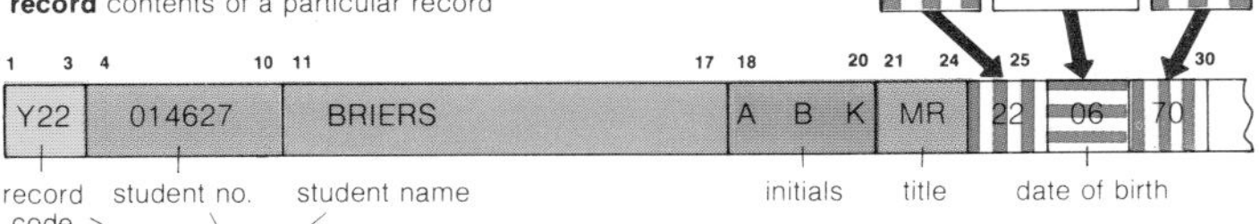

description of record layout

FIELD	POSITION START	END	FIELD NAME	FORMAT OR CONTENTS
1	**1**	**3**	RECORD-CODE	Y22
2	**4**	**10**	STUDENT-NO.	NUMERIC NO BLANKS
3	**11**	**17**	STUDENT-NAME	ALPHA LEFT JUSTIFIED
4	**18**	**20**	INITIALS	AS FLD 3
5	**21**	**24**	TITLE	MR, MRS, MISS, MME, MLLE
6	**25**	**30**	DATE OF BIRTH	DDMMYY

physical and logical records

physical record in two linked parts

field (*n*) a part of a record (↑) which contains one piece of data, such as a name or an amount. Sometimes the field has smaller parts. For example, a field might contain the date which could be used as a single piece of data or it could be separated into day, month and year.

elementary item a single piece of data which is complete in itself and which does not contain any smaller parts.

data element = elementary item (↑).

data unit = elementary item (↑).

logical record a record (↑) in the form it is used by a program. It is not necessarily stored in the same form on a disk (p. 66) or tape (p. 71) where records are usually blocked (p. 159). In data-bases (p. 174) the record as used by a program may in fact be stored in several different places on a disk.

physical record the actual data on a storage device (p. 199) which is transferred in a single read or write operation. It is hardly ever a single record (↑) since most files (p. 153) are blocked (p. 159). Except in sequential files the records are unlikely to be in the same order as they will be made available to a program.

control field the field (↑) in a record (↑) which is used to decide the sequence in which records are to be arranged. It is not exactly the same as a primary key (p. 156); it can be any part of a key (p. 156) but it can also be a field which is not part of a key but which decides the order in which records will be processed in a particular program.

key (*n*) a field (p. 155), or fields, in a record (p. 154) whose contents are used to decide the sequence in which a file (p. 153) is to be arranged. For several fields the order of importance has to be specified. The parts of the key are called control fields (p. 155) and the most important one is called the major control field (p. 169).

primary key the key (↑) which decides the sequence in which a file (p. 153) is normally held or processed. Each key usually appears only once.

primary and secondary key

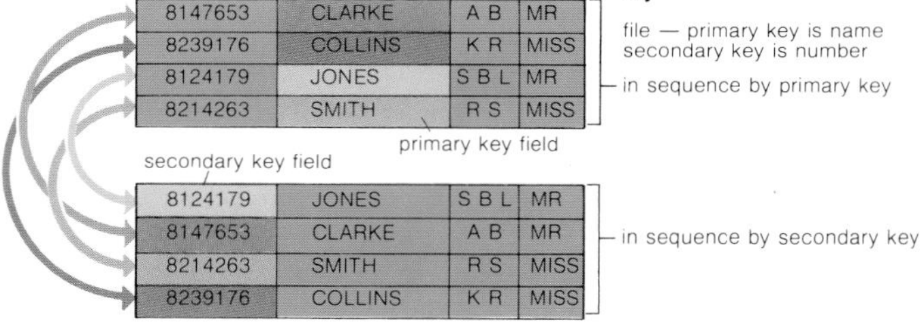

file — primary key is name
secondary key is number

in sequence by primary key

number	name	initials	title
8147653	CLARKE	A B	MR
8239176	COLLINS	K R	MISS
8124179	JONES	S B L	MR
8214263	SMITH	R S	MISS

primary key field

secondary key field

in sequence by secondary key

number	name	initials	title
8124179	JONES	S B L	MR
8147653	CLARKE	A B	MR
8214263	SMITH	R S	MISS
8239176	COLLINS	K R	MISS

secondary key a key (↑) which can be used to process a file (p. 153) but it is not the one which is used to sequence the file normally. The same secondary key can appear several times in a file and, in different programs, a different secondary key can be used. Sometimes a file is sorted (p. 169) to secondary key sequence, sometimes it is indexed (p. 145).

shared file a file (p. 153) on a direct access device (p. 67) which can be accessed by two or more separate computers.

variable length of records (p. 154) in a file (p. 153) which are of different lengths. There is usually an extra field (p. 155) at the front of the record, which is not part of the data. This gives the length of the record so that it can be checked by the operating system (p. 130). Sometimes the operating system, or a service program (p. 127), may not allow the use of files of variable length records, e.g. some will not allow them in random files (p. 166).

fixed length of records (p. 154) in a file (p. 153) which are all of the same length. There may be different record formats (p. 207).

file protection the process of protecting a file (p. 153) against accidental over-writing by a program, or damage while it is stored when not being used.

EOF end of file. A common name for a switch (p. 120) in a program which is set on when the end of a file (p. 153) has been reached.

file creation the process of running a program which first produces a file (p. 153). Once a file has been created it is usually updated (p. 202) whenever changes are made to its contents but it must first be created with correct header labels (p. 154), etc and sometimes records (p. 154) with empty fields (p. 155). The creation is not necessarily done just once, it may be done regularly. For example, a file which was to hold a week's transactions (p. 162) might need to be created each week.

creation date the date on which a version (p. 129) of a file (p. 153) was first produced. It is given in a field (p. 155) held in a header label (p. 154). It is entered into the header label when the file is first created but it will be changed on each update (p. 202) when the new version of the file which is output will show the date of the update.

generation number a number held in a header label (p. 154) which shows when a version (p. 129) of a file (p. 153) was produced. Each update (p. 202) produces an output file (p. 160) which has a generation number one higher than the input file (p. 160). The generation number can be used by an operating system (p. 130) to prevent accidental over-writing of a file.

retention period a date, or a number of days after a creation date (↑) which shows the earliest date on which a file (p. 153) is allowed to be over-written. It is held in a header label (p. 154), and is used to prevent the accidental erasure (p. 74) of a file..

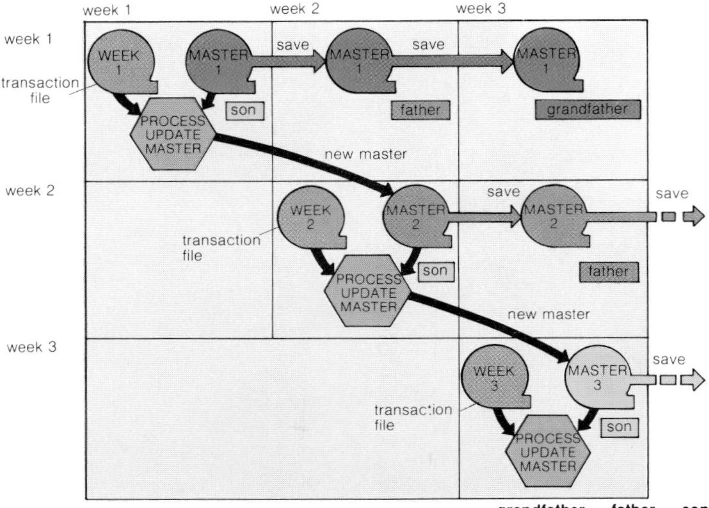

grandfather — father — son copies of master files

grandfather tape the third copy of a master file (p. 162) held on tape (p. 71). When a master file is updated (p. 202) the input is known as the *father*, and the output, i.e. the updated file (p. 153), as the *son*. The tape which was used to produce the father is the grandfather tape. It is kept in case the father tape is damaged or needs to be re-created. The idea can also be used with disk (p. 66) files.

file maintenance the work done on files (p. 153) which is not part of the actual processing of transactions (p. 162) but removes records (p. 154) which are no longer needed, corrects any errors which have been found, re-arranges the records to improve access, etc.

sequence check to check that a file (p. 153) has its records (p. 154) in sequence. Sequential files (p. 163) cannot be processed correctly if their records are not in sequence.

sequence error a fault in which a record (p. 154) is not in its correct place in a sequential file (p. 153).

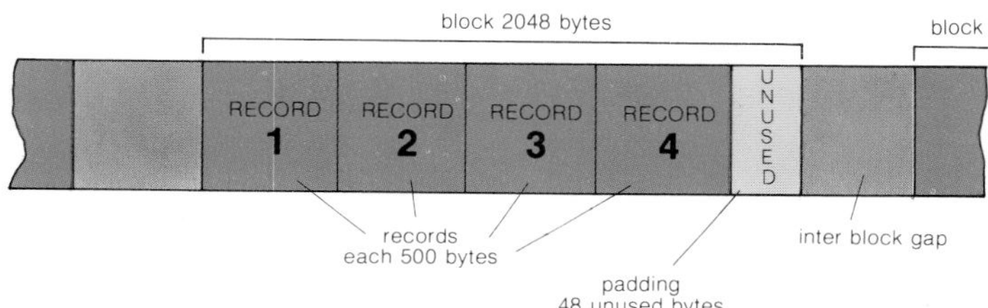

block (*n*) the smallest amount of data which is recorded in one continuous piece. It usually means data on a tape (p. 71) but is also sometimes used to mean the same as a sector (p. 69) on disk (p. 66). The size of a block, i.e. the amount of data it contains, tends to be fixed on disks, at least for a particular machine, but on tape the size tends to differ more widely depending on what the data is used for. Quite often the blocks are 256, 512, 1024 or 2048 bytes (p. 17) long since these sizes suit operating systems (p. 130). A block is therefore usually bigger than a single record (p. 154) and will hold as many records as can be fitted into it. If there is not enough space at the end of a block to fit in another complete record then the block is usually filled (↓). It is not usual to place a record so that parts are in two different blocks although this is sometimes done. **block** (*v*).

blocking factor the number of records (p. 154) in a block (↑). A blocking factor of 10 would mean that each block held 10 records.

unblocked (*adj*) of a block (↑) in which there is only one record (p. 154).

deblock (*v*) to take a block (↑) of records (p. 154) and make the records available to a program one at a time.

fill (*v*) to place some character, such as blanks, into the unused positions at the end of a block (↑) or record (p. 154).

pad (*v*) = fill (↑).

fill character the character which is used to fill (↑) out a block (↑) or record (p. 154).

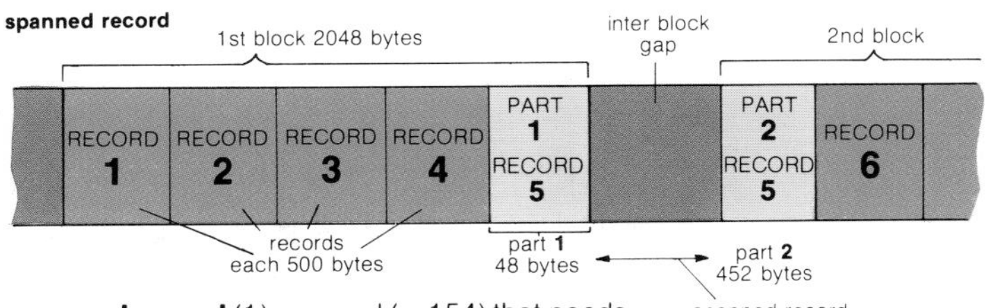

spanned record (1) a record (p. 154) that needs more than one block (p. 159) of a storage device (p. 199) to hold it; (2) a record, the first part of which is at the end of one block and the other part at the beginning of the next block.

bucket (*n*) (1) a block (p. 159) or sector (p. 69); (2) the amount of data which is read or written at one time. On tape (p. 71) this is the same as the block size but on disk (p. 66) it is often different from the sector size, i.e. more than one sector can be transferred with a single read or write command; (3) an area of memory or disk which is treated as a complete unit by some addressing method, particularly in a hash routine (p. 151).

input file a file (p. 153) which is input to a program. It is read but not usually written on to.

output file a file (p. 153) written out by a program.

input-output file a file (p. 153) which is read into a program, has changes made to some or all of the records (p. 154) which are then written back to the same place. The file must be on a direct access device (p. 67). The method saves space and can be faster than writing out a new output file (↓). A copy of the file is usually made before the start of the run in case of an error.

re-write (*v*) to write something again in the same place. It can mean writing back on a disk (p. 66) a record (p. 154) that has been read and changed in some way. It can also mean writing back the contents of memory following a destructive read (p. 43). **re-write** (*n*).

input area an area of memory into which a block (p. 159) of data is read from an input device (p. 12).

output area an area of memory where data is placed before being written to an output device (p. 13).

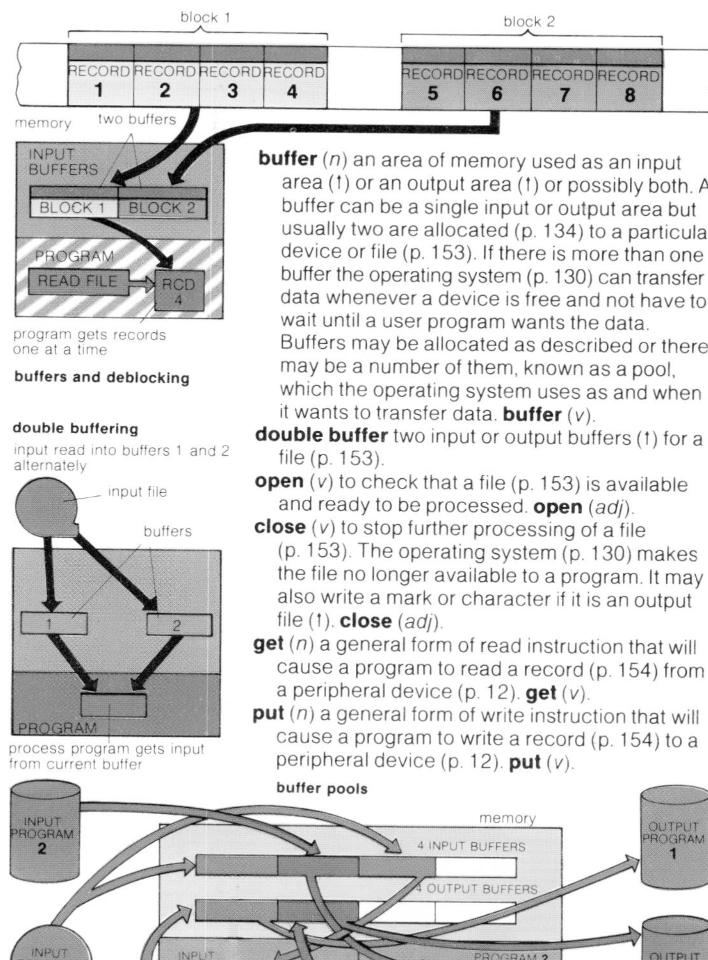

buffers and deblocking

double buffering

buffer pools

buffer (*n*) an area of memory used as an input area (↑) or an output area (↑) or possibly both. A buffer can be a single input or output area but usually two are allocated (p. 134) to a particular device or file (p. 153). If there is more than one buffer the operating system (p. 130) can transfer data whenever a device is free and not have to wait until a user program wants the data. Buffers may be allocated as described or there may be a number of them, known as a pool, which the operating system uses as and when it wants to transfer data. **buffer** (*v*).

double buffer two input or output buffers (↑) for a file (p. 153).

open (*v*) to check that a file (p. 153) is available and ready to be processed. **open** (*adj*).

close (*v*) to stop further processing of a file (p. 153). The operating system (p. 130) makes the file no longer available to a program. It may also write a mark or character if it is an output file (↑). **close** (*adj*).

get (*n*) a general form of read instruction that will cause a program to read a record (p. 154) from a peripheral device (p. 12). **get** (*v*).

put (*n*) a general form of write instruction that will cause a program to write a record (p. 154) to a peripheral device (p. 12). **put** (*v*).

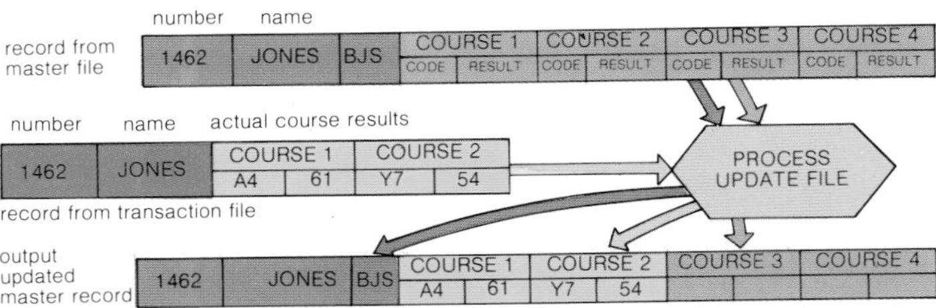

master file

master file a file (p. 153) whose records (p. 154) contain some data which is not changed very often, e.g. a person's name or address. This data is usually very important to a business. It may also contain transaction (↓) data which is changed quite often, e.g. sales to a customer. The file will usually be used by a number of programs in a system (p. 181).

master record (1) the main record (p. 154) where there are several records for a particular entry, e.g. it might hold a name and address and be followed by one or more records which hold transaction (↓) data; (2) = a control record (p. 183).

transaction (*n*) (1) an event that produces data which needs to be entered into a system (p. 181). For example, the sale of something would usually mean that an account number and the cost of the item would need to be entered into the computer at some stage; (2) the actual data which has been entered into the system.

transaction file a file (p. 153) whose records (p. 154) contain transaction (↑) data. It is used to update (p. 202) a master file (↑).

detail file = transaction file (↑).

update[2] (*v*) to change the contents of a master file (↑) with the transactions (↑) on a transaction file (↑). The data on the master file which is changed is usually data which changes regularly, such as sales for the week. Changes to the parts of the master file which contain data such as a customer's name are usually done by different programs, called amendment programs (↓). **updating** (*n*), **update** (*n*).

insertion (*n*) a record (p. 154) to be included in an existing file. If the file is in sequence then the record must be placed in its correct position. **insert** (*v*).

amendment (*n*) the changing of some of the data on a record (p. 154) which is already present in a file (p. 153). **amend** (*v*).

deletion (*n*) a record (p. 154) which has to be removed from a file (p. 153). **delete** (*v*).

amendment record a record (p. 154) which holds new data for the part of a master file (↑) which does not change very often, e.g. a person's name and address.

amendment program a program which is used to change parts of a master file (↑) which hold data that does not change very often, e.g. a person's name or account number. It could also add new records (p. 154) and mark records which are to be deleted later. An amendment (↑) is not the same as a transaction (↑) and although it is possible to handle them both in a single update (↑) program they are usually dealt with separately.

serial file a file (p. 153) whose records (p. 154) are not in any particular order. The contents are usually transactions (↑) which are often entered in the order in which they happen. It is possible to process a serial file against an indexed file (p. 165) or a random file (p. 166) but in practice serial files are often sorted (p. 169) to a sequential order first.

sequential file a file (p. 153) whose records (p. 154) are in sequence by a key (p. 156). Unless the file is also indexed (p. 164) it is usually necessary to read every record in the whole file in order to process any part of it.

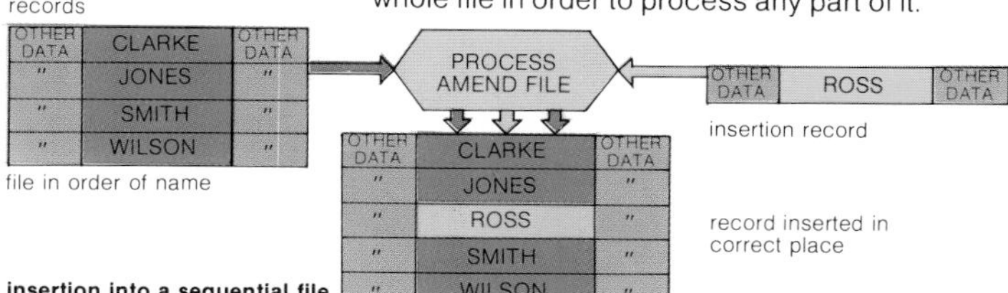

insertion into a sequential file

index[1] (*n*) a table (p. 144) in which each entry consists of a record key (p. 156) and the address of the record (p. 154). There may be an entry for every record in the file (p. 153) but more often only some of the record keys will be used, e.g. perhaps every tenth one. The file must be on a direct access device (p. 67) unless it is small enough to fit into memory. To find a record the programmer takes its key and uses it to search the index for the address of the record, or of a record which is near to the one which is wanted. For large files the index may have several index levels. **index** (*v*), **indexed** (*adj*).

dense index an index (↑) which has an entry for every record (p. 154) in the file (p. 153). This is needed only if the file is not in sequential order.

multi-level index an index (↑) in which the entries in the first, or top level of the index, point (p. 145) not to data records (p. 154) but to records which contain further index entries. There may be two or more levels and only the lowest one actually points to data records. It is used when the index is very large and only the upper levels can be kept in memory. The other levels are held on disk (p. 66) and only the part that is needed for access will be brought into memory.

index to file

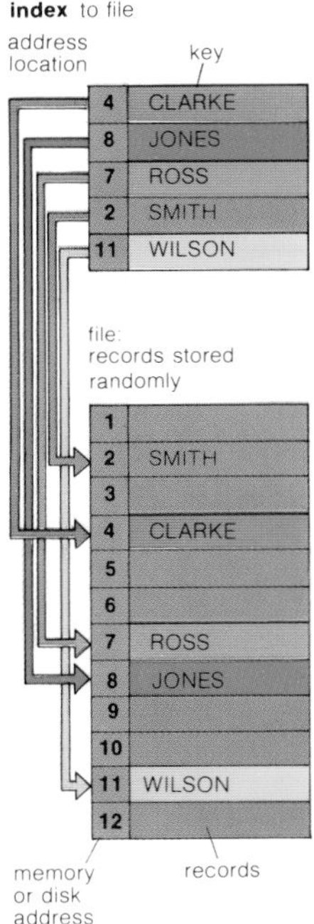

multi-level index

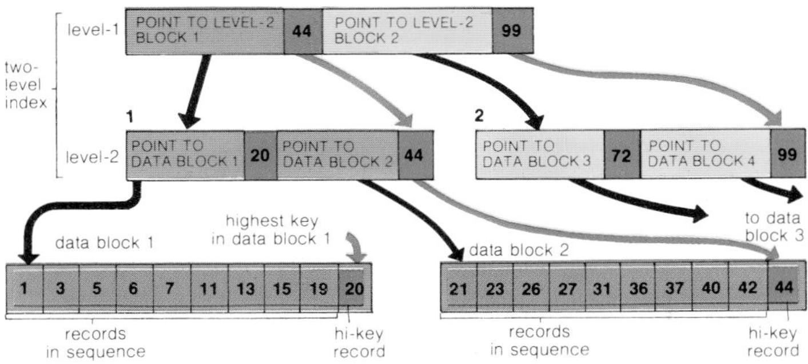

indexed file a file (p. 153) whose records (p. 154) can be in any order but which has an index (↑). The file must be on a direct access device (p. 67) or in memory. The index is in sequence by key (p. 156). To find a record the key of the record is used to search the index and get the record's address. It allows a program to access only those records it needs to, it does not have to read any others.

indexed sequential file a file (p. 153) whose records (p. 154) are in sequence by the primary key (p. 156) and which also has an index (↑). It can be accessed either in sequence or by use of the index. Because the records are in sequence it is not necessary to provide an index entry for every record, instead an entry is made for, say, every 100th record.

ISAM indexed sequential access method. A method of arranging an indexed sequential file (↑). Separate from the file (p. 153) there is an index (↑) with an entry for every cylinder (p. 68) of the file. On each cylinder there is an index for each track (p. 68) on the cylinder. If the file is large there can be further levels of index above the cylinder index. Records (p. 154) can be added or deleted and pointers (p. 145) are used to maintain the sequence but the indexes are not changed.

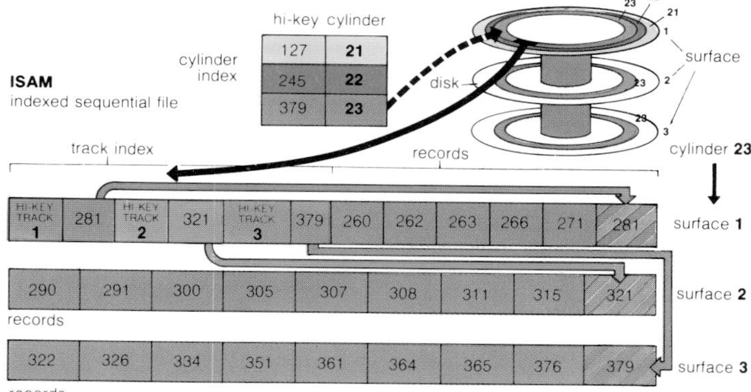

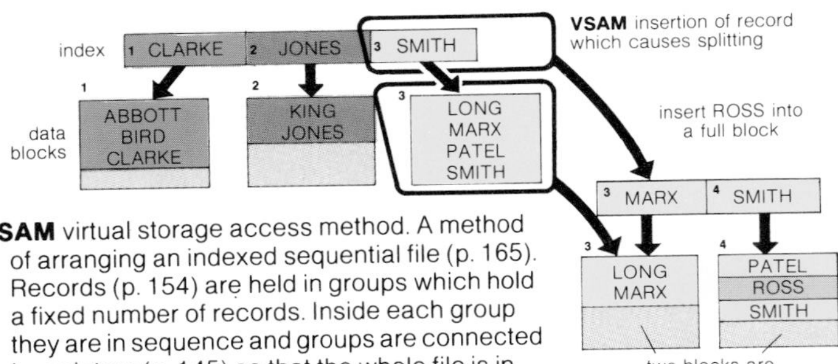

VSAM virtual storage access method. A method of arranging an indexed sequential file (p. 165). Records (p. 154) are held in groups which hold a fixed number of records. Inside each group they are in sequence and groups are connected by pointers (p. 145) so that the whole file is in sequence. An index (p. 164) has pointers to the groups of records. If records are added or deleted the groups can be split or joined to keep the whole file in sequence, but, unlike the ISAM (p. 165) method, the index is altered as well. The index is usually not a table (p. 144) but a form of B-tree (p. 150).

random file a file (p. 153) in which records (p. 154) are not in any particular order. Each record contains a key (p. 156) which is changed to an address by a hash routine (p. 151) and the record is placed at that address. The file must be on a direct access device (p. 67).

hash file = random file (↑).

relative file a random file (↑) or hash file (↑). The term is used because the address found from the hash routine (p. 151) is not a disk address (p. 69) but a number in the range 1 to N where N is the number of available disk addresses (not the number of records (p. 154)). Thus the address of a record is simply a number which is its position relative to the start of the file.

overflow area an area usually on disk (p. 66), but can also be in memory, in which to place records (p. 154) which cannot fit into the main file (p. 153) area. It is one way of handling collision (p. 152) records in a random file (↑) or records which have been inserted (p. 163) into an indexed sequential file (p. 165). A pointer (p. 145) to the collision record will be placed in a record in the main file or in the preceding record in the overflow area.

overflow record a record (p. 154) which is placed in the overflow area (↑) of a file (p. 153).

packing density the number of records (p. 154) in a random file (↑) divided by the total number of available address spaces. It usually ranges between 50% and 90% depending on the file.

average access the expected number of disk (p. 66) accesses needed to find a record (p. 154) in a random (↑) or indexed file (p. 165). It is not always possible to find a record with a single access, which for an indexed file usually gets part of the index (p. 164). Further accesses have to be made, which means moving the disk access arm (p. 70). For the file as a whole the number of accesses to find every record can be calculated and divided by the total number of records to give the average access. Common values are 1.1 to 1.6 for a random file and 2 to 3 for an indexed file.

inverted file a file (p. 153) which is in primary key (p. 156) order but needs to be accessed in a different order, specified by a secondary key (p. 156). Instead of sorting (p. 169) the file an index (p. 164) of the secondary keys is produced and the file is accessed indirectly using the secondary index.

inverted file

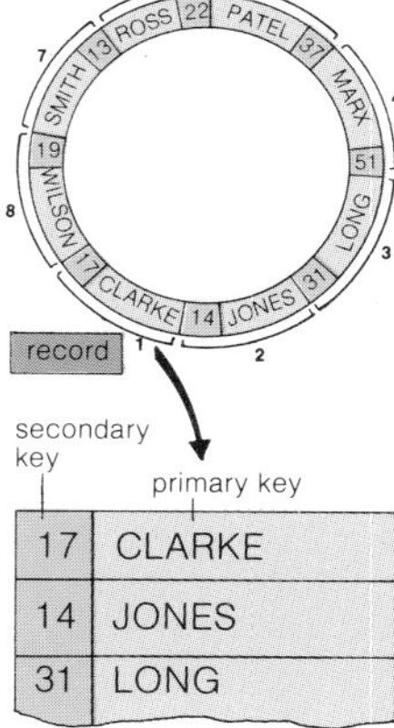

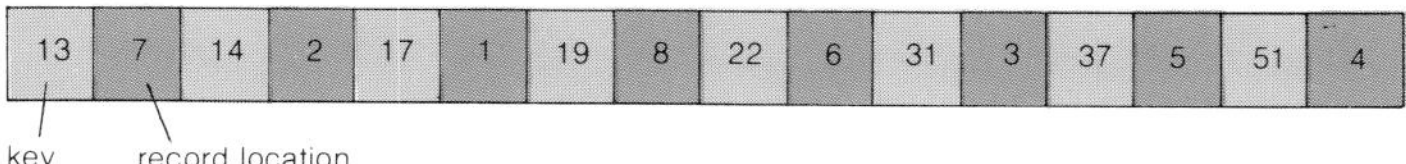

activity ratio the number of records (p. 154) in a file (p. 153) which are processed during a run divided by the total number of records in the file. Thus if, in a file of 100 records, only 5 need to be processed the activity ratio would be 5%. In random files (p. 166) and files which are processed using an index (p. 164) the activity ratio is usually less than 10% on any single run of the program. If an activity ratio is likely to be much higher, e.g. 50% up to 100% then it is usually quicker to process the file sequentially. Also known as **hit rate**.

activity (*n*) (1) = activity ratio (p. 167); (2) the number of times a record (p. 154) is accessed. Thus it is possible to find which records are used most often: files (p. 153) are sometimes arranged so that the most active records can be accessed more quickly.

multi-reel file a tape file (p. 153) which needs more than one reel (p. 71) to hold all the data.

multi-volume file (1) = a multi-reel file (↑); (2) a file (p. 153) which needs more than one disk pack (p. 66) to hold all the data.

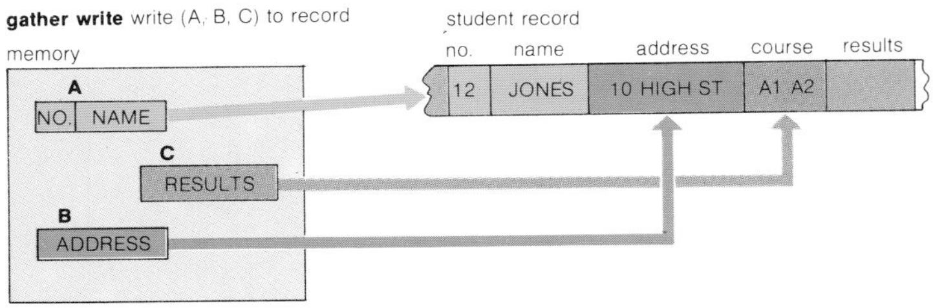

gather write an instruction which allows data in several different parts of memory to be written out to a peripheral device (p. 12) as a single continuous piece of data. It is faster than first collecting all the data together in memory before writing it.

scatter read an instruction that allows data, which is being read as a continuous stream, to be divided into pieces and placed in different parts of memory. This is faster than reading in a complete block (p. 159) of data and then using more instructions to move parts of the data to different areas of memory.

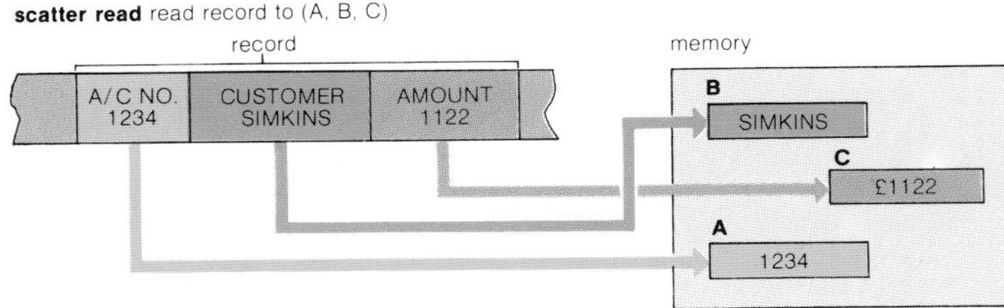

sort by name/initials

sort (*v*) to arrange data, usually the records (p. 154) of a file (p. 153), into a sequential order according to the values in one or more fields (p. 155) in the records. The fields used are called the sort keys (↓). The file may already be in sequence but not by the sort key. **sort** (*n*), **sorted** (*adj*).

sort key the field (p. 155) or fields in a record (p. 154) used to decide the order into which a file (p. 153) will be sorted (↑). The sort key is not usually the same as the key (p. 156) of the file, unless it is being sorted for the first time.

major control field the part of a key (p. 156) or a sort key (↑) which is most important in arranging a file (p. 153). If a file is being sorted (↑) then this is the field (p. 155) which is examined first and the sorted file will be in order by this field.

minor control field the part of a key (p. 156) or a sort key (↑) which is least important in arranging a file (p. 153). If a file is being sorted (↑) this field (p. 155) would be examined only if the major control fields (↑) were equal.

sort generator a general program which uses parameters (p. 112) to produce a sort (↑) for a particular purpose. Also known as **sort program**.

merge two strings

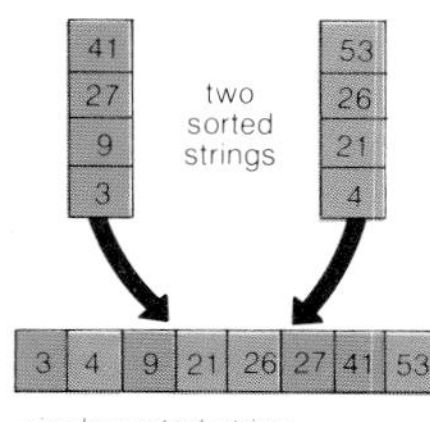

single sorted string

merge (*v*) to read two or more files (p. 153) or strings (p. 171) each of which is already sorted (↑) and write out a single file or string in sequential order. **merge** (*n*).

sort-merge (*n*) a sort generator (↑) which can merge (↑) files (p. 153) as well as sort (↑) them. Most sort generators can merge as well as sort.

internal sort a sort (↑) in which all the data to be sorted can be held in memory.

selection sort an internal sort (p. 169) which searches for the smallest entry in the list and, when it is found, places it in the first position. Then a search is made for the next smallest entry and so on. It is not as quick as other internal sorts but it can produce larger strings (↓) for merging (p. 169) in an external sort (p. 172). Also known as **linear selection**.

exchange sort an internal sort (p. 169) where pairs or records (p. 154) are examined and their positions changed if necessary, i.e records 1 and 2 are examined first and then records 2 and 3, etc. A complete examination of all the items in the list will leave the highest entry in the correct position. Another complete examination will leave the next highest in its correct position, and so on.

bubble sort an exchange sort (↑) which examines only the unsorted records (p. 154) each time. Once a record is in its correct position it is not examined again.

Shell sort a sort (p. 169) which does a bubble sort (↑) on pairs of entries which are a distance of half the total number of entries apart. For example, if there were 100 entries it would first compare entries 1 and 51, then 2 and 52, etc. It then bubble sorts entries which are a quarter of the number of entries apart and so on. It is much faster than a simple bubble sort.

selection sort

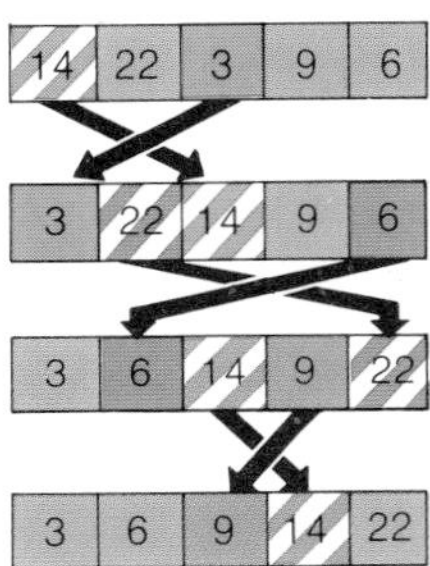

exchange sort

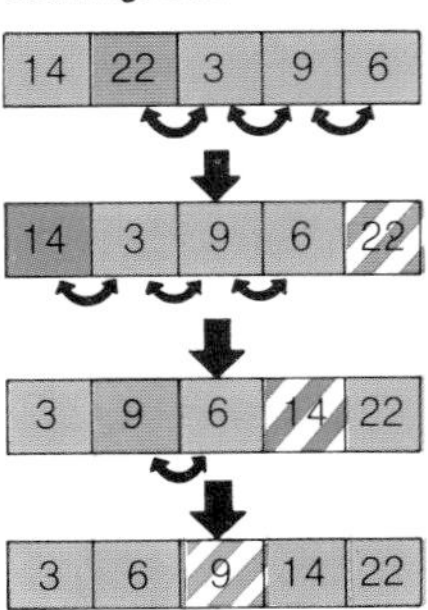

Shell sort

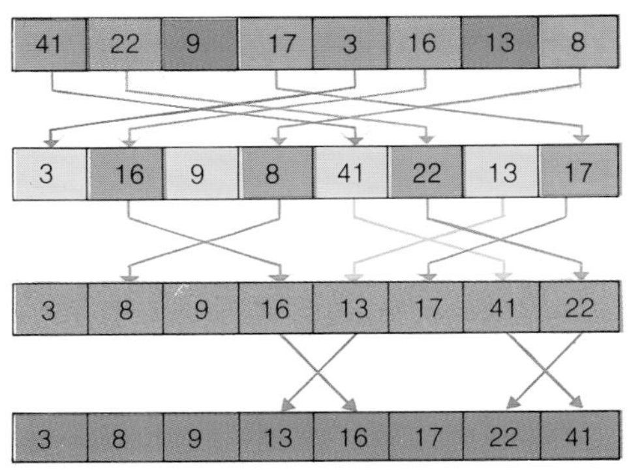

quicksort (*n*) an internal sort (p. 169) which chooses an entry which is likely to appear in the middle of the sorted list. This entry is called the key and it is put into its correct position by placing all the other entries into one of two smaller lists. The first list has entries which have values lower than the key, and the second has entries which have values higher than the key. New keys are then chosen for each of the smaller lists and they are each split into smaller lists in the same way. This is repeated until each list consists of only one entry.

heapsort (*n*) an internal sort (p. 169) where the list is treated as a binary tree (p. 149). Entries are rearranged so that each parent (p. 149) has a higher value than either of its children (p. 149). The highest value node (p. 149) is then exchanged with the right-most leaf (p. 149) which is then dropped from the tree. This is repeated until the tree is empty. It can also work so that the smallest number is removed from the tree and replaced by the next available one from an unsorted file (p. 153), thus acting like a selection sort (↑) which can build up longer strings (↓) for merging (p. 169).

detached keys of a sort (p. 169) where a copy is made of the sort keys (p. 169) of the records (p. 154) and their addresses. This is sorted separately into a table which then contains the keys in sequence. Using the record's address as a pointer (p. 145) the records can then be accessed sequentially without moving them. If necessary the records can be moved into the same order as the sorted keys. The keys are usually much shorter than the records so time is saved since the records are either not moved at all, or only at the end of the sort.

string[2] (*n*) a part of a file (p. 153) which has been sorted (p. 169) and placed on backing store (p. 12), ready to be merged (p. 169). Also known as **run**.

run[1] (*n*) = a string (↑). This use of the word should be avoided since it can be mixed up with the run of a program.

external sort a sort (p. 169) where there is too much data to be held in the available memory and so backing store (p. 12) has to be used to hold the data. Most files (p. 153) have to be sorted this way. It is actually done by reading some of the records (p. 154) of the file into memory and performing an internal sort (p. 169) on these records to produce a sorted string (p. 171). The sorted string is written to backing store and the same procedure is followed again until the file has been changed into a number of sorted strings. These strings are repeatedly merged (p. 169) into longer strings until finally there is a single sorted string with all the records in the correct sequence.

balanced merge an external sort (↑) in which the sorted strings (p. 171) of a file (p. 153) are placed on half of the peripheral devices (p. 12) available, with about the same number of strings on each device. They are then merged (p. 169) on to the other half. This produces a smaller number of strings, each of which contains more records. The merge is repeated until there is a single sorted file.

balanced 2-way merge sort

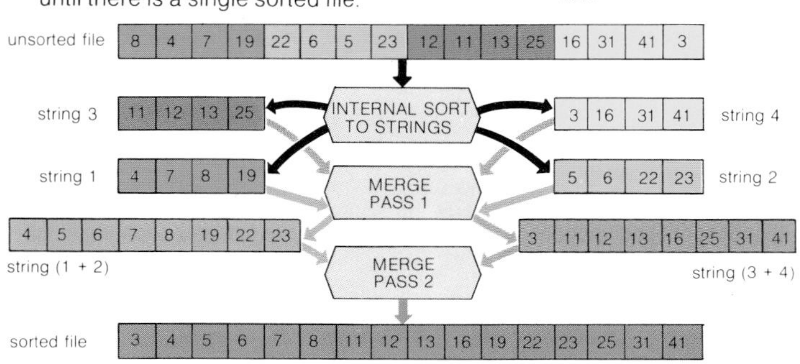

two-way merge a merge (p. 169) with two input files (p. 160) and, usually, two output files (p. 160).

N-way merge a merge (p. 169) which has N input files (p. 160). The number of output files (p. 160) will depend on the particular method of merging.

order of merge the number of files (p. 153) or sorted strings (p. 171) merged (p. 169) at one time.

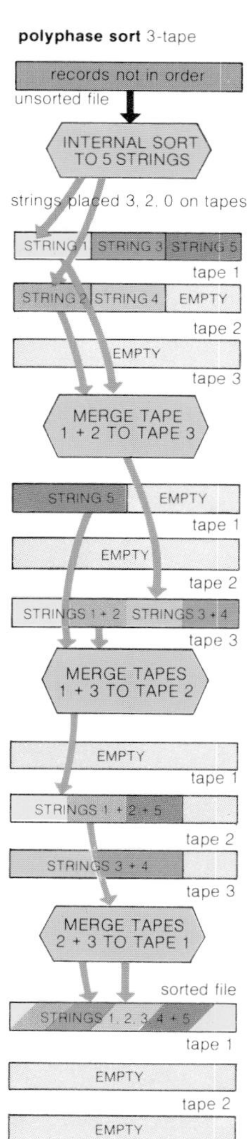

polyphase sort an external sort (↑) in which the sorted strings (p. 171) of a file (p. 153) are placed on all but one of the available peripheral devices (p. 12). The number of strings on each device differs and depends on the number of devices. A merge (p. 169) is started in which strings are merged on to the empty device, i.e. it has no strings. When one of the input devices (p. 12) has no strings left the merge is stopped. A new merge is started in which the device that is now empty becomes the new output device (p. 13) on to which all the others merge. The merging continues until there is one sorted file.

Fibonacci series a sequence of numbers which is used to decide how many sorted strings (p. 171) are to be placed on each of the available peripheral devices (p. 12) at the beginning of a polyphase sort (↑).

cascade sort an external sort (↑), similar to a polyphase sort (↑), but the merge (p. 169) is not stopped when the first input device (p. 12) becomes empty; any remaining inputs are merged on to this device, but the output from the first part of the merge is re-wound (p. 73) and then left until the next merge. Thus each stage of a merge has one less input than the preceding stage. The merge stops when there is only one device with any input strings (p. 171), and then a new merge is started.

oscillating sort an external sort (↑) that uses tapes (p. 71) which can be read backwards as well as forwards. This avoids re-winding (p. 73) the tapes between the merges (p. 169).

tag sort an external sort (↑) where a file (p. 153) is held on a disk pack (p. 66). The sort keys (p. 169) of the records (p. 154) and their addresses are sorted (p. 169), not the records. The output is a sequence of sorted keys and the address of the record containing that key.

own coding an extra code (p. 102) which can be added to a sort-merge (p. 169) to do some particular action which is not provided directly by the sort generator (p. 169). For example, a program might wish to change records (p. 154) in some way before they are sorted (p. 169).

information system any arrangement for producing information. Usually uses a computer, but parts of it may be manual.

management information system an information system (↑) where data is largely to help in the management of something. It is usually a business system (p. 181) and the data is mainly on costs, sales, etc.

information retrieval any process which has to be done to retrieve, i.e. get back, information from a collection of data.

data retrieval = information retrieval (↑).

information retrieval system a computer system (p. 181) whose main purpose is to get specific information from data stored, usually on disks (p. 66). There is usually no processing of transactions (p. 162) to produce results but the system may be a part of a larger one which does process them.

data-base (*n*) a collection of data, usually files (p. 153), which is so arranged that it is independent of any particular program or application. The files try not to contain more than one copy of the same data. Access to the files is not done directly by the application programs (p. 128), instead it is provided by a data-base management system (p. 181).

data bank a collection of files (p. 153) or records (p. 154) on a particular subject. It is not really the same as a data-base (↑) since it is not usually arranged so that it can be used independently of any program.

CODASYL conference on data systems languages. A group which defined the COBOL (p. 91) language and has defined a data description language (↓) as well as terms for describing parts of a data-base (↑). This is one of the two main definitions, the other is ANSI/SPARC (↓).

ANSI/SPARC a group within ANSI (American National Standards Institute) which defined terms for describing parts of data-bases (↑). This is one of the two main definitions, the other being the CODASYL (↑) one. They use terms which are similar but not exactly the same.

management information system

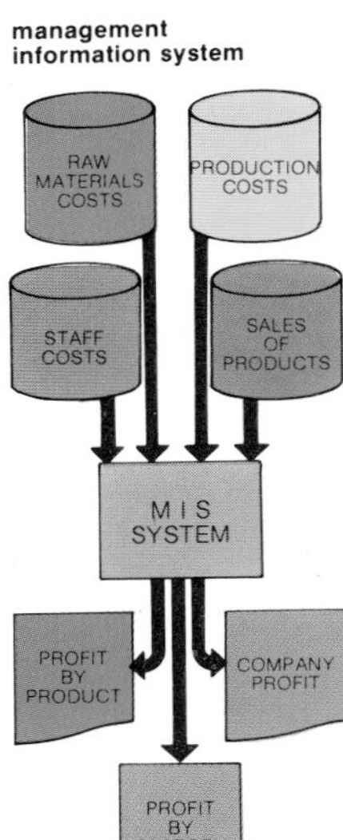

data-base

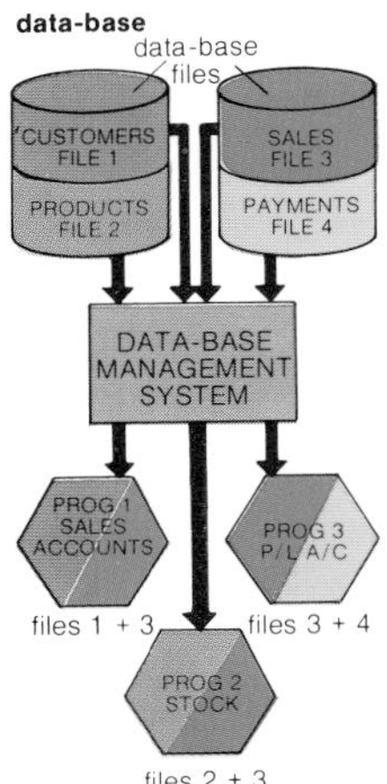

conceptual schema and internal schema
data-base model

external view

ACCOUNTANT'S VIEW

SALES VIEW

PRODUCTION VIEW

DATA DEFINITIONS AND RELATIONSHIPS

actual physical data-base files

schema (*n*) a complete description of the information contained in a data-base (↑): the files (p. 153), records (p. 154), their formats (p. 207), the way they are connected, rights of access etc.

conceptual schema = schema (↑).

conceptual model = schema (↑).

data description language DDL. A special language which is used to describe the schema (↑) of a data-base (↑).

subschema (*n*) the arrangement of just those files (p. 153), records (p. 154) etc, forming part of a data-base (↑), which are needed for a particular program.

external schema = subschema (↑).

physical data-base the arrangement of files (p. 153), records, (p. 154) etc in a data-base (↑) and the pointers (p. 145) which connect them, and how they are accessed.

internal schema = physical data-base (↑).

entity (*n*) something about which data can be collected and stored. It is similar to a record (p. 154). For example, a personnel record is a group of data about a person, and the person is the entity of the record.

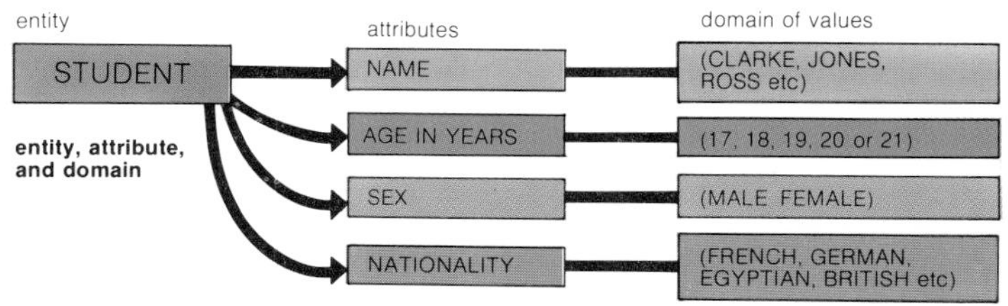

entity, attribute, and domain

attribute (*n*) the content of an entity (↑). For example, if the entity were a person then the attributes could be name, age, sex, etc.

domain (*n*) the set of possible values that an attribute (↑) may have e.g. if the attribute were the sex of a person then the domain would contain two values, male and female.

data item the smallest piece of data in an entity (↑): it is much the same as a field (p. 155) in a record (p. 154).

tuple (*n*) one of a collection or group of data items (p. 175) which describe an entity (p. 175). It is sometimes in the form N-tuple where N is the number of data items in the group. It is very similar to a record (p. 154) in a file (p. 153) or the row of a table (p. 144).

entity set a collection of entities (p. 175). It is very similar to a file (p. 153) or a data set (p. 153).

relation (*n*) a table (p. 144) in which the rows are the tuples (↑) and the columns are the attributes (p. 175). It can be thought of as a file (p. 153), or part of a file, but it may exist only for the time it is used in a particular program.

degree (*n*) the number of attributes (p. 175) in a relation (↑). A relation of degree 4 would have 4 attributes and any tuple (↑) in the relation would be a 4-tuple.

DBMS data-base management system. The programs needed to use a data-base (p. 174). They will handle accessing, insertion (p. 163), deletion and amendment (p. 163) of records (p. 154).

data-base path the sequence of accesses needed to get to an item or record (p. 154) within a data-base (p. 174).

data dictionary a list of the names and format (p. 207) of all the data items (p. 175) in a data-base (p. 174).

data-base administrator DBA. A person, or small group of people, whose job is to understand and maintain the complete description of a data-base (p. 174), i.e. all its data items (p. 175) and the connections between them.

non-key field an attribute (p. 175) which is not part of the key (p. 156) of a tuple (↑).

third normal form 3NF. A file (p. 153) in which the records (p. 154) are of fixed format (p. 207). Each record has a key (p. 156) and no two keys are the same. It is in effect a table (p. 144) with each entry being a tuple (↑) containing exactly the same attributes (p. 175), each of which appears once only in a tuple. Each non-key field (p. 155) can depend only on the whole of the key. This is the usual form used for data-bases (p. 175) but there are slight changes to produce a fourth and fifth normal form.

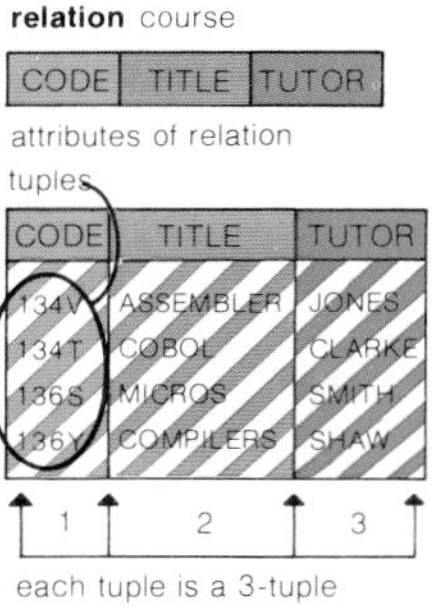

relation course

CODE	TITLE	TUTOR

attributes of relation

tuples

CODE	TITLE	TUTOR
134V	ASSEMBLER	JONES
134T	COBOL	CLARKE
136S	MICROS	SMITH
136Y	COMPILERS	SHAW

1 2 3

each tuple is a 3-tuple

normal form any one of the five possible normal forms, but especially the third normal form (↑).

normalize (*v*) to take a file (p. 153) and produce relations (↑) so that the relations are in normal form (↑), usually in third normal form (↑).

normalizing a relation

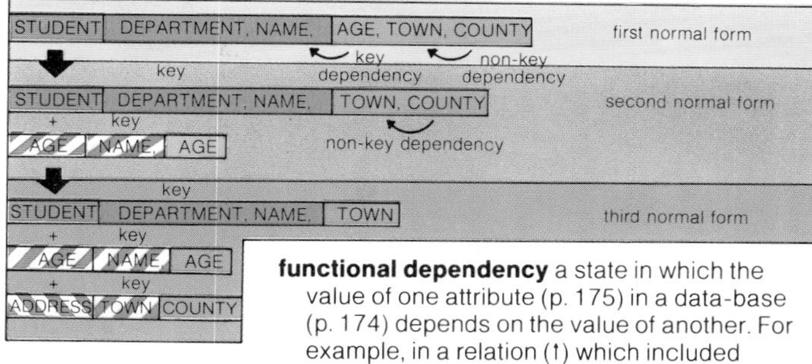

functional dependency a state in which the value of one attribute (p. 175) in a data-base (p. 174) depends on the value of another. For example, in a relation (↑) which included persons and their pay then the value of the pay in a record (p. 154) will depend on the person whose record it is.

select[2] (*v*) to form a new relation (↑) by choosing tuples (↑) from a relation which has a particular value in one of the attributes (p. 175). For example, if the tuples contained details of both men and women you might choose to select only those relations which dealt with men.

project (*v*) to form a new relation (↑) by selecting (↑) some attributes (p. 175) from an existing relation. If the new relation has tuples (↑) which are exactly the same then only one of them is kept. **projection** (*n*).

join (*v*) to create a new relation (↑) by joining two or more relations or, more usually, parts of relations together. **join** (*n*).

relational data-base a data-base (p. 174) where the data is held in relations (↑), usually third normal form (↑), and where operations such as select (↑), project (↑) and join (↑) are used to handle the data. The operations can be described either in words or by using relational algebra (a mathematical language which uses symbols (p. 98)).

hierarchical data-base a form of data-base (p. 174) in which relations (p. 176), or files (p. 153) containing records (p. 154) of the same type (p. 99), are arranged in the form of a tree (p. 149). Thus a record in one file may be the parent (p. 149) record; its children (p. 149) will be in another file. As in a tree there is only one possible path to any of the files or records.

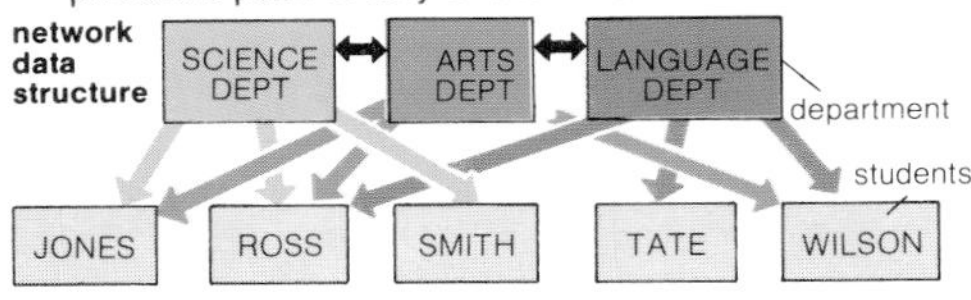

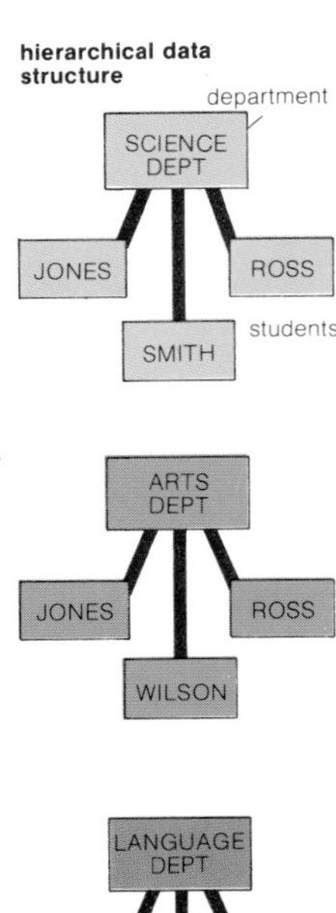

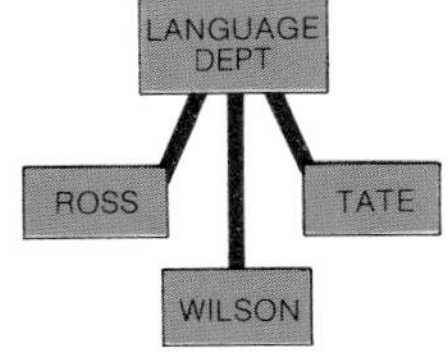

network data-base a form of data-base (p. 174) which is similar to a hierarchical data-base (↑) but it can include arrangements where records (p. 154) at one level may have several parent (p. 149) records in different files (p. 153). This means there is more than one possible path to such a record. It is not a relational data-base (p. 177).

IMS information management system. A hierarchical data-base (↑) produced by IBM.

query language a language designed (p. 121) to make it easier to specify exactly what information a user wishes to get from a data-base (p. 174).

SQL structured query language. A query language (↑) produced by IBM for use with relational data-bases (p. 177).

data compression a method of storing less data, but without losing any of the information it contains. The data actually stored may not be in a suitable form for use by a person or by the computer and so it may have to be converted (p. 194). For example, the number +12345 would take six bytes (p. 17) if stored in this form but if converted to packed decimal (p. 48) it needs only three bytes. The idea is used quite often to reduce the size of large files (p. 153) and also indexes (p. 164). It saves space on backing store (p. 12) and can reduce the total time needed to read or write records (p. 154).

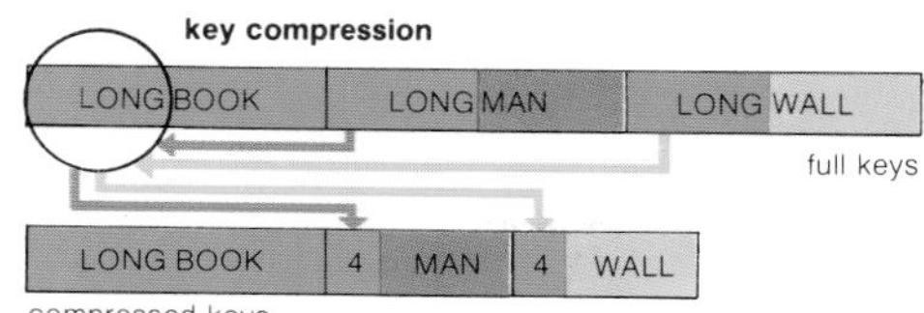

data compaction = data compression (↑).

key compression a form of data compression (↑) used in the key (p. 156) fields (p. 155) or index (p. 164) entries. It is widely used on large indexes. Usually only the part of the key which is different from the last one is stored. For example, if the full keys were longbook, longman, longwall they could be stored as longbook, 4man and 4wall, the 4 meaning that the first 4 characters were the same as those in the first key.

key word[1] a word in the title of a document which gives information about the data it contains. In a title such as the 'The Illustrated Dictionary of Computing Science' the words 'Illustrated', 'Computing' and 'Science' are key words, they tell us that the book is about computers and that it is illustrated.

key word in context KWIC. A method of sorting (p. 169) key words (↑), with the rest of the title, to make it easier to search a list of titles or documents. The title 'The Illustrated Dictionary of Computing Science' would appear twice, once under 'Computing' and a second time under 'Illustrated'. The list of titles produced in this way is usually called a KWIC-index.

index word = key word (↑).

part of a KWIC index book titles

	COMPUTING	MADE EASY
INTRODUCTION TO	COMPUTING	
PRINCIPLES OF	COMPUTING	
START	COMPUTING	TODAY

data processing the work necessary to prepare data, operate machines, run programs on a computer and send the results back to the users. It usually refers to computing in the business world where the files (p. 153) which are used tend to be much larger than in other forms of computing. There are often as many persons working on preparing and checking the data as there are in operating or programming the computer and, in a company, the complete operation is usually placed under the control of one person.

DP = data processing (↑).

EDP electronic data processing. Data processing (↑) especially by electronic machines i.e. those operating mechanically would not be included.

ADP automatic data processing or administrative data processing. Data processing (↑) by mechanical or electronic machines.

centralized data processing data processing (↑), especially where there is a single place where all the computing for a company is done, usually on a mainframe (p. 8). All the data is brought to the mainframe and the results or reports (p. 185) produced are sent back to the users.

decentralized data processing data processing (↑) which is done at more than one place in a company. There can either be separate computers at different places or intelligent terminals (p. 83) connected to one or more mainframes (p. 8).

distributed data processing data processing (↑) especially using intelligent terminals (p. 83) rather than separate computer installations (p. 10).

distributed data processing

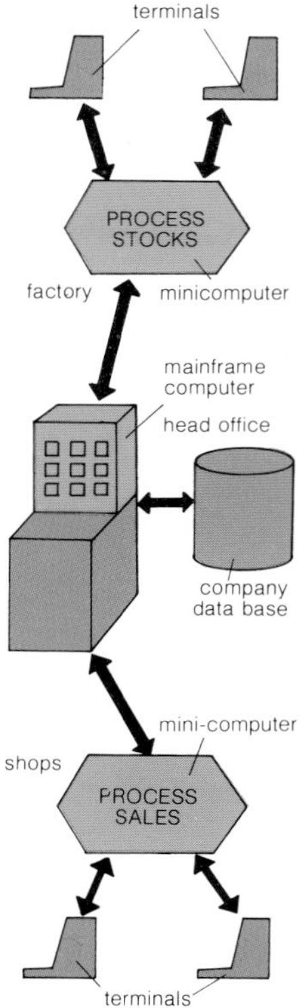

organisation of computer department

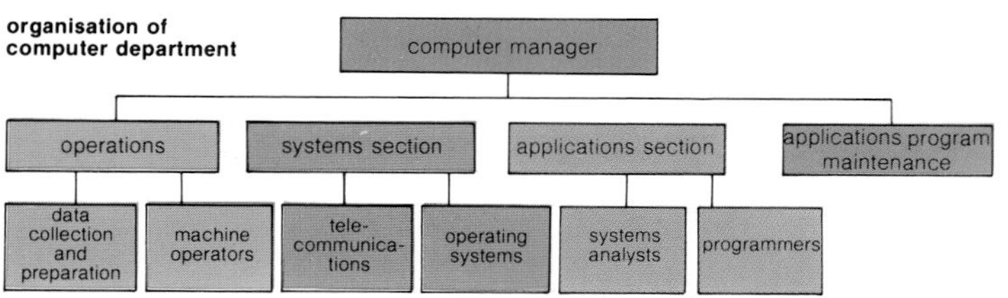

batch processing

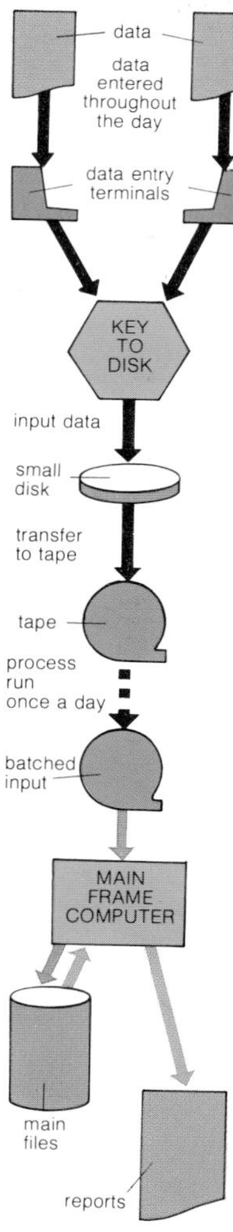

management services the part of a company that deals with data processing (↑) and other work needed to support it such as collection and transmission (p. 76) of data, studies, etc. In a company these are quite often placed under the control of a single person.

system (*n*) a complete set of programs needed to do all the work for some particular application in data processing (↑). For example, a pay system would have weekly pay, monthly pay, end-of-year print-outs (p. 19), etc. and might contain 50 programs. Also used to describe a part of a system, e.g. the monthly pay system.

end-user (*n*) the person, or group of persons, for whom a system (↑) or application is designed (p. 121) in data processing (↑). The person is said to use the system but does not operate the computer and often cannot program and may have very little knowledge of computing.

software house a company or group which designs (p. 121), writes, and sells programs or systems (↑) for use by other companies.

production program a program which is part of a user's system (↑) and produces results which are used, as opposed to a program which is still being tested, or a service program (p. 127).

production run a run which is producing actual results which are going to be used by someone. It is not a run which is just testing or compiling (p. 105) a program, or carrying out the file maintenance (p. 158).

batch processing processing in which all the data for a run is first collected and prepared before being entered into the computer. The amount of data can be quite large and there is always a delay between the data being collected and being processed. Quite often the data is processed regularly, once a day or once a week, regardless of how much data there is to be dealt with. This form of processing is very common in large business applications where there is not the need to process everything in real-time (p. 94). For example, customers may be sent their bills once a week, people may be paid once a month.

batch (*n*) a part of the data needed for a run. If the amount of data is quite large the input documents (↓) are grouped in batches of 25–50 transactions (p. 162). Data preparation (p. 184) and control totals (↓) are prepared for each batch as well as for the total of all the batches. It makes things easier to control and any errors can be found more quickly. **batch** (*v*).

batch total the total of a field (p. 155) which is present in every transaction (p. 162) in a batch (↑) of data. For example, if the data were the sales to customers then the total of all the sales would probably be used. The total is used for control (↓) purposes.

check total the total of a field (p. 155) which is present in every transaction (p. 162) in the data to be processed. It can be a total for a batch (↑) or for all the batches in a run.

hash total a total which is produced by adding up a field (p. 155) which is present in every transaction (p. 162) but which would not be added up as part of the usual processing, e.g. the total of customers' account numbers. It is used as a batch total (↑) or control total (↓) when there is no other suitable field to use. It can be used for control of the input data but is often used as a control total for a file (p. 153).

check sum = hash total (↑).

control total the total of a field (p. 155) which is present in every transaction (p. 162) of data, or a total which can be calculated from it. The total can be for input documents (↓) or a file (p. 153) but it often means the complete set of totals needed to control a run. They are used to make sure that every transaction is processed and that the programs are working correctly.

control (*n*) anything which is used to control the correct preparation and processing of data. It will include batch totals (↑), retention periods (p. 157), numbers of records (p. 154) processed, etc.

control data data whose purpose is to provide a way of checking or producing control totals (↑). It is often stored in a separate record (p. 154) in a file (p. 153).

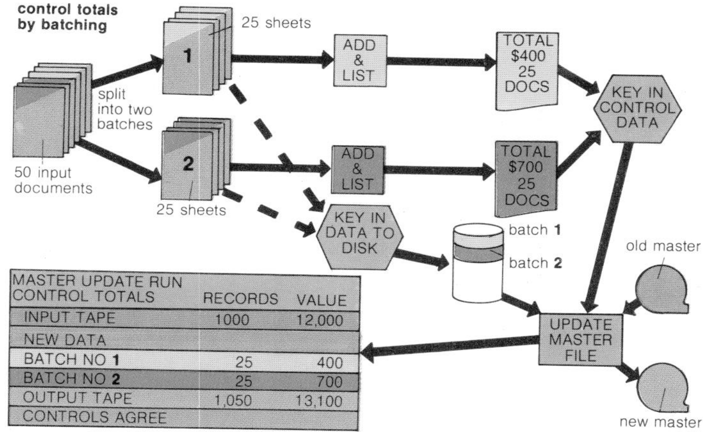

MASTER UPDATE RUN CONTROL TOTALS	RECORDS	VALUE
INPUT TAPE	1000	12,000
NEW DATA		
BATCH NO **1**	25	400
BATCH NO **2**	25	700
OUTPUT TAPE	1,050	13,100
CONTROLS AGREE		

control record a record (p. 154) in a file (p. 153) which is not part of the normal data but holds control data (↑) or control totals (↑) for the file.

source data the data on a document which needs to be entered into a computer for processing.

source document one or more sheets of paper which contain the data for each transaction (p. 162) to be entered into a computer. Usually only part of the data is needed.

input document (1) = source document (↑); (2) = a document which can be read by a machine such as an optical character reader (p. 88).

data capture the process of collecting data so that it can be used for processing. It tends to mean the actual recording of the data that is needed, close to the place where it is created, to avoid having to move source documents (↑) about.

data collection data capture (↑), especially when the data is entered into remote terminals (p. 82) and transmitted (p. 76) to a central processing (p. 31) installation (p. 10).

data gathering (1) = data collection (↑); (2) = data capture (↑).

data preparation the work done in taking data from source documents (p. 183) and changing it into a form which can be read into a computer: batching (p. 182) the source documents, entering the data or using a document reader, preparing control totals (p. 182) and making sure that all transactions (p. 162) are accounted for. It is an important part of the work of data processing (p. 180) in any company.

edit (*v*) to check data to see that it is correct. It can be a manual operation in which people check to see that all input documents (p. 183) have been collected and that they have been properly completed. It also means checking the data by the use of edit programs (↓).

validate (*v*) to edit (↑), especially by computer rather than a manual edit.

data vet = validate (↑).

edit program a program whose purpose is just to edit (↑) data so that it can be used by other programs. It checks that fields (p. 155) contain only the kind of data they are supposed to contain, e.g. that numeric (p. 15) fields hold only digits (p. 16) not letters. It also checks that the range of values is acceptable, e.g. in a date the month could not be greater than 12. It calculates and checks control totals (p. 182).

validation program = edit program (↑).

GIGO garbage in garbage out. If a program is given bad or wrong data then it will produce bad or wrong results.

error report a report (↓), usually from an edit program (↑), which lists errors found in the data.

raw data data which has not been checked or examined for errors or correctness. Also data which has not yet been processed.

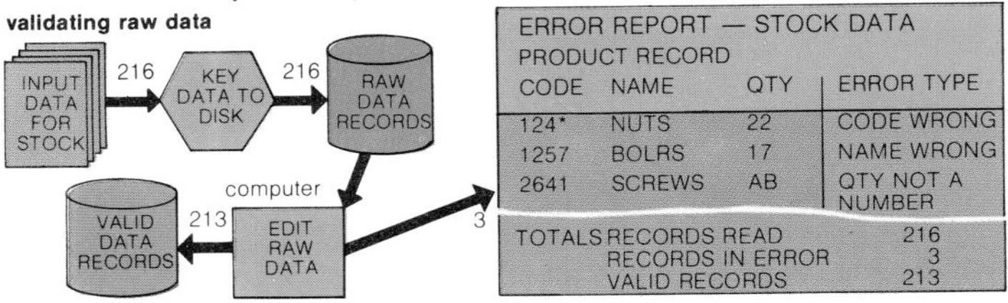

ERROR REPORT — STOCK DATA

PRODUCT RECORD CODE	NAME	QTY	ERROR TYPE
124*	NUTS	22	CODE WRONG
1257	BOLRS	17	NAME WRONG
2641	SCREWS	AB	QTY NOT A NUMBER

TOTALS		
	RECORDS READ	216
	RECORDS IN ERROR	3
	VALID RECORDS	213

validating raw data

report (*n*) a display or print-out (p. 19) from a program. It is a very general word and, particularly in data processing (p. 180), can mean almost anything readable produced by a program.

exception report a report (↑) which contains only those items where something unusual has happened. No other items are printed. It saves time and paper as well as allowing a user to see quickly the things which need attention.

exception report

full list

STUDENT LIST		
NO.	TUTOR	STUDENT
1241	JONES	KHAN
1246	SHAW	SMITH
1251	----	ROBERTS*
1262	JONES	DAVIES
1274	CLARK	WILSON
1283	SHAW	BIRD
xxxx	JONES	COYLE*
1316	JONES	HOGG
1317	SHAW	KING
TOTAL	STUDENTS	128
	ERRORS	2

STUDENT LIST			
NO.	TUTOR	STUDENT	NOTES
1251	----	ROBERTS	NO TUTOR.
xxxx	JONES	COYLE	INVALID NUMBER
EXCEPTIONS		2	
TOTAL STUDENTS	128		

group printing a report (↑) which prints totals and other data only on the change in a control field (p. 155) in the data.

audit (*v*) to check and verify (p. 56) that the results of a system (p. 181) are correct. It is usually a business system and the original source documents (p. 183) are used to check the results. **audit** (*n*).

audit trail a means of following transactions (p. 162) through a system (p. 181) from source documents (p. 183) right through to the results. It is commonly needed in data processing (p. 180) so that results can be checked and to test either that unpermitted changes have not been made to programs, or that permitted changes in one program do not cause errors elsewhere in the system.

suite (*n*) a group of programs which do some particular piece of work. For example, the programs needed to calculate pay would be called the payroll suite.

suite

student registration suite
programs STU.XX.X

program number	function of program
STU.01.2	REGISTRATION LIST IN STUDENT NUMBER ORDER
STU.02.3	SORT LIST TO STUDENT NAME
STU.03.1	LIST IN ALPHABETICAL ORDER
STU.04.6	SORT BY TUTOR/STUDENT
STU.05.1	LIST STUDENTS BY TUTOR
STU.06.1	UPDATE TUTORS MASTER FILE
STU.07.2	UPDATE DEPARTMENT FILE

transcription error a mistake in entering a number or data. The data entered is not correct, usually one of the characters is wrong, e.g. data written as A1234 but keyed as B1234.

transposition error a mistake in entering data. The correct characters are entered but not in the right order, i.e. A1234 entered as 1243A.

self-checking number a number which has one or more check digits (↓) and so can be checked for possible errors.

check digit a digit (p. 16), sometimes two, placed at the end of a number and which can be calculated from the number. If a mistake is made in recording or entering the number then the calculation will produce the wrong value for the check digit and so the mistake will be found. Very often used in data such as account numbers to make sure they are correct.

modulus-11 (*adj*) of a very common way of calculating a check digit (↑). Each digit (p. 16) of the number is multiplied by another digit, called the weight, which depends on the position of the digit. The results, added to the check digit, should divide exactly by 11.

check-restart (*n*) the starting of a run again. Sometimes means that the run failed to work correctly the first time but more often means starting again after a checkpoint (p. 117).

run[2] (*n*) the set of programs needed to do some particular piece of work in data processing (p. 180). For example, a pay run would consist of all the programs needed to calculate pay, print details, etc. **run** (*v*).

run chart a diagram whose purpose is to show the order in which programs in a system (p. 181) are to be run, usually with notes which say what each program does and which files (p. 153) it uses. It is used both in designing (p. 121) a system and also as part of the documentation. *See* opposite.

throughput (*n*) the amount of work done by a computer system in a certain time. It is used as a general measure to compare how well systems (p. 181) have been designed (p. 121), or the power of one computer against another.

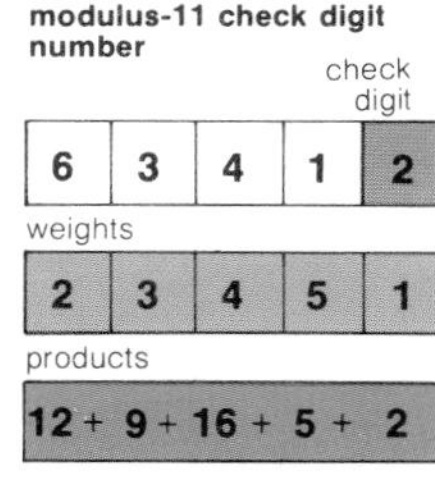

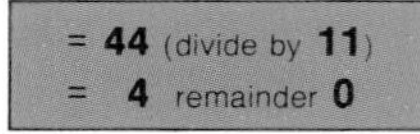

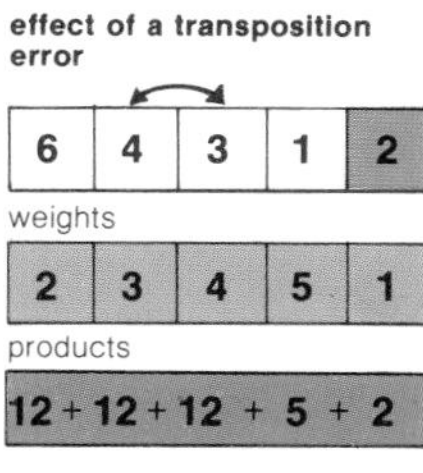

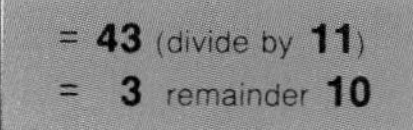

non zero remainder therefore number is invalid

part of a run chart

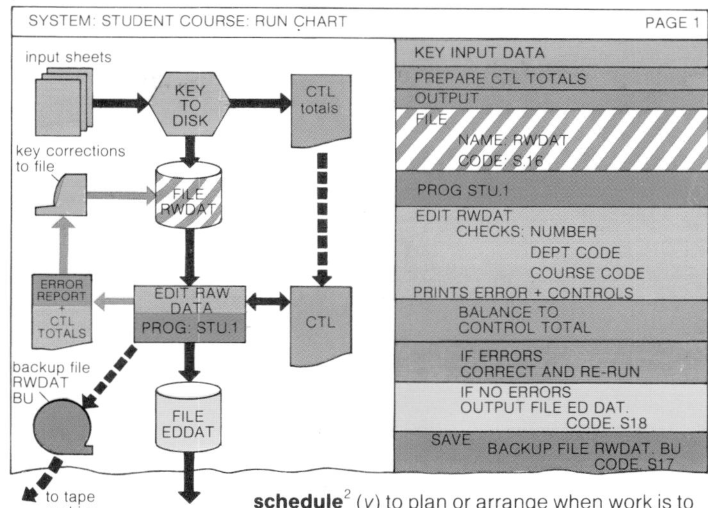

schedule[2] (*v*) to plan or arrange when work is to be done on a computer. In data processing (p. 180) much of the work consists of repeating runs at regular intervals, i.e. daily, weekly or monthly, together with file maintenance (p. 158), testing, etc. The various runs are planned to take place at particular times according to the importance of the work.

part of computer room schedule

SCHEDULE BOARD — DAYSHIFT OPERATORS: JONES, SMITH

DAY \ TIME (MORNING)	8 a.m.	9 a.m.		10 a.m.	11 a.m.	noon
MONDAY	BACK-UP ALL SYSTEM DISKS		WEEKLY PAY INPUT EDIT RUN		PROGRAMMERS' TEST SLOT	RUN WEEKLY SALES
TUESDAY	BACK-UP CUSTOMER DISK	EDIT MONDAY'S SALES		RUN WEEKLY PAY SLIPS	RUN MAIN LEDGER	PROG TEST
WEDNESDAY	BACK-UP PAYROLL DISK	PREVENTIVE MAINTENANCE			ENGINEERS	EDIT TUESDAY'S SALES
THURSDAY	BACK-UP SALES					M/C FREE

back-up (*n*) (1) a copy of the files (p. 153) used by a system (p. 181). It is usual to take copies of files regularly in case of error or accidental damage to the file; (2) a second computer installation (p. 10) which is suitable for running a user's work, i.e. it has enough memory, input and output devices (p. 13), etc. The second computer is usually owned by someone else and would only be used if there was serious delay or damage to the user's own computer. Companies often agree to provide this arrangement for each other. **back-up** (*v*).

maintenance[2] (*n*) work done to repair faults or to prevent them. It is particularly used for work on computers or the peripheral devices (p. 12). **maintain** (*v*).

preventive maintenance work such as cleaning parts, testing devices, etc. which is done to make sure that a computer will continue to run properly. It is usual to have such work done regularly.

scheduled maintenance = preventive maintenance (↑).

maintenance contract an arrangement between the person who owns a computer and a specialist company who maintains the computer and other equipment in working order. The arrangement can simply be to repair any faults but it can also include preventive maintenance (↑).

MTBF mean time between failures. A measure of the dependability of a piece of equipment. It is the interval of time after the equipment fails before it is expected to fail again.

degradation (*n*) a slowing down in the speed of a computer because there is a fault in some part. For example, if some of the input-output devices (p. 12) are not working the computer may still be able to run programs but it will usually do so more slowly. Also known as **graceful degradation**.

diagnostics (*n*) (1) a group of diagnostic routines (↓); (2) a set of circuits in a computer whose purpose is to find or report faults in the computer. **diagnose** (*v*).

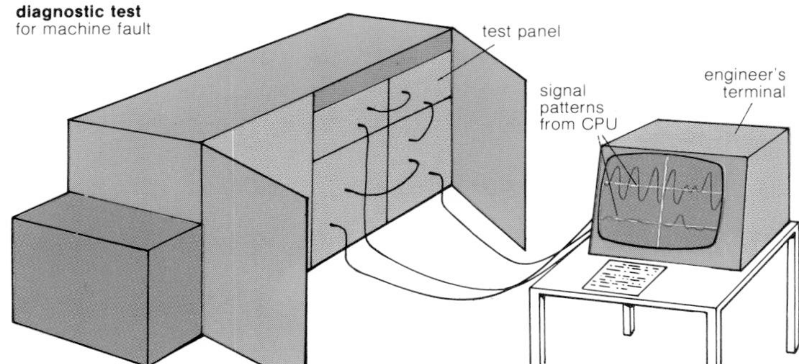

diagnostic routine a routine (p. 111) whose purpose is to test whether the computer or its peripheral devices (p. 12) are working correctly. There are usually a number of routines for each part of the computer. Sometimes means a routine to test other programs.

diagnostic test a test using diagnostics (↑) particularly for machines and equipment. It can either be one which is to find a fault which has already happened or one which shows where a fault is likely to happen fairly soon.

down time the time when a computer is not working either because of a fault or because of preventive maintenance (↑).

idle time time when a computer is available for work but there is none to do.

turn around time the time interval between sending a job (p. 133) to a computer and getting the results back.

machine room the room where the computer is installed (p. 10).

open shop a machine room (↑) into which anyone is allowed to go. It is particularly used to mean that programmers can go in and test their programs.

closed shop a machine room (↑) into which only the persons needed to operate the machines are allowed to go. It is particularly used to mean that neither programmers nor users are allowed to operate the computer.

part of operating instructions

OPERATOR INSTRUCTIONS
PAYROLL EDIT RUN
NUMBER: 164 DATE: 12 OCT

prog no.	tape unit A	tape unit B	disk drive 01	disk drive 02	possible halts
PAY 01	REEL 802 RING OUT UNLOAD AFTER PROGRAM		PACK C.02	PACK D.01	STANDARD LIST PAPER MESSAGES P.01: WRONG INPUT FILE CORRECT RE-RUN P.02: UNREADABLE TAPE ABANDON RUN
PAY 02		LOAD SCRATCH RING IN	PACK C.02	PACK D.01	NO PRINT OUTPUT MESSAGES P.16: INPUT CONTROL ERROR ABANDON P.17: NOT SCRATCH TAPE

operator (*n*) a person who is employed to operate the computer and its peripheral devices (p. 12) or other equipment. The operator will load (p. 106) tapes (p. 71), disks (p. 66), paper, etc. and handle messages from the operating system (p. 130). **operate** (*v*).

computer operator = operator (↑).

machine operator = operator (↑).

operating instructions a set of instructions on what programs, files (p. 153), etc. are to be used to run a job (p. 133). They are written by the programmer but are used by the computer operator (↑). They should also include notes on what is to be done in case of data errors or program failure.

set-up (*v*) to prepare a device or computer so that it can do its work, i.e. load (p. 106) tapes (p. 71), paper, etc. **set-up** (*n*).

tape library a room which holds the tape reels (p. 71) used by an installation (p. 10). The reels will be on racks usually in order of the volume (p. 13) numbers, or arranged by application. For safety the room is often protected against fire.

tape librarian a person whose job is to record the use of tape reels (p. 71), to make sure that they are properly stored in a tape library (↑), and to give them out when needed.

systems analysis
steps in life of a system

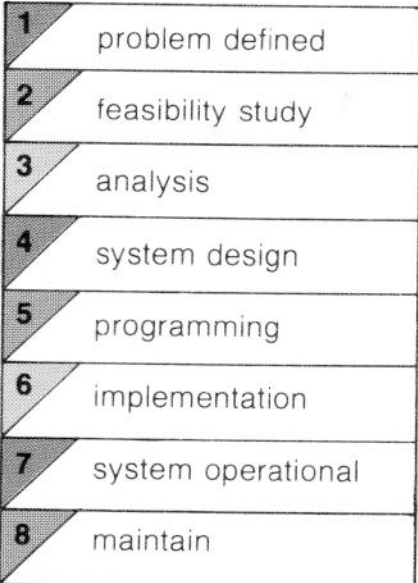

systems analysis the work done in studying a problem to decide how best it can be handled by a computer. It can cover a wide area, e.g. the way a company works, how data moves from one part of a company to another, the design (p. 121) of forms and reports (p. 185), etc.

feasibility study a short form of systems analysis (↑). The purpose is to do a quick analysis, not a full one, in order to decide not only whether a problem can be done on a computer but also whether the cost of doing it will be acceptable.

pilot study a feasibility study (↑) especially when the study is longer and examines things in more detail but is not a full systems analysis (↑).

systems analyst a person who does systems analysis (↑). A systems analyst must also be able to prepare the specifications (p. 203) and design (p. 121) the resulting system (p. 181) for a computer, specify the programs, control the testing of the programs and the systems test (p. 192) and train the users in the use of the system.

analyst (*n*) = systems analyst (↑).

data flow the way data, i.e. forms, details of what is bought or sold, etc, moves from one part of a company to another. In systems analysis (↑) it is nearly always used to describe the path followed by data which is not on a computer.

data flow diagram a diagram which shows data flow (↑). It usually contains the paths which the data follows, where it starts from and where it stops, how much data is moved and how long it takes.

data flow diagram

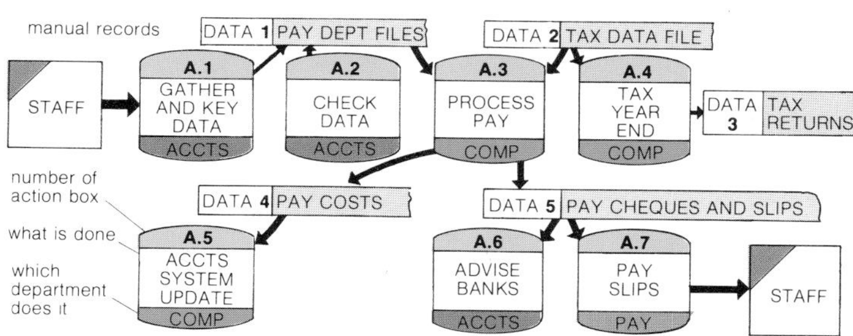

problem definition the description of a problem in a manner which is clear to a user. It is quite often difficult to decide what a user's problem really is and a clear description of it should be agreed before any attempt is made to decide how it can be done on a computer.

boundary (*n*) the furthest point to which a systems analysis (p. 191) goes in studying a problem. It is usual to decide what areas are to be included within a study and this decides its boundary.

method study the examination of the way things are done particularly in a manual system (p. 181). It is often used in systems analysis (p. 191) to determine the data flow (p. 191).

O and M organisation and methods. It is sometimes used to mean the same as method study (↑) but more generally it means a wider form of study which includes matters not connected with computing. Quite often the persons who do the work will form part of a management services (p. 181) group.

system specification the specification (p. 203) of a system (p. 181). It can either be one which the user is able to understand, i.e. written with very little use of computing terms, or one whose purpose is to set out how a problem is to be handled on a computer, the formats (p. 207) of the files (p. 153) and records (p. 154), what each program is to do, etc. It is meant to be used by programmers and systems analysts (p. 191) to guide them in producing the system.

system flowchart a diagram which shows how data is meant to move through a system (p. 181). It will include details showing where data arises, how it is collected and what reports (p. 185) are produced as well as the programs that use the data.

system test the test of a whole system (p. 181). The aim is to make the data follow the path from data collection (p. 183) to data entry and then through all the programs in the system. Each program will have first been tested by itself with test data (p. 124), but a system test uses all the programs together for the first time and also tries to use actual data.

parallel run

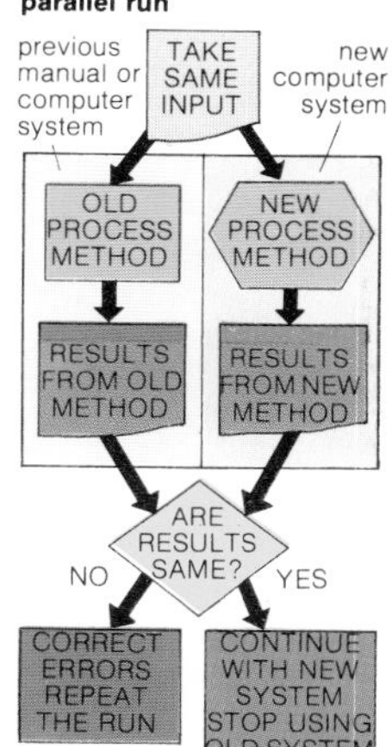

walk through a process of checking that a system (p. 181) is likely to do what it should. The systems analyst (p. 191) who designed (p. 121) the system describes it to other analysts who try to see if there are any faults in the design and also offer ideas to improve it. The same can be done with large programs.

parallel run a test of a new system (p. 181), or part of a system. Both the old and the new system are run at the same time and the results compared to make sure they agree. It is a common way of testing a new system. The old one may be a computer system or a manual one.

pilot run a test of a system (p. 181) by trying it out on some but not all of the data. Quite often used where a number of places will use the final system. The pilot run would consist of running the system at one or two places, until it was satisfactory.

pilot run

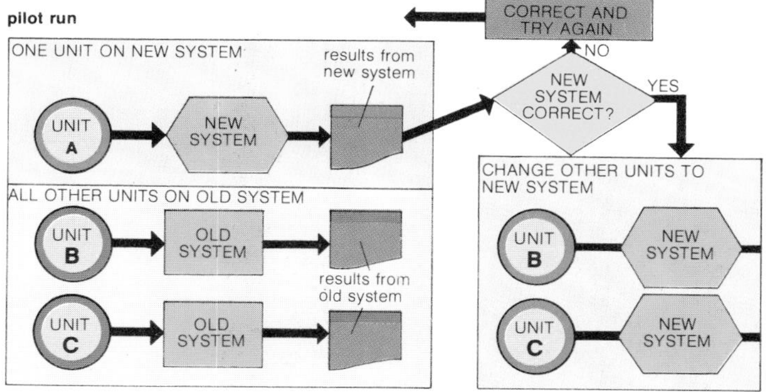

prototype (*n*) a system (p. 181) which will do most of the work needed but not all of it and whose programs and documentation are not to the normal standards (p. 194). The purpose is to produce quickly a working system to allow the user to try the main features to make sure the design is satisfactory. Any changes wanted by the user can then be made for the proper working system. **prototype** (*v*).

standard (*n*) one of a set of rules which describe how the documentation of systems (p. 181), programs, operating instructions (p. 190), etc, is to be set out, what is to be included, and what terms and diagrams are to be used. Most installations (p. 10) have a set of such rules.

bar chart a chart (p. 204) whose lines show how much work has been done and how much is still to be done on a system (p. 181). There is usually a line, or bar, for each program, often in several colours to show the different stages, e.g. design (p. 121), coding (p. 102), testing, etc.

bar chart

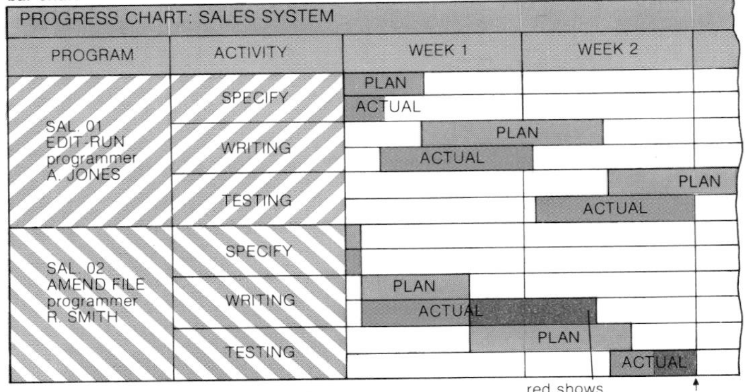

conversion² (*n*) the process of changing a program and data so that they can be used on another computer. Also changing data in files (p. 153) so that they can be used by different programs or on a different computer. If a system (p. 181) is moved from one computer to another then the files and programs usually need to be changed. **convert** (*v*).

conversion program a program whose purpose is to change files (p. 153), or other programs, so they can be used on a different computer.

conversion cost the cost of converting (↑) a system (p. 181). This can be quite large if the system is being moved from one computer to another.

information science the study of transmitting (p. 76) and processing data using computers.
information technology = information science (↑).
informatics (*n*) = information science (↑).
queuing theory the study of events which happen at a place, e.g. a terminal (p. 79). The events are usually messages and they may arrive at random or in some particular manner. The theory is used in information theory (p. 77) and also in simulation (↓).
simulation[2] (*n*) the representation (p. 45) of a real life problem in mathematical terms. The representation is used to produce a program which can calculate the results that would be obtained in real life. For example, we could simulate persons wanting to pay at a supermarket and see the effect of changing the number of pay points. **simulate** (*v*).

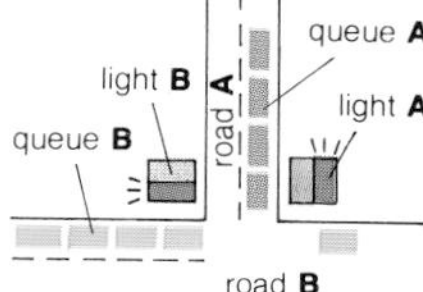

simulation of queues and traffic light timings

SIMULATE TRAFFIC JUNCTION							
TIMES LIGHT **A**		TIMES LIGHT **B**		CARS IN QUEUE **A**		CARS IN QUEUE **B**	
STOP	GO	STOP	GO	AVE	MAX	AVE	MAX
10	5	5	10	18	22	0	2
10	6	6	10	13	14	3	6
10	7	7	10	5	5	4	8

cybernetics (*n*) the study of the systems (p. 181) used to control machines and the comparison of such systems with the way persons and animals operate.
heuristic (*n*) a method of trying to find an answer to a problem by trial and error rather than use an algorithm (p. 122). An attempt is made to find an answer using simple rules and after each attempt the result is examined to see if it can be improved. For example, if we were trying to find a way through a network (p. 76), at any node (p. 76) there might be several possible paths and the rule might be to take the path which leads to the greatest number of paths at the next stage. It is a method used either because there is no satisfactory algorithm or because the algorithm would take too long to compute. **heuristic** (*adj*).

numerical analysis the use of mathematical methods for describing problems and then using programs to calculate the results.

numerical control the use of special programs which produce data, usually sequences of numbers, which can then be used to control the way a piece of equipment operates. The data is often stored on paper tape (p. 64) which can be fed into part of the machine.

linear program a method which solves a particular class of numerical analysis (↑) problems. It is very useful where problems of allocation (p. 134) arise and values of variables (p. 119) must lie between certain lowest and highest levels, e.g. we might wish to hold goods at several places to reduce the costs of moving them and so would try to make the total cost of storage and moving as low as possible.

LP = linear program (↑).

model (*n*) a representation (p. 45) of a problem using mathematical forms. **model** (*v*).

operational research a study to try to describe a problem, or an existing arrangement, in mathematical terms to see if a better solution can be found. It is not particularly a computing method but the calculations are quite often large enough to need a computer.

control computer a computer used specifically for process control (↓). It is usually an analog (p. 8) or hybrid computer (p. 8).

process control the use of a computer to control an operation which either makes something or operates some form of equipment.

feedback (*n*) data from one step of an action which is used to control what is done on the next step. Used a lot in process control (↑) but disk (p. 66) access arms (p. 70) also use the idea to make sure that the read-write head (p. 202) is kept exactly over the track (p. 68) being transferred.

computer aided design CAD. A system (p. 181) which allows people to design (p. 121) using a computer. The results are printed out or shown on a VDU (p. 83), or both, and changes can be made to see what effect they will have.

computer aided design

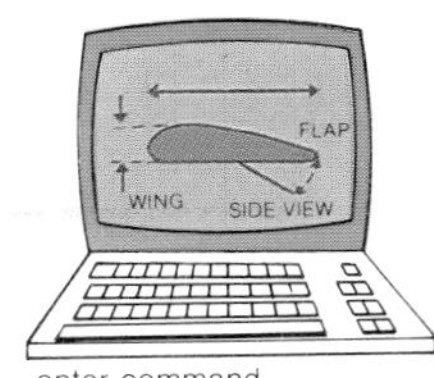

enter command for different view

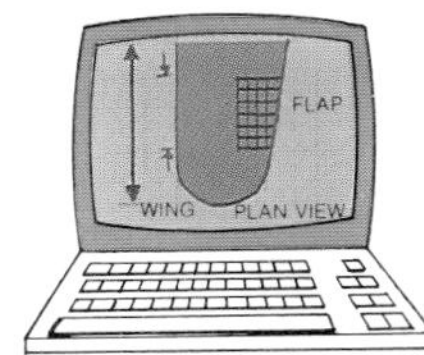

computer aided manufacture CAM. The use of a computer to help make something, usually a piece of equipment which has been the subject of computer aided design (↑).

computer aided instruction CAI. A method of teaching a person a subject by using a computer, usually with a VDU (p. 83) which is programmed to ask questions, examine the answers, tell the person of mistakes and try to help the learner.

PERT program evaluation and review technique. A method which uses a special form of diagram called a network to help in controlling the work in jobs such as building projects where there are a large number of events which need to take place in a particular order and may take time to complete. The nodes in the network are the events and the lines between the nodes show the time available. By using a computer it is possible to help in organizing the project, detect likely delays, etc.

critical path method = PERT (↑).

critical path the path through a PERT (↑) network which takes the longest time. This is how long the work will take.

artificial intelligence the use of a computer to try to simulate (p. 195) the thought processes of human beings, by trying to write programs which are able to learn from their mistakes and so improve their performance.

expert system a system (p. 181) whose purpose is to use a computer to follow specific rules for finding solutions to problems. Special languages may be used, e.g. PROLOG (p. 94), rather than the normal processing ones.

functional programming a form of programming that solves problems by describing them in terms of expressions (p. 18) or functions (p. 18).

combinatorics (*n*) the study of how things can be grouped together or arranged. It covers whether arrangements are possible and, if they are, how many arrangements can be made. This type of problem is often handled by programming a computer to examine or search for all the possible solutions.

computer (*n*) a machine which can read data (↓) presented in electronic (p. 203) form, can process (p. 201) the data by both moving it or doing calculations (p. 208) according to a set of instructions (p. 200), and produce results in a form which can be read by a human being, or in electronic form for further processing. Most computers are not a single piece of equipment but consist of a number of separate machines which are connected together. There are different types of computer, the main ones being digital (p. 8), analog (p. 8), and hybrid (p. 8). By itself the word computer is taken to mean a digital computer. **compute** (*v*), **computation** (*n*). *See also* Note on computer working p. 213.

program (*n*) a number of instructions (p. 200), and data (↓) which the instructions use. A computer carries out the instructions in sequence (p. 206) in order to do some particular action. The word may mean either a program written by a person, and called the source program (p. 103), or one in a language (p. 103) which a computer can understand, called the object program (p. 104). In either case the instructions and data are those necessary to complete some particular part of the work which is to be done. Any complete piece of work usually needs a number of programs to be run in sequence with each program doing a different part of the work. **program** (*v*), **programmer** (*n*).

machine (*n*) (1) a computer or any separate part of the computer; (2) a piece of equipment, such as a guillotine (p. 63), which is part of a computer installation (p. 10) but not connected to the computer.

device (*n*) any machine or part of a machine which can perform some specific (p. 203) action or piece of work, e.g. printing, or writing to a tape (p. 71). It may be possible to see what is happening, e.g. if the device were a printer (p. 58), but sometimes, as with a computer, there is very little to show that something is being done.

devices

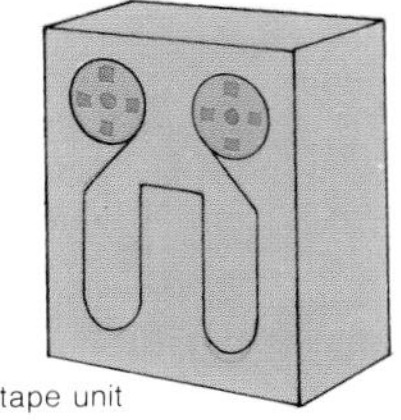

tape unit

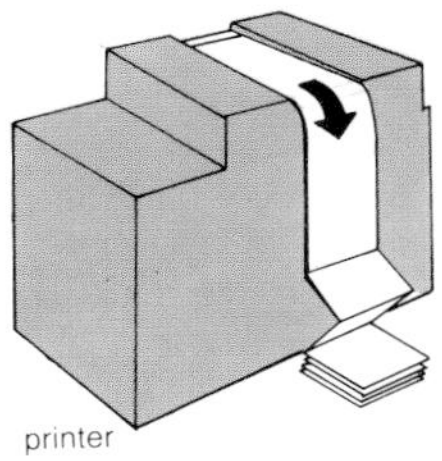

printer

VDU screen and keyboard

printing characters

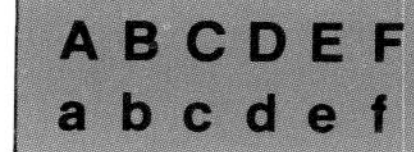

alphabetic

digits

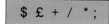

special characters

part of a keyboard

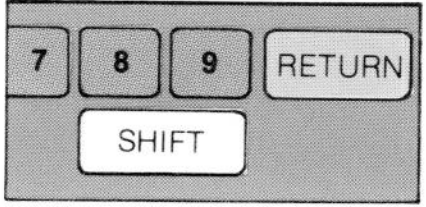

pressing the RETURN key sends a non printing character to computer

unit (*n*) a piece of equipment, a machine or a device (↑) which does some particular action or work. Computers are collections of devices some of which are the same. For example, there may be several tape drives (p. 71) and a tape unit would be any one of the tapes.

data (*n*) information (↓) in the form of numbers, characters or electrical signals (p. 22) on which a computer can act. It means both the information in a form which can be used directly by a computer and information, usually on paper, which has to be changed into a form which can be used by a computer.

character (*n*) a character is something which can be stored in a single byte (p. 17). It may be a letter such as A, B or C, it may be a decimal digit (p. 16) such as 1, 2 or 3, or it may be a special character (p. 46) such as ?, + or $. It may also be one which has a special meaning for a computer, but which has no printed form although it has a binary notation (p. 49).

information (*n*) data (↑), or more correctly the meaning of the data, or the results which can be obtained from working on the data.

store[2] (*n*) a part of a computer where it is possible to hold data (↑). By itself the word usually means the same as memory (p. 200), but it can also mean a disk (p. 66) or backing store (p. 12). **store** (*v*).

storage (*n*) = store (↑), especially the storing of data (↑) on disk (p. 66) or tape (p. 71) rather than in memory (p. 200).

storage device a device (↑) such as a tape (p. 71) or disk (p. 66) on which data can be placed and then later be read back into the computer.

contents (*n*) the actual data (↑) held in a memory location (p. 200) or backing store (p. 12) as opposed to its address (↓).

address (*n*) (1) a number which identifies a location (p. 200) in memory (p. 200) or a peripheral device (p. 12); (2) a number which identifies the exact location of a sector (p. 69) on a disk (p. 66); (3) part of an instruction (p. 200) which specifies (p. 203) the location of an operand (p. 15). **address** (*adj*), **address** (*v*).

memory (*n*) a part of a computer that holds the instructions (↓) and data (p. 199) so that they are immediately available. The instructions are used by the control unit (p. 27) to act upon the data either by calculation (p. 208), or by moving it to other parts of memory or between the CPU (p. 31) and the peripheral devices (p. 12).

location (*n*) a part of memory (↑), or sometimes backing store (p. 12), which can be identified exactly using an address (p. 199). **locate** (*v*).

memory location a term (p. 205) which tends (p. 206) to be used to refer to (p. 206) a specific (p. 203) part of memory (↑) with a particular address (p. 199). It is usually a small area of 1, 2 or 4 bytes (p. 17).

instruction (*n*) the basic element of a computer program (p. 198). It specifies (p. 203) the particular operation (↓) to be carried out, where the data (p. 199) is to be found, and where the result is to be placed.

operation (*n*) (1) the part of an instruction (↑) which describes what the computer is to do. It may be an action such as addition (p. 207), which is to be carried out on some data (p. 199), or an action such as rewind (p. 73) which is to be carried out on some peripheral device (p. 12); (2) an action done by a computer when it executes (↓) a group of instructions. **operate** (*v*).

execute (*v*) (1) to carry out an instruction (↑); (2) to carry out a program (p. 198). **execution** (*n*).

run[3] (*n*) the execution (↑) of a program (p. 198), or several programs, on a computer. **run** (*v*).

layout on magnetic tape

0	0	1	0	
1	0	1	0	
1	0	1	1	
0	1	0	1	
0	1	0	0	
1	1	1	0	
0	0	1	0	
1	1	0	0	
0	0	1	0	

parity track

strongly magnetized areas record **1**

other areas record **0**

process (*n*) a general word for an operation (↑) or group of actions carried out on a computer with the purpose of obtaining a result. In computing it can be the execution (↑) of a group of instructions (↑) which are a part of a program (p. 198), a complete program, or several programs. Also the action of a machine. **process** (*adj*), **process** (*v*), **processor** (*n*).

magnetic (*adj*) of materials which can accept and hold electrical patterns. The patterns can be read or written by special pieces of equipment called read-write heads (p. 202). The surface of suitable materials can be covered with a magnetic film and used to hold data (p. 199) which a computer can use.

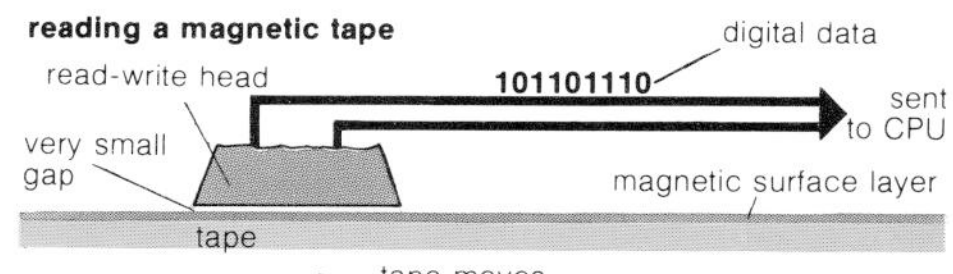

reading a magnetic tape

transfer of data

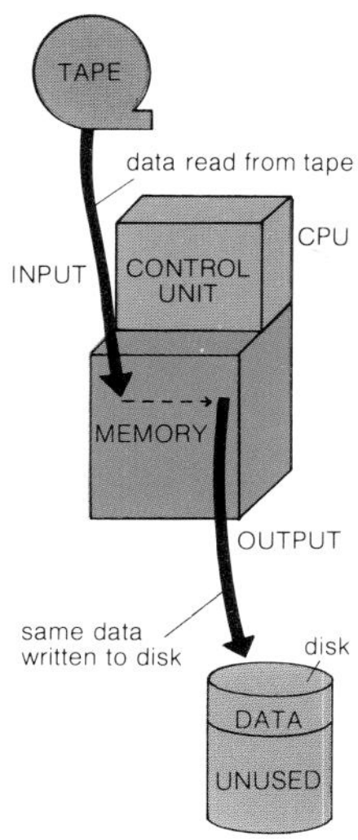

read (*v*) to get data (p. 199) from a peripheral device (p. 12) into memory (↑) or to get data from memory into the control unit (p. 27) of the CPU (p. 31). The data must be in a form that the computer can understand; it can be holes in a card (p. 52), magnetic signals (p. 22) on tape (p. 71) or disk (p. 66), or the shape of specially printed letters. Data which can be read by a computer is said to be machine readable. **read** (*adj*), **read** (*n*).

write (*v*) (1) to take data (p. 199) from memory (↑) and place it on an output device (p. 13) such as a printer (p. 58) or disk (p. 66); (2) to take data from a control unit (p. 27) of the CPU (p. 31) and place it in memory (↑). **write** (*adj*), **write** (*n*).

transfer (*v*) to move something from one place to another. It is commonly used to describe the movement of data (p. 199) between different parts of a computer, especially between the CPU (p. 31) and its peripheral devices (p. 12). Any read (↑) or write (↑) operation (↑) is a transfer of data. **transfer** (*adj*), **transfer** (*n*).

update[1] (*v*) to change the contents of something such as a variable (p. 119), a record (p. 154) or a file (p. 153) so that it holds the newest information available. **update** (*n*). *See also* update[2] p. 162.

delete (*v*) to take away data (p. 199). The data may be removed or over-written (↓) with spaces but often it is marked to prevent it being used again. **deletion** (*n*).

over-write (*v*) to write new data (p. 199) or spaces on top of old data. The old data, which can be in any part of a computer, is lost. It is not quite the same as delete (↑). In both cases whatever data was there before is lost but data which is over-written has new data put in its place, data which is deleted does not have new data put in its place.

read-write head the part of a unit (p. 198) which can either read (p. 201) or write (p. 201) data (p. 199) which is held in magnetic (p. 201) form on the surface of a device (p. 198) such as a tape (p. 71) or disk (p. 66). It may be fixed in position or it may be possible to move it. Also known as **head**.

magnetic head = read-write head (↑).

read head a read-write head (↑), that can only read (p. 201) data (p. 199). It is often used to describe the reading part of a read-write head.

write head a read-write head (↑), that can only write (p. 201) data (p. 199). It is often used to describe the writing part of a read-write head.

head (*n*) a read-write head (↑), a read head (↑) or a write head (↑).

access (*v*) to set up a path (p. 28) or a link (p. 77) between the control unit (p. 27) of the CPU (p. 31) and memory (p. 200), or between the CPU and any peripheral device (p. 12) and, usually, move data (p. 199) along it. Within the CPU a path can be set up just by use of electronic switches (p. 24). This may also be possible when some peripheral devices are accessed but with others, such as tapes (p. 71) or disks (p. 66), parts of the device usually have to be moved. **access** (*n*).

input (*n*) data (p. 199) which is read (p. 201) from one part of a computer, such as a terminal (p. 79) or a tape (p. 71) or disk (p. 66), into memory (p. 200). **input** (*adj*), **input** (*v*).

output (*n*) data (p. 199) which is written (p. 201) from one part of a computer, usually from memory (p. 200), to a tape (p. 71) or disk (p. 66), or to a screen (p. 84) or a printer (p. 58). **output** (*adj*), **output** (*v*).

input-output (*adj*) of input (↑) or output (↑) or both. Sometimes it means the peripheral devices (p. 12) which contain data (p. 199) for input or output, sometimes it means the part of a program (p. 198) which deals with the working of these devices (p. 198).

I-O (*adj*) = input-output (↑).

input-output unit a piece of equipment which can either be an input device (p. 12) or an output device (p. 13), e.g. a tape (p. 71) or disk (p. 66) as opposed to one like a card reader (p. 54) which can only provide input (↑).

record[2] (*v*) to write (p. 201) some data (p. 199) into a store (p. 199) so that it can be read (p. 201) back again at a later stage.

electronic (*adj*) of any device (p. 198) which uses electricity to control its action and method (p. 204) of working. It is particularly used where the device is small, i.e. no larger than can be fitted into a room, and usually very much smaller, and which uses a lot of circuits (↓).

part of a circuit diagram

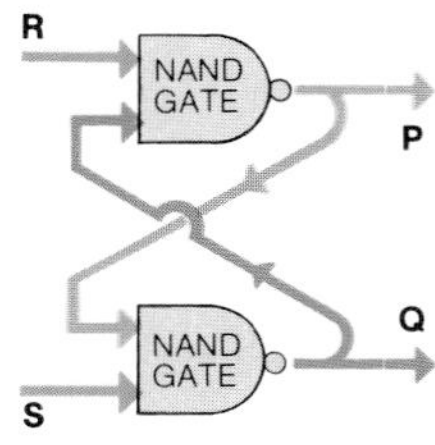

circuit (*n*) one or more complete paths (p. 28) along which electricity can flow from one point to another. The particular path chosen will depend on switches (p. 24) in the circuit which can direct the electricity in different directions. The machine which contains the circuit, and is controlled by it, will do different things or actions depending on which path is taken. **circuitry** (*n*).

specify (*v*) to set out an exact statement of the things that have to be done in order to perform some particular piece of work. It can refer (p. 206) to data (p. 199), a program (p. 198) or a machine. **specific** (*adj*), **specification** (*n*).

define (*v*) to state or describe the exact meaning of a word or a term (p. 205). **definition** (*n*).

diagram (*n*) a drawing using lines, shapes and words to show how something works, or is arranged, or is used. It can be used to describe the paths (p. 28) in a circuit (p. 203), how a program (p. 198) should work, or how data (p. 199) is moved from one part of a business to another.

chart (*n*) = diagram (↑).

method (*n*) a particular way of doing an action or a piece of work according to rules which are well known and understood.

method to find a square root

TO FIND A SQUARE ROOT OF A NUMBER METHOD	
SET-UP	
1 CHECK NUMBER IS POSITIVE **2** SET ROOT (R_0) TO 1	$N > 0$ $R_0 = 1$
CALCULATE	
3 DIVIDE R_0 INTO N	$\frac{N}{R_0}$
4 ADD R_0 TO RESULT FROM 3	$R_0 + \frac{N}{R_0}$
5 DIVIDE SUM BY 2 CALL RESULT R_1	$R_1 = \frac{1}{2}(R_0 + \frac{N}{R_0})$
6 CALCULATE $R_1 \times R_1$	R_1^2
7 IF THIS IS NEAR ENOUGH TO N STOP. OTHERWISE GO TO STEP **3** AND USE NEW VALUE OF R_1	$R_1^2 \approx N$??

request (*v*) to ask for something. It is commonly used in computing to show that one part of a computer wants another part to take some particular action. **request** (*n*).

available (*adj*) of something that is obtainable, or can be accessed (p. 202), or made use of.

test (*v*) to try using something, such as a program (p. 198) or a piece of equipment, to see whether it works correctly, with the aim of removing any errors (↓) that are found. **test** (*adj*), **test** (*n*).

error (*n*) a fault in the working of a machine, or a mistake in a program (p. 198) or the data (p. 199) which is being used.

check (*n*) (1) an examination of data, or a program (p. 198) or a signal (p. 22) to see whether there is an error (↑). It may either be done manually (p. 207) by a person, or by circuits (p. 203) in a machine; (2) an error which causes a program or a machine to stop. **check** (*v*).

detect (*v*) to find an error (↑) as the result of a test (↑) or a check (↑). It does not mean that the error is corrected. **detection** (*n*).

term (*n*) a word (or a group of words) commonly used to describe something, or which means the same, or almost the same, as another group of words. For example, 'human beings' is a term which is often used to describe people.

solve (*v*) to find, or to calculate (p. 208), the answer to a problem. **solution** (*n*).

item (*n*) a single thing in a collection or list of things of the same sort. For example, in a list of telephone numbers an item would be any one of the numbers.

display (*v*) to show something so that a person can see it. Information (p. 199) can be shown on a screen (p. 84) in the form of numbers, letters or diagrams (↑) or it can be printed. **display** (*n*).

unique (*adj*) having only one form, or only one way or method (↑) of doing something. For example, there are several ways in which numbers can be represented (p. 45) in a computer, they could be in binary (p. 16) or decimal (p. 16) but there is only one way of representing the letter A, so it is said to have a unique representation.

immediate (*adj*) of things or events which follow without anything happening in between, e.g. this page comes immediately after the page in front of it.

interval (*n*) the length of time between two events.

normal (*adj*) of the most common way or manner of doing something, or the most likely thing which will happen. There may be other ways but they are not very likely. It is very similar in meaning to the word 'usual'.

original (*n*) the first event, action or process (p. 201) as opposed to any later one.

precede (*v*) to come immediately (↑) before something, such as an event or a number, in time or place, e.g. in the numbers 1, 2, 4, 8, 10 the number 8 precedes the number 10. **preceding** (*adj*).

previous (*adj*) of events or numbers which come before the present event or number in time or place. The difference between previous and preceding (p. 205) is that preceding usually means an earlier event in a sequence (↓) of events, previous means an earlier event when there is no particular sequence.

sequence (*n*) things or numbers which are in a particular order, either by time or by size, e.g. the numbers 1, 2, 4, 4, 6, 9 form a sequence of numbers, each number being as large or larger than the one in front of it. There is usually no rule which says what the next number in the sequence should be; in this case, for example, all we can say is that it must be 9 or a larger number. It is possible to enter a number into the sequence but it must be in the correct place. If we enter the number 7 then it must go between 6 and 9. Some sequences do not allow a number to be repeated, i.e. the second 4 would not be allowed. In computing it is very common to deal with things in sequence, starting with the first item (p. 205) and then taking each item in turn, e.g. a sequential file (p. 163) is one whose records (p. 154) are in sequence by the key (p. 156) of the record. **sequential** (*adj*).

simultaneous (*adj*) of two events which happen at the same time. In computing the word is often used when events appear to take place together although they are in fact being done one after the other very quickly.

refer to (*v*) to say that something is particularly used to describe an event, a machine, a program (p. 198) or a memory location (p. 200), e.g. by itself the word computer means, or refers to, a digital computer (p. 8) not to any other type of computer.

tend (*v*) to be likely to or to lean towards. The word computer can mean a digital computer (p. 8) or an analog computer (p. 8) but it tends to mean a digital computer; if any other sort of computer is meant then the full name is usually given in order to make it clear. **tendency** (*n*).

sequences

1, 2, 3, 4, 6, 8

ascending sequence — each number higher than the previous one

22, 16, 5, 4, 3, -2, -6

descending sequence — each number lower than the previous one

1 ABBOTT
2 ARNOLD
3 BAKER
4 COLLINS
5 DAVIS
6 ERICSON

names in alphabetic sequence

user (*n*) (1) a person who uses a computer in the sense that they may get it to do something for them, such as a calculation (p. 208), by using programs (p. 198) which have been written by someone else. It is not the same as a computer operator (p. 190) who is a person who puts other people's work through a computer but does not use it to do anything for him or herself; (2) a person, in practice a group of persons, for whom some programs are written for their particular work but who never actually use the computer themselves. Their work is run (p. 200) for them by a computer operator. Quite often these users know very little about computing.

application (*n*) connected pieces of work that are done on a computer, e.g. a payroll application would be a set of programs (p. 198) which could be run (p. 200) on a computer to deal with all pay matters.

format (*n*) the way that data (p. 199) has to be arranged if it is to be used successfully, i.e. the order in which the items (p. 205) must appear and the allowable contents of each item. It can be used to refer to an instruction (p. 200), a printed report (p. 185), data held on cards (p. 52), tape (p. 71) or disk (p. 66).

manual[1] (*adj*) done by a human being and not by a computer (p. 198).

false (*adj*) not true.

addition (*n*) finding the sum of two or more numbers **add** (*v*).

division

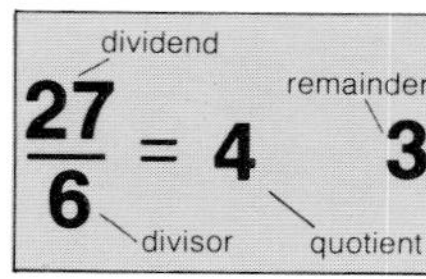

subtraction (*n*) finding the difference between two numbers. **subtract** (*v*).

division (*n*) repeated subtraction (↑). Most computers carry out division by subtracting the divisor (↓) from the dividend (↓) as many times as this can be done without the result becoming less than 0. **divide** (*v*).

dividend (*n*) the number into which some other number is divided (↑).

divisor (*n*) the number which is divided into the dividend (↑).

quotient (*n*) the number of times that the divisor (↑) can be subtracted from the dividend (↑).

remainder (*n*) the part of the dividend (p. 207) which is left when it is no longer possible to subtract the divisor (p. 207). It will always be less than the divisor.

ratio (*n*) the result of a division (p. 207), i.e. a ratio of 9/4 would be 2.25. A ratio is often written as a percentage, which is the ratio times 100, for example a ratio of 2/5 = 0.40 is the same as 40%.

multiplication (*n*) repeated addition (p. 207), e.g. 3 × 4 = 4 + 4 + 4. Most computers do multiplication by repeated addition and the order of the numbers is not important as long as they are nearly the same size. However if one is much larger than the other then it may affect the speed of execution (p. 200). For example, 2 × 1000 = 1000 × 2 but the first form will need only two additions, whereas the second form would need a thousand additions. **multiply** (*v*).

multiplier (*n*) the number which multiplies (↑) another one.

multiplicand (*n*) the number which is multiplied (↑) by the multiplier (↑).

calculate (*v*) to perform operations such as addition (p. 207), multiplication (↑), division (p. 207) etc. **calculation** (*n*).

scientific (*adj*) of programs, calculations (↑), or languages (p. 103) which tend to deal with large calculations where the numbers quite often range from the very large to the very small. Medium and larger size computers usually have special instructions, and registers (p. 14) which use a floating point (p. 51) format (p. 207) to handle this sort of work.

mathematical (*adj*) of methods which make use not only of the usual calculations (↑) to solve problems but can use a wider range of functions (p. 18), e.g. ones which can handle matrices (↓), equations etc.

dimension (*n*) the size of something, especially the number of items or possible entries which can be held in an array (p. 145) or table (p. 144).

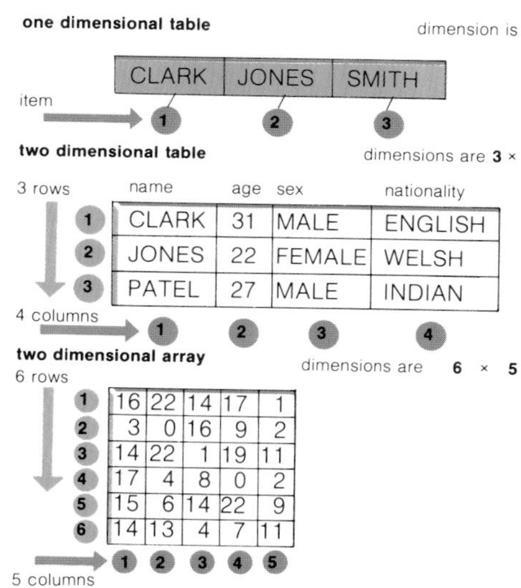

dimensional (*adj*) of the number of subscripts (p. 145) which is needed to access a table (p. 144) or an array (p. 145). A one dimensional table needs one subscript, a two dimensional table needs two subscripts, one for the row and another for the column. The first subscript is usually for the row and the second for the column. In data processing (p. 180) a single entry in a table may have several data elements (p. 155), each with its own name, allowing any element to be accessed with a single subscript but this is not usually the case with arrays in scientific work.

matrix (*n*) (1) an array (p. 145) of numbers used in scientific (↑) calculations (↑). It is usually two dimensional (↑), i.e. rows and columns; (2) an array of any number of dimensions (↑); (3) a diagram of a circuit. **matrices** (*n. pl.*).

integer (*n*) a whole number such as 1 or 2 etc. It does not have a decimal point (p. 16).

real number a number which is not an integer (p. 209). It has a decimal point (p. 16) and there are one or more digits (p. 16) after the decimal point, although these may be 0's, e.g. 1.0 to show they are not integers. In many program languages (p. 103) they are handled differently from integers, and the actual machine language (p. 104) instructions may be different as well.

real (*n*) = real number (↑).

scale (*v*) to change the range of values that is used to measure something to another range which can be more easily handled. For example, 0.123 might be changed to 123, i.e. to an integer (p. 209). It could be used in this form for calculation and the result changed back to the correct form at the end.

scaling factor the number used to scale (↑) something, e.g. a scaling factor of 1000 would change 0.123 to the integer (p. 209) 123.

significant digits the digits (p. 16) in a number which are needed to give the accuracy (↓) of a result. The number 123 has three significant digits; a number such as 123,000, which had an accuracy of 1 part in a thousand, would also have three significant digits.

precision (*n*) the number of digits (p. 16) used in a result. The normal range used in a particular computer is known as *single precision*. It is often possible to use twice as many digits for extra accuracy, *double precision*, but processing time is longer.

accuracy (*n*) the nearness of a number to its correct value. The result of a large calculation (p. 208) is hardly ever exactly the correct value. There is usually a small difference which arises from rounding (↓) or truncation (↓). The accuracy is a measure of the size of the difference and is usually given in the form of a ratio (p. 208).

truncate (*v*) to cut off. If a number has more digits (p. 16) than can be held in a register (p. 14) or word (p. 47) then the extra ones are dropped and not used, e.g. the number 2/3 = 0.666666 . . . and there is no end to the digits. In a computer whose register can store only four digits it would be truncated to 0.666. **truncation** (*n*).

rounding and truncation

NUMBER	ROUND TO 3 DEC PLACES	TRUNCATE TO 3 DEC PLACES
12.34562	12.346	12.345
21.45551	21.456	21.455
31.12143	31.121	31.121

round (*v*) to truncate (↑) but at the same time the last digit (p. 16) which is kept is made to be the nearest to the correct result. For example, 2/3 = 0.6666 . . . and if it were rounded as four digits it would be 0.667 which is nearer to the actual value than 0.666. When the first digit which is going to be dropped is 5 it is usual to round up (↓). **rounding** (*n*).

round up (*v*) to round (↑) so that the last digit (p. 16) is increased if the part truncated (↑) is greater than zero. For example, 1.2 rounded up would be 2.0.

truncation error an error caused by truncating (↑) a number. It is not a mistake, it is the difference between the exact value of a number and the nearest possible value which can be held in a computer.

rounding error an error caused in rounding (↑) a number. It is not a mistake, it is the difference between the exact value of a number and the nearest possible value which can be held in a computer.

absolute error the actual size of the difference between the exact answer and the one actually calculated (p. 208); no attention is paid as to whether the difference is positive or negative.

relative error the size of the error compared with the size of the correct value, i.e. the error divided (p. 207) by the correct value.

types of error

CORRECT VALUE	COMPUTED VALUE	DIFFERENCE FROM CORRECT	ABSOLUTE ERROR	RELATIVE ERROR
10.00	10.00	0	0	0
20.00	19.99	− 0.01	0.01	− 0.05%
20.00	20.05	+ 0.05	0.05	+ 0.25%

arithmetic overflow the result of a register (p. 14) or an accumulator (p. 15) not being large enough to hold the result of an arithmetic instruction (p. 35). For example, if a register can hold only four digits (p. 16) and already contains 9999 then any further addition (p. 207) will cause the register to overflow. The overflow is detected by the CPU (p. 31) and, if necessary, a program can take special action.

arithmetic overflow

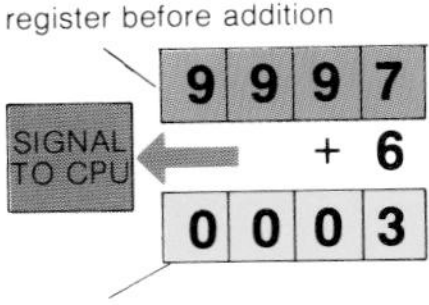

overflow and underflow

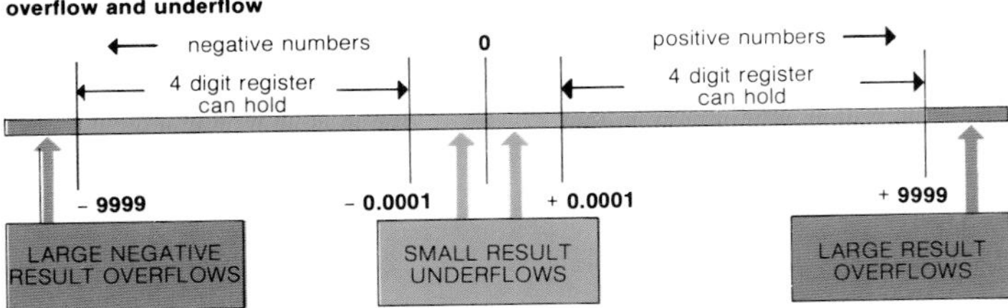

arithmetic underflow the result of a calculation (p. 208) being too small for the register (p. 14) or accumulator (p. 15) to measure. For example, a register which held four digits (p. 16) could not store 1/100,000 = 0.00001. An underflow can cause loss of data or incorrect results. It is detected by the CPU (p. 31) and the program can take special action to deal with it.

random number a number, usually one of a set, which is not connected in any way to any other number in the set; the numbers are considered to be produced purely by chance.

pseudo-random number a number which is almost a completely random number (↑), and for the purpose for which it is going to be used it can be treated as such. Most random numbers are really pseudo-random numbers.

random-number generator a routine (p. 111) whose purpose is to produce random numbers (↑). The routine is started by giving it a number, called a seed, which it uses to calculate a random number. It can continue to generate more numbers without using another seed. The numbers produced are really pseudo-random numbers (↑) and it is quite common to use a fresh seed fairly often.

Note on computer working

the terms are explained in the dictionary

A computer is simply a piece of equipment which has the ability to do a small number of things very quickly, and with complete accuracy. It can in fact really only do nine things:

- read data
- write data
- store data
- move data from one place to another
- add numbers
- subtract numbers
- compare two things, numbers or characters
- decide what to do next as the result of the comparison
- start/stop

A computer has instructions which can do each of these things; each instruction has also to say where any data is to be found and where any result is to be placed. A computer with just these nine instructions would be very slow and difficult to program, but it would work. Notice there are no instructions to multiply or divide two numbers; they are not strictly necessary. Multiplication is simply repeated addition and can always be done by using the add instruction the necessary number of times. In fact some of the computers sold in the early 1960s had no instruction for multiplication or division; they used repeated addition or subtraction. Nowadays computers have anything from 40 to 180 instructions, depending on the size, but they are simply to make the computer work faster and be easier to use. Most of the instructions are, like the multiply instruction, groupings of some of the basic instructions which experience has shown to be useful; a manufacturer therefore provides a new single instruction, such as multiply, which will do easily in one instruction what could be done more slowly with a suitable sequence of the basic nine.

To do any work the computer needs a program. This is just a long series of instructions which are carried out one after the other. The program will also usually contain some data on which the instructions are to work. The program, data and instructions, are held in a store, nowadays usually called memory, and a second part of the computer, the control unit, is responsible for fetching one instruction at a time, getting the data needed to do whatever the instruction wants to do, and then storing the result and getting the next instruction. If calculations, or tests, have to be done then there is a third part of the computer called the arithmetic logic unit, ALU for short, which actually does them. These three parts, memory, the control unit and the ALU form what is commonly called the central processing unit, or CPU for short.

A program has somehow to be brought into memory before it can be run and there is not often enough memory to hold the program and all the data it needs to use. Thus there has to be a separate form of storage, (secondary storage), which can hold programs and large amounts of data and which the control unit of the CPU can read from. Secondary storage can take different forms - cards, paper tape, disk, magnetic tape. Programs and data can be held on any of these but most commonly they are kept on disk or tape. Instructions in a program can ask the control unit to bring in data from one of these storage devices whenever it is needed. Data which is moved into memory in this manner is called input. Results of programs may have to be made available in a form a person can use, and this normally means using a screen or a printer. Results can also be written out to secondary storage so that they can be used as input to another program.

A computer is thus a machine which reads programs containing instructions and data into memory, does what the instructions in the program say, including reading and writing more data, and then gets the next program. Larger computers can run several programs at the same time.

The CPU uses small electrical signals to do its work and can only use data which is in this form. Thus data in the form of holes in cards has to be converted into the right type of signal; data which is to be shown on a screen or printed has to be converted from signals into numbers and letters which people can read. The CPU has special parts which allow it to make the necessary changes. Tapes and disks store data in a magnetic form which is very similar to the way it is required by the computer and so by using special reading and writing heads, data can either be written to them or read from them, i.e. they can be used as both input and output devices. They can also store very large amounts of data in a small space and the data can be moved, very quickly, between the device and memory. Data which is being entered into memory for the first time is usually keyed into cards, paper tape or through a terminal, data which is being stored for use again at a later stage is almost always kept on tape or disk because they are much faster and can hold more information.

As a rough guide, depending on their size, computers can do anything from 10,000 to several million instructions every second. Input from cards, or output to a fast printer takes place at about 1000 characters a second but transfer of data to or from tape or disk takes place at speeds of from 50,000 to 500,000 characters a second. Once in memory a character can usually be moved to the control unit, or to another part of memory, in less than a millionth of a second.

Index

keyboard and control mnemonics

EBCDIC 8-bit code part I

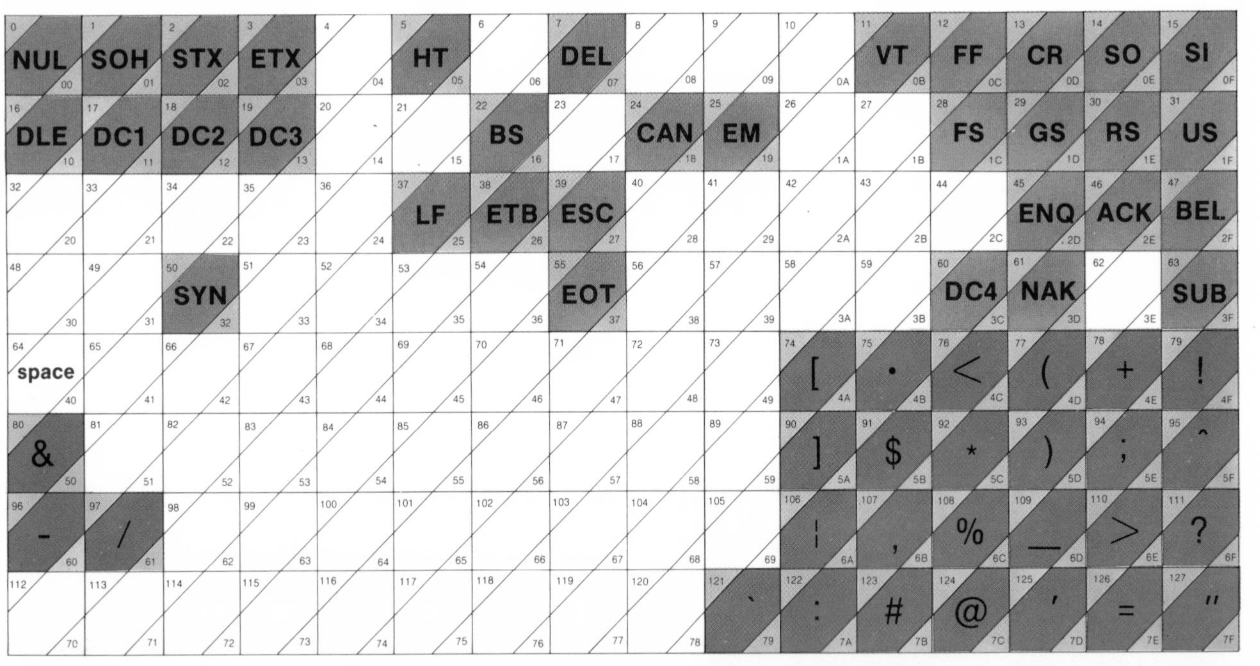

0 NUL 00	1 SOH 01	2 STX 02	3 ETX 03	4 04	5 HT 05	6 06	7 DEL 07	8 08	9 09	10 0A	11 VT 0B	12 FF 0C	13 CR 0D	14 SO 0E	15 SI 0F
16 DLE 10	17 DC1 11	18 DC2 12	19 DC3 13	20 14	21 15	22 BS 16	23 17	24 CAN 18	25 EM 19	26 1A	27 1B	28 FS 1C	29 GS 1D	30 RS 1E	31 US 1F
32 20	33 21	34 22	35 23	36 24	37 LF 25	38 ETB 26	39 ESC 27	40 28	41 29	42 2A	43 2B	44 2C	45 ENQ 2D	46 ACK 2E	47 BEL 2F
48 30	49 31	50 SYN 32	51 33	52 34	53 35	54 36	55 EOT 37	56 38	57 39	58 3A	59 3B	60 DC4 3C	61 NAK 3D	62 3E	63 SUB 3F
64 space 40	65 41	66 42	67 43	68 44	69 45	70 46	71 47	72 48	73 49	74 [4A	75 • 4B	76 < 4C	77 (4D	78 + 4E	79 ! 4F
80 & 50	81 51	82 52	83 53	84 54	85 55	86 56	87 57	88 58	89 59	90] 5A	91 $ 5B	92 * 5C	93) 5D	94 ; 5E	95 ^ 5F
96 - 60	97 / 61	98 62	99 63	100 64	101 65	102 66	103 67	104 68	105 69	106 ¦ 6A	107 , 6B	108 % 6C	109 _ 6D	110 > 6E	111 ? 6F
112 70	113 71	114 72	115 73	116 74	117 75	118 76	119 77	120 78	121 ` 79	122 : 7A	123 # 7B	124 @ 7C	125 ' 7D	126 = 7E	127 " 7F